THE
EVERYTHING®
STEM HANDBOOK

Dear Reader,

"STEM" has become a buzzword in education recently, but it's so much more than just a buzzword. The fastest-growing careers these days are in STEM. The companies and organizations that are changing the way we live are STEM related. In the very near future it will be difficult, if not impossible, for an individual to get through life without some knowledge of technology, science, and mathematics.

This book won't teach your child everything he or she needs to know about science, technology, engineering, or math. The purpose of the book is to help plant and nurture the seeds that may one day develop into a passion in your child—a passion for studying some STEM field, or possibly several. Our hope is that some activity or resource contained in these pages will fire your child's imagination and set her off in search of more information or additional hands-on activities. We also hope that you'll enjoy trying out these activities with your child.

We encourage you to approach these activities with a creative spirit. Look for ways you can alter the experiments and activities to make them more fun, more interesting, or more educational for your child given his specific interests and aspirations. If some of the activities in this book help your child see how exciting and interesting STEM can be, he'll understand why millions of scientists, mathematicians, engineers, computer programmers, and so on have chosen a career in STEM, just as we did long ago.

Best Wishes on Your Learning Adventure,

Rihab Sawah and Anthony Clark

Welcome to the EVERYTHING® Series!

These handy, accessible books give you all you need to tackle a difficult project, gain a new hobby, comprehend a fascinating topic, prepare for an exam, or even brush up on something you learned back in school but have since forgotten.

You can choose to read an Everything® book from cover to cover or just pick out the information you want from our four useful boxes: e-questions, e-vocab, e-alerts, and e-ssentials. We give you everything you need to know on the subject, but throw in a lot of fun stuff along the way, too.

We now have more than 400 Everything® books in print, spanning such wide-ranging categories as weddings, pregnancy, cooking, music instruction, foreign language, crafts, pets, New Age, and so much more. When you're done reading them all, you can finally say you know Everything®!

QUESTION

Answers to
common questions

VOCAB

Important terms
to know

ALERT

Urgent
warnings

ESSENTIAL

Quick
handy tips

PUBLISHER Karen Cooper

MANAGING EDITOR, EVERYTHING® SERIES Lisa Laing

COPY CHIEF Casey Ebert

ASSISTANT PRODUCTION EDITOR Alex Guarco

ACQUISITIONS EDITOR Hillary Thompson

DEVELOPMENT EDITOR Brett Palana-Shanahan

EVERYTHING® SERIES COVER DESIGNER Erin Alexander

THE
EVERYTHING®
STEM
HANDBOOK

Help your child learn and succeed in the fields of science, technology, engineering, and math

Rihab Sawah, MS, MA, and Anthony Clark, PhD

Aadamsmedia
Avon, Massachusetts

For Widad Fakir and Mamoun Sawah—two
of the greatest teachers we've ever known.

An Everything® Series Book.
Everything® and everything.com® are registered trademarks of F+W Media, Inc.

Published by
Adams Media, a division of F+W Media, Inc.
57 Littlefield Street, Avon, MA 02322. U.S.A.
www.adamsmedia.com

ISBN 10: 1-4405-8979-8
ISBN 13: 978-1-4405-8979-9
eISBN 10: 1-4405-8980-1
eISBN 13: 978-1-4405-8980-5

Printed in the United States of America.

10 9 8 7 6 5 4 3 2 1

Readers are urged to take all appropriate precautions before undertaking any how-to task. Always read and follow instructions and safety warnings for all tools and materials, and call in a professional if the task stretches your abilities too far. Although every effort has been made to provide the best possible information in this book, neither the publisher nor the author is responsible for accidents, injuries, or damage incurred as a result of tasks undertaken by readers. This book is not a substitute for professional services.

Many of the designations used by manufacturers and sellers to distinguish their products are claimed as trademarks. Where those designations appear in this book and F+W Media, Inc. was aware of a trademark claim, the designations have been printed with initial capital letters.

Cover images © Diego Alies, Andrey Skaryna, ppbig/123RF.
Illustrations by Dave Forbes.

This book is available at quantity discounts for bulk purchases.
For information, please call 1-800-289-0963.

Contents

Acknowledgments

Rihab: A special thanks to my former colleague, Dr. Dan Meininger, Professor of Chemistry at Moberly Area Community College, for sharing his valuable expertise and insights in physical chemistry. I am also thankful for Dr. Keith MacAdam, Professor Emeritus at the University of Kentucky, Lexington, for having supported me in pursuing a career path in physics. The journey has been most rewarding.

I would like to especially acknowledge my dear friend and former math professor at Damascus University, Yahya Alsayed, for inspiring me to think outside the box and to seek uniquely creative solutions to complex problems.

A huge thanks to my family for their love and unwavering support. A tender thanks to my mother, Widad Fakir, for modeling to me the path of education as the foundational brick of the future. I am grateful to my father, Mamoun, for teaching me to be humbly proud and self-honoring. I'd like to thank my nephews, Abed and Mamoun Traboulsi, for providing me with the motivation to bring science to life in their lives and into their classrooms, and to make science relevant for the young. I would like to also thank my sister, Khaula, who has supported me all my life in my pursuits in science and education, and for being a true cornerstone in my heart.

Finally, my deepest gratitude goes to my precious life companion and husband, Anthony, for constantly challenging me to live my highest potential, and for always, always believing. The pages in this book would not have seen the light without him.

Anthony: I'd like to thank all my teachers from all throughout the years, but most especially my dissertation advisor, Tony Prato. I'd also like to thank my colleagues Marie Gunn and Laura Westhoff for helping make my workdays productive and fun. A special thanks to Brendan Clark for being who he is and for always helping me see the world in new ways. And I extend my heartfelt gratitude to my wife and coauthor of this book, Rihab, who continuously inspires me to be a better teacher and a better man.

Introduction

STEM IS A WELL-KNOWN acronym in the education arena, and it's rapidly on its way to becoming a household word. Short for Science, Technology, Engineering, and Mathematics, STEM represents more than a collection of school subjects or classes. STEM has become a way of life for many people, and it represents a pathway to the future for society.

The intense focus on STEM in recent years has occurred due to the broad acknowledgment of STEM's importance to the future of all nations. As technology continues to advance, the need for highly skilled workers will only continue to rise. Although not every student will ultimately become a computer programmer or engineer, every future citizen will need to understand how to interact with technology. In order to carry out their duties, most future workers will need a firm grasp of mathematics. Many future jobs will require specialized training in some STEM field. Already employers place a premium on the kind of critical thinking skills developed in math and science classes, and that trend will only intensify as workplace technology becomes more and more complex.

Over the decade spanning 2000 to 2010, employment in STEM fields grew by 7.9 percent, compared to just 2.6 percent for non-STEM fields. The Bureau of Labor Statistics projects a continued faster-than-average growth rate in STEM jobs. Not surprisingly, unemployment rates are lower and average wages are higher in STEM fields than in non-STEM fields. In addition, entry-level jobs in STEM pay roughly 28 percent more on average than entry-level jobs in other fields.

Clearly, based on the facts, any young person would benefit from a solid grounding in a STEM subject or subjects. Although students are introduced to a number of STEM subjects in school, the curriculum presented is not enough for some young learners. Despite the healthy job prospects in science, engineering, technology, and math, many young people choose other paths. Some kids likely steer clear of STEM because the subjects are difficult.

Others possibly avoid STEM areas because they haven't seen STEM's relevance to their lives.

Every young person deserves the chance to be successful in school, and every student deserves the extra mentoring and support necessary for success in science and math classes. One way parents can help their kids face challenging coursework is by providing opportunities for learning outside the classroom. A child who develops a love of science and math at a young age is more likely to succeed in those subjects in subsequent grades, even when the work becomes more challenging.

The Everything® STEM Handbook offers over sixty-five activities you can use to engage your young learner beyond the classroom. The activities cover a broad range of STEM subjects, with sections relating to physics, chemistry, biology, astronomy, engineering, and math. All the activities can be done in your home—no laboratory needed. In some cases, your child will benefit from your involvement in the activity. Depending on your child's age and aptitude, she may enjoy exploring some of the activities on her own. One strategy is to try each activity with your child, and then invite her to try it again on her own, or with a friend or sibling. The basic purpose of each activity is to provide you with a means of introducing your child to a science or math principle in a way that's fun and hands-on. As she progresses through the activities, your child will also learn something about the scientists and mathematicians who first discovered the key theories and principles in their respective fields.

In addition to the activities, *The Everything® STEM Handbook* offers information about other STEM-related learning resources, including afterschool classes, summer camps, learning apps, science kits, and more. The "Additional Resources" section also includes a number of websites and other resources you'll want to investigate after your young learner has attempted all the activities—and hopefully mastered all the principles—presented in the chapters.

CHAPTER 1

Thinking Like a Scientist

Some people believe that you're born either a creative type or a science/math type. The truth is that most science/math types are also highly creative. The process of conducting scientific research requires a great deal of imagination. It can be argued that scientists and mathematicians have been among the most creative people in the history of humankind. Their contributions have enriched human life at least as much as the contributions of artists and writers. This chapter offers a basic introduction to science and its various fields, a discussion of the scientific method, and a hands-on science activity you can do with your child that illustrates the scientific method.

What Is Science?

When you hear the word "science," a number of images probably come immediately into your mind. You might think of a laboratory featuring beakers and Bunsen burners, or a scientist in a white lab coat looking through a microscope, or a tweed-coated professor peering at the stars through a telescope. Perhaps the word conjures up images of the periodic table, or high school biology students dissecting a frog. Science certainly includes images like those, but it's a broader concept than many people realize.

QUESTION

Where does the word "science" come from?
The word "science" comes from the Latin word *scientia*, which means knowledge. Many science terms are Latin, or derive from it, because at one time Latin was the universal or common language.

Science is a systematic process for discovering knowledge or uncovering general truths based on observation and experimentation. Science also refers to the body of knowledge that results from that process. You can think of science as a process of discovery, along with all the discoveries that are made along the way. Science also entails the application of scientific knowledge, so an individual could work in a scientific field and not necessarily be involved in discovering new breakthroughs.

ESSENTIAL

Not all scientific discoveries arrive through experimentation. Some very important breakthroughs have come more or less by accident. A happy accident like that is called **serendipity**, and there are many examples of it occurring in science throughout the years. Alexander Fleming, a Scottish scientist, left a Petri dish open by mistake and it became contaminated by a bacteria-killing mold. That "accident" marked the discovery of penicillin. While testing radar equipment for the Raytheon company, a worker noticed that a candy bar had melted in his pocket, leading to the development of the microwave oven. Safety glass came about when a lab worker forgot to wash out a glass beaker and the plastic that it had contained coated the inside of the beaker.

There are a couple of ways in which science can be broadly categorized. One of the most basic distinctions is to divide scientific work into basic science and applied science. *Basic science* involves the discovery of new knowledge or fundamental principles. *Applied science* involves utilizing already existing knowledge for some purpose. The discovery of x-rays would be considered basic science. The use of x-rays to examine fractured bones is applied science. All fields of science have basic aspects and applied aspects, and sometimes applied science can lead to advancements in basic science.

ESSENTIAL

Basic research and **applied research** are terms synonymous with basic science and applied science, respectively. Basic research is also sometimes referred to as *fundamental research* or *pure research* ("pure" because it's done without concern for practical application or commercialization of the end results of the research).

Fields of Science

Science is divided into a number of scientific disciplines or fields. The major scientific fields are then further divided into subfields. The main scientific fields, and some of the subfields, are listed here. Some will be very familiar to you, while others you've probably never heard of.

Life Sciences

The life sciences are those fields involving the study of living organisms. The life sciences include biology and its many branches and subfields. Some of the life science subfields are biochemistry, anatomy, evolutionary biology, genetics, botany, horticulture, forest management, zoology, microbiology, food science, and environmental health. Medicine and its many subfields are also part of the life sciences. Some emerging fields in life sciences are bioinformatics and systems biology.

ALERT

Zoology is the study of animals, but there are more specialized fields involving the study of animals. *Entomology* is the study of insects, *ornithology* is the study of birds, *ichthyology* is the study of fish, *primatology* is the study of primates, and *herpetology* is the study of amphibians and reptiles.

Physical Sciences and Mathematics

The physical sciences focus on the study of nonliving matter and energy. The physical sciences include all the subfields of physics, chemistry, earth science, oceanography, and atmospheric sciences. Mathematics also has a number of divisions and subfields. The computers sciences are also grouped under this broad category.

Physics

Physics involves the study of matter and energy. Some of the subfields in physics are fluid dynamics, optics, nuclear physics, quantum physics, nonlinear dynamics, and astronomy and astrophysics. Physics principles are employed in many other science and technology fields.

Chemistry

Chemistry focuses on the composition and properties of substances, as well as the interactions among substances. Some of its subfields are organic chemistry, analytical chemistry, biochemistry, physical chemistry, and medicinal-pharmaceutical chemistry.

Earth Science

Earth science includes all the subfields related to the study of the earth's makeup. Geology, paleontology, soil science, volcanology, glaciology, geophysics, and seismology are among the subfields in earth science.

ESSENTIAL

Some fields of science are known as **interdisciplinary fields**. An interdisciplinary field is one that incorporates concepts or tools from multiple disciplines. A good example of an interdisciplinary field is *environmental science*. Environmental science focuses on the interaction of the living and nonliving parts of the environment, including the impact of humans on the environment. The field uses concepts from natural sciences like biology, ecology, soil science, and chemistry, but it also incorporates ideas from the social sciences.

Oceanography, Atmospheric Sciences, and Meteorology

Oceanography is the study of oceans and marine life. The atmospheric sciences and meteorology involve the study of the weather and climate and its impact on the earth.

Mathematics, Applied Mathematics, and Statistics

The field of mathematics involves the study of numbers, equations, shapes, and their relationships. Some of its subfields are algebra, number theory, set theory, and logic and foundations. Applied mathematics focuses on the use of math concepts in other fields, such as engineering and business. Control theory, partial differential equations, and dynamic systems are examples of subfields in applied mathematics. Statistics involves gathering, analyzing, interpreting, and presenting data. Some of its subfields are probability, statistical theory, and biostatistics.

Computer Sciences

Computer sciences deal with computers and their practical applications. Computer science subfields include databases/information systems, programming languages, graphics/human computer interfaces, and artificial intelligence/robotics.

ESSENTIAL

Artificial intelligence is a fascinating area of computer science focusing on the development of intelligent machines. Researchers working in artificial intelligence attempt to create machines that can emulate certain human abilities, such as speech recognition, reasoning, and learning. The fields of artificial intelligence and robotics are highly related, since robots require artificial intelligence to function.

Engineering

Engineering involves the practical application of science and math for the purpose of designing and building physical structures and machines, or otherwise managing resources. Some engineering fields include mechanical engineering, civil engineering, aerospace engineering, biomedical engineering, materials science, industrial engineering, ergonomics, nuclear engineering, environmental engineering, electrical engineering, and computer engineering.

ESSENTIAL

An emerging area of engineering is **nanoscience**, which involves the creation of **nanotechnology**. According to the Center for Responsible Nanotechnology, nanotechnology is "the engineering of functional systems at the molecular scale." The National Nanotechnology Initiative claims that, "[n]anoscience and nanotechnology are the study and application of extremely small things and can be used across all the other science fields." Just to give you an idea of how small the nanoscale is, there are 25,400,000 nanometers in an inch.

Social and Behavioral Sciences

The social and behavioral sciences are those that examine how humans behave, either as individuals or as part of a group or community. Some examples of social and behavioral sciences are anthropology, psychology, economics, sociology, geography, political science, and criminology.

ALERT

Some people think of economics as the study of money. In fact, economists—those who study or practice economics professionally—are interested in *human* behavior. A pile of money does nothing on its own but sit and collect dust. What's interesting to economists are the decisions people (consumers, businesses, or governments) make with regards to that pile of money. As a field, economics is more closely related to psychology and other social sciences than it is to business disciplines like finance and accounting.

The Scientific Method

Early humans developed many theories about why the world works the way it does. There were fanciful explanations for various natural phenomena, many of them involving unseen forces like gods and goddesses. Lightning storms, earthquakes, even the rising and setting of the sun all had explanations based on the actions of various deities. Those explanations may have made for entertaining stories, but there was nothing scientific about them.

The scientist Ibn al-Haytham (also known as Alhazen), who lived and worked primarily in Cairo during the tenth and eleventh centuries, made one of the earliest statements about the scientific method in his book *Doubts Concerning Ptolemy*.

The seeker after the truth is not one who studies the writings of the ancients and, following his natural disposition, puts his trust in them, but rather the one who suspects his faith in them and questions what he gathers from them, the one who submits to argument and demonstration and not to the sayings of a human being whose nature is fraught with all kinds of imperfection and deficiency.

Ibn al-Haytham's statement captures the basic idea behind scientific inquiry, or what has come to be known as *the scientific method*. The theories and principles that are widely accepted in each of the various sciences were not accepted immediately. Each was subjected to a great deal of analysis and verification. In some cases, the theories were only partially correct as originally proposed, and had to be corrected or completed by later scientists. The scientific method has been employed in the discovery of most of the important findings in science. The method is used in all fields and subfields of science.

Steps of the Scientific Method

The particular application of the scientific method may differ some from field to field, but the basic process is the same in all sciences. The scientific method can be broken down into a few fundamental steps.

Ask a General Question

Scientific inquiry begins with a researcher asking a general question. For example, suppose you begin to wonder about the new chemical factory that was just built in your neighborhood close to the banks of your favorite fishing stream. In particular, you wonder if the factory will impact the stream in some way. That's your general question: Will the new chemical factory affect the local stream?

Gather Background Information

As a researcher, you always want to know what other research has been done on your subject. Most researchers want to read a lot about their subject, particularly any work that was published relatively recently. Researchers also need to have a good understanding of the fundamental science, or the widely accepted principles, relating to their research focus. To analyze the question about the chemical factory and the stream, it would be good for the researcher to have a background in environmental science or some related field.

Form a Hypothesis

A hypothesis is a proposition about the cause or nature of something. For it to be used as part of the scientific method, a hypothesis must be testable. For example, a man who lost his car keys could form the hypothesis that his keys were stolen by leprechauns. Since there's no obvious way to scientifically test whether or not leprechauns stole his car keys, the man's hypothesis can't be explored with the scientific method. The man's hypothesis would be considered highly *nonscientific* in light of the fact that science doesn't generally acknowledge the existence of leprechauns!

ALERT

Hypothesis is one of those words that has a unique plural form. The plural of hypothesis is not hypothesise. The plural of hypothesis is actually hypotheses (pronounced hī-pŏth'ĭ-sēz).

You also can't test hypotheses that are statements of value judgment. For example, the statement "people who drive yellow cars have poor taste" is not a testable hypothesis, because good taste and poor taste are all in the eye of the beholder.

Following are some examples of testable hypotheses.

EXAMPLES OF TESTABLE HYPOTHESES:
- Cigarette smokers are more likely to develop lung cancer than nonsmokers
- Married people tend to live longer than unmarried people, all else equal
- Kids tend to become hyperactive when they eat too much sugar
- Plants grow faster when exposed to classical music
- People who take regular vacations have lower stress levels than people who rarely vacation

QUESTION

What's the difference between a hypothesis and a theory?
Sometimes people use the terms *hypothesis* and *theory* interchangeably, but they're actually different concepts. A hypothesis is a specific prediction about a natural or social phenomenon. Some might say that a hypothesis is a sort of educated guess. A theory, on the other hand, is a hypothesis that has been tested and proven repeatedly, and is generally accepted as true by practitioners in a given scientific field.

Test the Hypothesis
After stating your hypothesis it's time to look for a way to test it. Some tests of hypotheses are easy to conduct. Others take a lot of time and resources.

For example, you could state the following hypothesis: "A one-pound brick dropped from 5 feet will reach the ground in less than two seconds." Such a hypothesis would be easy to test by performing a simple experiment. You could simply drop the brick from 5 feet and time how long it takes the brick to reach the ground. Usually scientists will want to repeat an experiment a number of times to verify the results. If you dropped the brick several times in a row and each time it reached the ground in less than two seconds, you could be pretty certain of your results.

Experiments are used to gather data about the hypothesis being tested. Each time you drop the brick you record the length of time it takes the brick to reach the ground. Each time you repeat the experiment and record the result, you're making an *observation*. The data or observations you're recording—generated by repeated trials of your experiment—are what you'll analyze to determine whether your stated hypothesis is true or not. But experiments are not the only method used to gather data. Social scientists often use surveys to collect information. For example, if you wanted to find out how people feel about a particular political candidate, you wouldn't conduct an experiment. You would conduct a survey, asking people their opinion of the candidate.

Sometimes scientists use data that already exists. For example, if you needed to know the population of the United States in order to test your hypothesis, you would not be required to count the number of people living in the country yourself. The U.S. Census Bureau spends a lot of time and resources gathering population data for the nation, and the data is free for anyone to use. When you utilize data that's been gathered by someone else it's known as *secondary data*.

ESSENTIAL

Primary data is data that is collected from the original source. If you conduct an experiment, then you're gathering primary data. If you collect data using a survey, you're also working with primary data. **Secondary data** is data that someone else collected. Some companies specialize in collecting and selling or renting out secondary data. A great deal of secondary data is made available by various government agencies.

Analyze the Data and Make a Conclusion

The final step in the scientific process is to analyze the data you've gathered and make a conclusion about your stated hypothesis. If your hypothesis turns out to be false, you might want to repeat your procedure to be sure you didn't make any errors in conducting the experiment or recording the data. Even if you prove your hypothesis, it's a good idea to review your procedure to be sure it's error free.

After reaching a conclusion about your hypothesis, you'll want to communicate your results. You can let people know what you discovered, either in the form of an oral presentation or a written report. For as long as the scientific method has existed, scientists have communicated the results of their work so that others could build upon it and advance the sciences.

The Scientific Method in Action: An Activity You Can Do at Home

This famous experiment that kids have been doing for decades involves only an eyedropper and coins. The basic purpose of the experiment is to introduce kids to the scientific method and to scientific thinking in general.

MATERIALS NEEDED:
- A penny, a dime, and a quarter
- A clean eyedropper
- Water
- Two other kinds of safe liquids
- A pencil or pen
- A table for recording observations (see following example)

There are several ways to approach this activity. One is to begin with the smallest coin, a dime, and an eyedropper filled with tap water. Invite your child to squeeze one drop of water onto the dime and then observe the behavior of the water. After your child has observed the water for a moment, ask her to make a prediction about how many drops of water will fit on the dime before the water spills off the edge of the coin. Help her craft her prediction into a testable statement of hypothesis before she proceeds with the experiment.

After your child records the number of water drops the dime held, ask her to make a conclusion about whether her hypothesis was correct or not. Then ask her to make a prediction (i.e., state a hypothesis) about the number of water drops a penny will hold. After she has completed her experiment and made her conclusion about the penny, have her repeat the process for a quarter.

If your child is particularly inquisitive, invite her to repeat the entire process (penny, dime, and quarter) using two other safe liquids. Some possible choices include milk, soda, rubbing alcohol, and cooking oil. She'll want to be sure to clean the coins and the eyedropper after each round. For these subsequent rounds involving other liquids, encourage your child to form statements of hypothesis that include some comparison to water (e.g., fewer drops of milk will fit on the penny than drops of water).

RECORD YOUR RESULTS: THE COIN AND LIQUID EXPERIMENT

Liquid	Number of Drops		
	Dime	Penny	Quarter
Water			
Milk			
Soda			
Oil			
Alcohol			

The actual science underlying the eyedropper activity is somewhat advanced. If your child is deeply interested in science, encourage her to seek out the scientific explanation online, or in the library. The point of the activity is to introduce her to the basic steps of the scientific method, and expose her to some basic STEM vocabulary.

The Limits of Science

Science has led to breakthroughs and innovations that have enriched human life tremendously over the centuries. Despite all that it's done for humanity, however, science does have its limitations. Science can't answer questions of value judgment, and it can't prove or disprove the existence of supernatural phenomena. Scientific results may also be impacted by the biases of the scientists conducting the research, as well as the assumptions they make about their subjects.

Value Judgments

Earlier in this section it was mentioned that statements of value judgment can't be tested. The scientific method can be used to test the impact of automobile emissions on the environment, for instance. But the scientific method can't answer the question of whether or not should drive SUVs. That question is a matter of personal opinion.

Sometimes scientists are criticized when their findings appear to run afoul of someone else's personal view on a particular issue. The well-known economist Steven Levitt (coauthor of the bestselling book *Freakonomics*) and his co-researcher John Donohue angered a number of individuals and groups with the results of an economic study. Their study concluded that legalized abortion contributed significantly to a drop in the crime rate eighteen years later. Abortion is a politically charged issue, so any conclusion Levitt and Donohue reached would be controversial. But the researchers never argued that legalized abortion was a good thing, or that more abortions should occur. They simply offered statistical evidence of a hypothesis—the hypothesis being that legalized abortion had a long-term impact on the crime rate. Science can't answer questions of morality; those types of questions are best addressed through the political and legal systems.

One can't say that morality has no place in science. In fact, ethics are very important in the conduct of science. If science isn't conducted in a scrupulous manner it will bear questionable results. The outcomes of scientific processes must be reported as accurately and as objectively as possible. Although it's rare, scientists are occasionally found intentionally fudging their results. Such scientists are discredited by peers, and ultimately lose all credibility within their fields.

Supernatural Phenomena

Recall the example from earlier in the chapter concerning a hypothetical man who believes that his car keys may have been stolen by leprechauns. An assertion like that can't be tested using any kind of scientific process because it involves an element of the supernatural. Many people believe wholeheartedly in supernatural phenomena. In some cultures, the majority of people believe in certain supernatural beings and events. By definition such phenomena can't be tested; it's the lack of scientific proof that makes them "supernatural." Science can't prove or disprove the existence of leprechauns, ghosts, fairies, Bigfoot/abominable snowman creatures, or any kind of deity.

Assumptions and Biases

All scientific studies are subject to certain assumptions the researchers make when conducting them. Scientific models are simplifications of the world, and simplifying any aspect of the real world requires some simplifying of assumptions. Sometimes those assumptions are valid and lead to reliable results, but other times the assumptions are faulty. Trends are a good example. It's not uncommon for scientists in some fields to assume that future events will follow trends, based on historical data. A demographer might consider projecting future population figures based on the population growth rate from the previous twenty or thirty or fifty years. But some factors change over time that affect the population growth rate, such as the fertility rate, the infant mortality rate, life expectancy, and so on. Many of those changes have occurred as a result of cultural shifts or advancements in technology. Even in the life sciences and physical sciences, assumptions are sometimes made that lead to faulty research results. For any field of science to advance, its underlying assumptions must be chosen with care and improved upon where possible.

At times, the assumptions scientists make are influenced by cultural or personal biases. These biases may affect the way some scientists frame research questions, or their interpretations of the results. It's not uncommon for scientists to approach a research question anticipating a particular answer, or an answer that lies within a given range of possibilities. If a researcher in a particular field discovers a result outside of that expected range of possibilities, he may dismiss the result as inconsequential when in fact the result may have been important. Scientists should always strive to remain objective and to make reasonable assumptions; their research is weakened when they fail to do so.

ESSENTIAL

Pseudoscience is any set of beliefs or practices that has the appearance of being scientific, but in fact lacks scientific foundation. Pseudoscience includes claims that aren't provable, or that have yet to be proven. To cite an example, some "experts" assert that aliens visited the earth long ago and built ancient civilizations on the planet. Although such assertions may be entertaining, they lack scientific evidence. Some pseudoscience, despite having no scientific merit whatsoever, is widely regarded as fact among the general population.

Despite its limitations, the scientific method has endured for centuries thanks to the millions of insights and advances it has yielded. Without the advent of the scientific method, the pursuit of scientific knowledge would not have followed the trajectory it has. Human life would not be the same as you know it today. The scientific method has become so embedded in the research practices of scientists in all fields that it's impossible to imagine what scientific endeavor would be like without it.

CHAPTER 2

Everyday Physics

Physics is everywhere around you. You have always had a direct experience of it, even if you were not aware. You've experienced physics every time you sat in a bathtub full of water, every time you moved a box or heavy object, any time you've played with a ball. Even when you've tuned in to the evening news to hear the weather, you've heard physics splashed all over that forecast. This chapter will help you explore some examples of physics, some of which show up right in your own home.

Pressure, Temperature, and the Weather

If you've ever been in a crowd of people trying to exit a place very quickly (like when there is an emergency), you know about pressure. You might also know that it feels hotter when there are so many people pushing through a door or a gate. This is exactly how the air molecules "feel" when the pressure is high: The heat is turned on (the temperature goes up).

VOCAB

Pressure: Pressure is the amount of force applied to a surface area.

But what happens when the pressure is low? Does the temperature go down?

Try This Experiment

MATERIALS NEEDED:
- Balloons (have several handy in case one pops)
- Freezer
- Video camera to document the event (optional)

PROCEDURE:
1. Ask your child to inflate a balloon using your own breath. Make sure he inflates to a point where the balloon is stretched to the limit without popping. (You might need to do this more than once if the balloon pops.)
2. Place the balloon on an empty rack in the freezer for at least 24 hours.
3. Remove the balloon from the freezer. If you are videotaping, start filming the balloon before you remove it from the freezer. What do you observe?

Does the balloon look different than when you first placed it in the freezer? Does it look smaller and wrinkly? What begins to happen to it the instant you pull it out of the freezer and into the warmer environment of your kitchen? Does the balloon begin to expand back to the size it was when you first put it in the freezer?

If you have videotaped the entire event, you can replay that video rather than place the balloon back in the freezer for another 24 hours to see the effect again.

In order to understand the relationship between temperature and pressure, you need to zoom down to the level of the air molecules inside the balloon.

QUESTION

What is a molecule?
A *molecule* is made of two or more atoms (the smallest building block in nature). For example, an oxygen molecule is made of two oxygen atoms that are bonded together. When you breathe in oxygen, you are breathing oxygen molecules. A water molecule is made of one oxygen atom bonded with two hydrogen atoms.

You can think of the air molecules as little balls constantly moving and bouncing off each other. They also bounce off the inside wall of the balloon. The arrows in the drawing show the motion of the air molecules. When those molecules bounce off the walls of the balloon, they apply pressure to it.

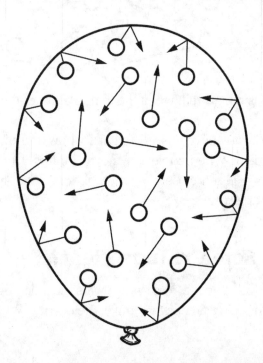

What does it mean to apply pressure? When you press against a surface, you apply pressure. For example, if you stand on a trampoline, you are applying pressure (or force) to the surface of the trampoline. You can see the effect of that pressure on the trampoline because its surface stretches down.

Similarly, the air molecules press against the balloon surface as they bounce off it. This pressure makes the balloon stretch out.

Once inside the freezer, the air inside the balloon cools down. When the air is cooler, its molecules don't move around and bounce as much. They basically slow down and get closer to one another. They're cold! In a way, they're like you when you're cold: You just want to move less and cuddle close to someone. Notice how the arrows in the drawing get smaller, showing a slower motion of the air molecules. And when they slow down, they're not bouncing as hard off each other and off the balloon surface. They don't push as hard. This makes the balloon less inflated.

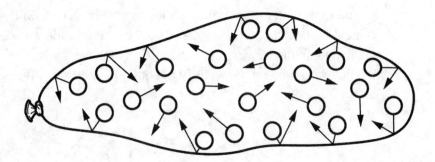

This means that when the temperature of the air goes down, so does its pressure.

Do you think this is similar to how the air behaves in the weather? Absolutely. When cooler air moves in, it is usually accompanied with low pressure. Listen closely to what the forecaster says next time you hear the weather forecast.

Why Do Some Things Float?

When you throw a rock in the water, it sinks. But huge, heavy objects like ships float in water as they travel the oceans. Why is that?

It is all about buoyancy. But what is buoyancy? And what factors have an effect on buoyancy?

QUESTION

What is the name of the scientist who figured out buoyancy? Archimedes was a Greek scientist who lived in the third century B.C. He was the first scientist to understand buoyancy and how to apply it to real-life dilemmas that required solutions. For example, using his understanding of buoyancy, Archimedes was able to detect that the king's crown was not made of pure gold, but was mixed with a cheaper metal like silver.

When an object is placed in a fluid like water, the object is pushed up by a force from within the water called the *buoyancy force*. There is more than one factor that makes the buoyancy force larger or smaller. One such factor that you can investigate here is the surface area with which the object touches the fluid. The following experiment will help your child specifically explore the relationship between the buoyancy force and the surface area of an object placed in water.

Try This Experiment

MATERIALS NEEDED:
- Aluminum foil roll
- Big plastic tub 14" (L) × 14" (W) × 6" (H)
- Vise grip
- Pliers
- Scissors

PROCEDURE:
1. Using scissors, cut 2 sheets of aluminum foil that are 12" × 7".
2. Assist your child in filling the tub about ¾ full with water.
3. Give your child 1 of the aluminum foil sheets. Carefully help her place the flat sheet on top of the water. Take caution not to bend the sheet so that you don't let any water float on top of the sheet. What do you both observe?

4. Now let your child crumple the second aluminum sheet into the tiniest ball she can muster. Then, using the vise grip and the pliers, assist her in squeezing the aluminum foil ball down to an even tinier ball. Keep squeezing it until it becomes a small ball with a diameter of no more than ½".

5. Have your child place the ball of crumpled aluminum on top of the water. What do you both observe?

Did the aluminum sheet float? What about the aluminum ball? Did it sink? Why do you suppose they behaved differently even though they're made of the same material (aluminum foil)? Ask your child what the difference is between the flat and the crumpled aluminum foil. Remind her they were identical to start with; they were the same size and are made of the same stuff. Does she think it matters that the flat sheet has a larger surface than the crumpled one?

If she guesses yes to that last question, she is absolutely right. The crumpled aluminum ball sinks straight to the bottom of the tub. The flat sheet, with its larger surface area, floats on top of the water.

Take a few moments to consider and discuss how the water influences the flat sheet as it floats on top of it. The water pushes up on every part of the sheet's surface. This is the buoyancy force. The larger the sheet's surface the water can push against, the more *distributed* the force is over that surface, as shown in the picture, and the larger the buoyancy force.

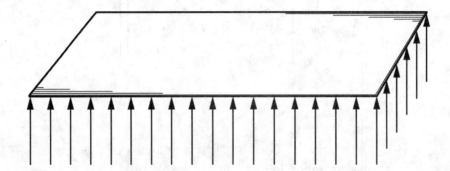

When the aluminum foil is crumpled to the size of a small ball, the water can only push up against a tiny, tiny surface area. The smaller the surface the water can push against, the smaller the buoyancy force.

As long as the upward buoyancy force on an object is equal to the weight of the object, it will float. That's exactly why ships have a large surface area. The buoyancy force pushing the ship up—so it can stay at the surface—must be just as big as the weight of the ship, or else it would sink.

How a Magnifying Glass Works

Gazing through the glass of a magnifying lens makes tiny things look bigger. Letters on a page appear much larger, and the eye of a needle becomes easier to see. Magnifying lenses come in different strengths; some can magnify a little, and some can magnify a lot. But if a magnifying lens is made of glass, what is the difference between it and the glass of a window? And why do you have to hold the lens a certain distance from the object? What else can you do with a magnifying glass that's fun?

Look closely at a magnifying glass and you'll notice how the front and the back of it bulge out; both surfaces of the lens have an outward curvature. This type of lens is called a *convex* lens, which is thicker at the center of the lens than its edges.

VOCAB

Convex: Something that is convex has a surface that is curved outwardly similar to the way a sphere is.

If you look closely at the glass of a window, you'll notice those surfaces do not bulge out. They are totally flat. When placing a sheet of paper with written words on it behind a window, the letters don't seem any bigger.

The difference in glass in terms of magnification (or not) is the bulge in the surface. Only a convex lens can magnify letters. This is true only if you hold the paper with the words (or the object to be magnified) closer than a specific distance beyond the lens. If you hold the object further from the lens, it becomes a blur. What is this special distance from the lens behind which objects look blurry? It is called the *focal length*. This length measures how far the focal point of a lens is from the center of the lens. And the focal point (on either side of the lens) focuses all the light coming through the lens.

Here is how the focal point works. Imagine the light coming in from the left side of the lens. The curved surface the light arrives at bends the light toward a point that focuses that light. That's why it is called the focal point.

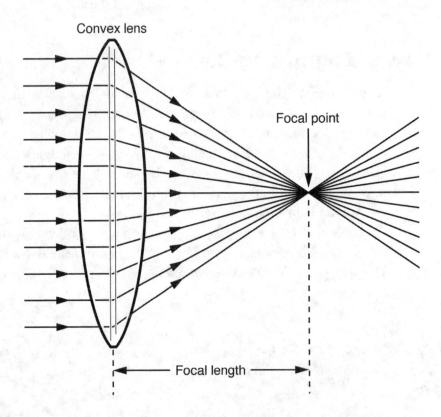

Here is the trick for using a magnifying glass to make small things have a larger appearance. You must hold it such that the object you are attempting to magnify is between the lens and its focal point. But how do you determine where the focal point of a convex lens is?

QUESTION

Is there another name for a convex lens?
The other name is a converging lens. The name is given to this type of lens because, as light passes through a convex lens, it bends the light rays toward each other. The bent light rays converge, or meet at a single point (the focal point) on the other side of the lens.

Try This Experiment

MATERIALS NEEDED:
- 1 sheet of printer paper
- 1 matchstick
- 1 magnifying glass (convex lens)

You will need to have your child do this experiment on a sunny summer day at exactly noon.

PROCEDURE:

1. Assist your child in holding the paper underneath the lens of the magnifying glass. This might need two hands. Point out to him how the sun's bright disk forms a circular image on the paper.
2. Now tell your child to move the lens closer to the paper, then further from the paper. Ask him to notice how the bright circle on the paper gets bigger and smaller.
3. Help your child move the lens such that the bright circle on the paper becomes the smallest it can be, almost a point. Once that point is identified, hold the paper still. What do you both observe happening?
4. Eyeball the distance between the lens and the paper when the bright circle has become a pinpoint.
5. Put the paper down, and switch to holding the matchstick for your child. Help him place the center of the lens above the head of the matchstick so that it is at about the distance you eyeballed in the previous step. Hold the matchstick steady. What do you both observe?

Your findings might be startling at first because you'll see the paper begin to turn brown at that one spot where the sun's rays coming through the lens were focused. If you held the lens over the paper longer, the brown spot would light up as the paper starts to burn. The same happens with the matchstick when you hold the head of the match right at the focal point of the lens! Because it is tiny, like a point, the head of the matchstick helps you pinpoint exactly where the focal point of the magnifying glass is.

Here is something your child can do with a magnifying glass that's fun. The next time you visit the hardware store, buy some balsa wood. On the next sunny day, take your child outside with his magnifying glass and the balsa wood and help him etch some fun shapes onto the wood. Your child might end up with a beautiful piece of artwork made by the sunlight, crafted by a lens.

Balloons, Spoons, and Density

When you throw a penny in the water, it sinks. But when you throw in a twig, it floats. Even if the wood is much larger than the penny—say a log—the wooden log still floats. Why is that?

It is all about the density of the material you're using.

One way you might test the density of a material is by squeezing it. If it takes more effort to compress it when you squeeze it, it is denser. For example, a metal toolbox is far denser than a loaf of bread.

Is there a more scientific way to test the density of material rather than trying to squish it? Indeed there is. Here is the bottom line for the method of measuring density: When you attempt to place an object in a cup full of water, depending on the object's density, it will spill more or less water. This phenomenon happens because everything occupies a certain amount of space. The water in the cup occupies the entire space inside the cup. If you attempt to add more things into that space, some of the water has to spill— be displaced.

Try This Experiment

MATERIALS NEEDED:
- Several different-sized rocks (a size that fits in your fist, some slightly smaller, some slightly larger)
- Child's rubber duck
- Electronic kitchen scale (with a "grams" setting available)
- Bucket
- Plastic tub the bucket can easily fit into
- 2 measuring containers or glasses
- Water hose connected to a faucet
- Pencil and paper

VOCAB

Mass: Mass is a measure of how much matter is in an object. Mass is measured in grams, the abbreviation for which is g.

PROCEDURE:

1. Ask your child to place the kitchen scale on a flat surface, then turn it on. Make sure the scale is set to the "grams" setting. Make sure to tare (reset to zero) the scale properly.
2. Have your child place the rubber duck onto the scale. Ask her to record, in grams, the mass of the duck on her paper. For example, *25 g.*
3. Have your child place each of the rocks on the scale one by one, measuring and recording the mass of each one of them, also in grams.
4. Ask your child to choose the rock that has a mass close to that of the rubber duck. Have her set the other rocks aside so she doesn't accidentally use them.
5. Have your child place the bucket into the plastic tub, and place the tub on the ground. Using the water hose, your child can now fill the bucket with water to the very top. You can assist her in filling the bucket so that no water spills out of it. It is important that the water reaches the very top of the bucket, to the point just before it spills.
6. Using the chosen rock, ask your child to drop the rock inside the bucket. Ask her to observe whether the water spills out of the bucket. Assist your child in emptying the spilled water from the tub into one of the measuring containers.
7. Ask your child to pull the rock out and place the bucket back into the tub. Assist her in refilling the bucket to the very top without overfilling it.
8. Have your child take the rubber duck and submerge it totally into the bucket by pushing it down with her hand just far enough to where the duck's head is just below the surface of the water. Ask her to observe whether the water spills out of the bucket into the tub. Assist your child in emptying the spilled water from the tub into one of the measuring containers.

VOCAB

Was there water that spilled out when the rock went into the bucket? What about when the rubber duck was submerged? Check the two water levels in the two measuring containers. Was it the same amount of water in both cases? Which one displaced more water out of the bucket, the rock or rubber duck?

Your child most likely figured out that the rubber duck displaces far more water than the rock. The rubber duck has a mass similar to a rock, so it must be something else about the rubber duck that made more water spill. Ask your child what she thinks is different about the rubber duck than the rock. Is it perhaps the material it is made of? Is it possibly its size (volume)?

If she guessed yes to either of those two questions, then she guessed right. Discuss with your child the answer to the first question. The duck is made of rubber, but the rock is made of a material called silicates. Rubber is not as dense as rock. In other words, the density of rock is much greater than that of rubber. The greater the density, the more matter is *compacted* into the object. For example, the density of the rubber in the duck is about 0.5 g/cm^3, while the density of rock is well over 2 g/cm^3.

Now discuss with your child the answer to the second question, the one pertaining to the size of the two objects. Because the densities of rubber and rock are different, the sizes (volumes) of the rubber duck and the rock have to be much different in order for their masses to be the same. Recall that you had your child pick the rock that measured closest in mass to the duck, using the kitchen scale. The greater the density of an object is, the smaller its size. The rock has a much greater density; that's why its size is smaller than the rubber duck.

Since the size of the duck is larger than the rock, this means it would need to displace more water if it is going to sit in the space inside the bucket. Stated differently, the rubber duck takes up a lot more space than the rock does. So when you submerge it, it has to move more water out in order to make room for itself. The rock doesn't need to move as much water out.

The denser an object is the less water it displaces when it is submerged than an object with lesser density but equal mass.

What is the density of water?
Water has a density of 1 g/cm³. This means there is one gram of mass—which is a measure of how much "stuff" water is made of—in a volume of one cubic centimeter of water.

So why does a penny sink in water when a wooden log floats? When a material has density greater than that of water, it sinks. Copper's density is almost 9 g/cm³, much greater than the density of water. When a material has density less than the density of water, it floats. The density of most wood is under 1 g/cm³.

You can test the density of other things compared to water. Drop a spoon in the water bucket. If it sinks, its density is greater than water's density. Drop an inflated balloon in the water bucket. You will find that it floats on top of the water. That's because the air inside the balloon (if you discount the thin walls of the balloon) is much less dense than water. The density of air is very close to zero in density (0.001225 g/cm³)!

Searching for Newton

You might have heard the phrase "for every action there is an equal and opposite reaction." This statement spells out Newton's third law. If you wonder where in your daily life can you observe this principle, here are a few hints: Newton's third law is what makes a space shuttle fly up away from the earth, and it is also what makes you able to stand up from a seated position. So how does this principle work?

ESSENTIAL

The *law of force pairs* is what we call Newton's third law. This is because when a first object acts on a second object with a force, the second object automatically does the same back, but in the opposite direction. Specifically, the force from Object 1 cannot show up on its own without the opposite force from Object 2 showing up as well. They are always *paired*.

Try This Experiment

MATERIALS NEEDED:
- 1 balloon
- Masking tape
- 1 drinking straw
- 1 bag clip sealer

PROCEDURE:
1. Tell your child to insert the straw about 1½" into the neck of the balloon.
2. Assist your child in securing the straw at the opening of the balloon, so that the opening is totally taped onto the straw with no gaps.
3. Tell your child to blow through the straw to inflate the balloon so that it is full to its maximum.
4. Once the balloon is fully inflated, help your child clip the straw with the clip sealer so that the air is sealed tight inside the balloon.
5. Ask your child to stand at one end of a long table or wooden floor (a hallway is ideal), and place the balloon so that the straw is lined up parallel to the length of the hall or table.
6. Now tell your child to block the end of the straw with her finger to prevent the air from escaping, and release the clip sealer. Ready, set . . . tell her to let go. What do you both observe?

Did the balloon move along the floor like it had a small turbo engine attached to it? Well, in a way it does! But what exactly happened? Here is where Newton's third law comes to the rescue.

When the air inside the balloon begins to release and move out through the straw, the air is actually being forced out by the balloon's deflation. In other words, the balloon pushes the air out. This is the *action* force. The *reaction* force is the force that the air pushes back on the balloon, so the balloon begins to move. Those two action and reaction forces are what Newton's third law is all about. Without the *reaction* force showing up, the balloon would never have moved!

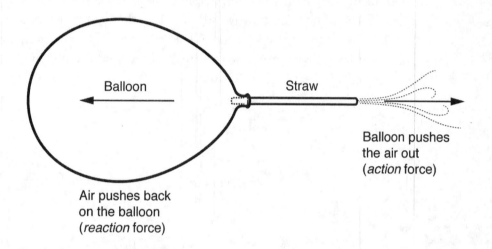

Balloon

Straw

Balloon pushes the air out (*action* force)

Air pushes back on the balloon (*reaction* force)

This is exactly how the space shuttle is able to move up into the sky. The engine attached to the shuttle pushes the exhaust gases out <u>downwardly</u> (*action*). In response, the gases push back <u>upwardly</u> on the shuttle and its attached engine (*reaction*). The *action* force acts *on the gases* as they are being expelled downward, and the *reaction* force acts *on the shuttle* being propelled upward.

QUESTION

What is Newton's cradle?
Newton's cradle is a set of steel balls (often five or seven balls) that are hanging right next to each other at the same height. When you lift an end ball off to the side then release it, it strikes the ball adjacent to it, transferring the action and reaction forces to the ball on the far end. That ball, in turn, moves off to the side.

Here is another example from your everyday life where you will find Newton's third law at work. Next time you find yourself attempting to stand up from being seated in a chair, become aware of Newton's third law *action* and *reaction* force pairs. As you attempt to stand, you actually push downward on the floor with your feet. This is the *action*. The *reaction* is that the floor pushes back on your feet, helping you to stand up. Think about this: If your feet were pushing downward on a floor that can't push back up, like a thick layer of mud, would you be able to stand up? If the floor's *reaction* that pushes back on your feet were to vanish, you would be stuck in your chair!

CHAPTER 3

The Physics of Moving Objects

Moving objects are everywhere around you. You walk down the sidewalk alongside other pedestrians, a skateboarder passes you as you're riding your bicycle, you catch a ride in an automobile through heavy traffic, maybe you even take to the skies in an airplane. Floating kites, swimming fish, skidding tires, robotic arms . . . all the movement you see in the world is physics in action. All movement occurs according to a few basic principles. This chapter will help you explore some of those basic but important principles.

Racing Juice Cans

According to Newton's first law, when an object is in motion it wants to stay in that same motion, unless a force acts on it to make it change. This also means that if an object is *not* moving, it wants to remain still unless a force acts on it. For example, if you place an ice cube on a horizontal surface—perhaps in a baking pan on your kitchen countertop—it will stay put. But if you tilt the pan and let the force of gravity act on the cube, it will most definitely move.

QUESTION

Who was Isaac Newton?
Sir Isaac Newton was an English physicist and mathematician who is considered by many physicists to be the father of classical physics. He was born in England in 1643 and died in 1727. He was once sitting under an apple tree when an apple fell on his head and led him to formulate the universal law of gravitation.

It's a property of matter to want to keep moving if already in motion, or to remain still if it's not moving. In other words, when it comes down to motion or stillness, matter always, always, always *resists* change.

The motion of the ice cube moving across the baking pan is called sliding, or translational, motion. But what if an object rolls instead of slides? Does Newton's first law still apply? A simple experiment will yield the answer.

Try This Experiment

MATERIALS NEEDED:
- 2 identical cans of frozen fruit juice concentrate
- 1 wooden board 1.5' × 4'
- Stack of books or magazines

The question this experiment will investigate is whether matter—in this case, the juice inside the can—resists change in its motion more when it's in liquid form or when it's in solid form. The real question is whether it's easier for the juice to go downhill when it's *sliding* inside the can because it's a liquid, or when it's *rolling* with the can because the juice is frozen.

To prepare for the experiment, keep one of the frozen fruit juice concentrate cans in the freezer, and allow the other to sit on your countertop for a day so that it completely thaws.

When the cans are ready, prop the wooden board up on one end using a stack of books or magazines. This will create the incline necessary for racing the two cans.

Before proceeding with the experiment, ask your child to make a prediction about the results. Which do you think will reach the bottom of the incline first, the frozen juice or the liquid juice? Remember that the frozen juice will *roll* down the incline, while the liquid juice will *slide* inside the can. Talk with your child about how this could impact the movement of the cans.

After you've made your prediction, place the two cans side by side at the top of the incline. Use a ruler to line up the two cans so that when you remove the ruler, the cans will begin their downhill descent at the same time.

Ready . . . set . . . let go!

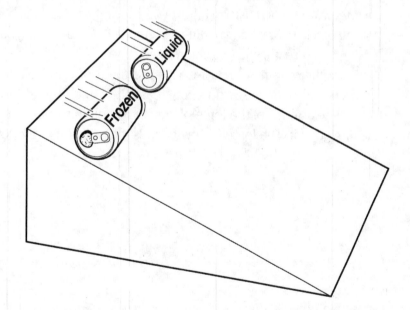

The result might surprise you both. You might have predicted that the frozen can would reach the bottom first, but it turns out to be the opposite!

Since the liquid juice can reaches the bottom faster, the conclusion can be made that it's easier for the juice to *slide* inside the can than it is to *roll* inside the can. Since it's easier for the can containing the liquid juice to get to the bottom, the conclusion can also be made that the liquid-juice can resists change in its motion *less* than the frozen-juice can.

The result of this experiment reveals that it's easier to slide than to roll, which is something you can definitely feel when a car's tires lock up and start sliding on an icy road.

Repeat the racing juice cans experiment for a friend or family member. See if your friend or family member can predict which juice will win the race.

The Physics of Floating Feathers

If you've ever dropped a feather, you've noticed that it seems to float or sway in the air as it falls to the ground. Most other objects, such as books and toys and keys, don't behave the same way when dropped. Why do feathers appear to float or sway when many other objects don't?

To answer this question, it's first necessary to understand the concept of a force. When you push on a box, you're using a force. When you pull on the string of a kite, or when you lift up a cup of water, or when you blow bubbles using your breath, you're using a force.

Another example of a force is the force of gravity. Earth pulls on all objects with a downward force—that's the force of gravity. Your child can test the existence of the force of gravity by holding a pencil in her hand and letting go of it. The force of gravity pulls the pencil straight down.

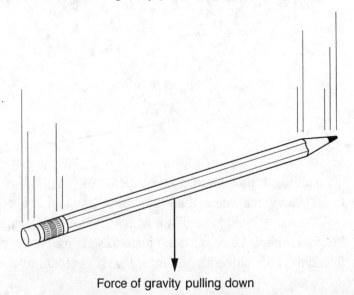

Force of gravity pulling down

Consider what happens to another object—say a box resting on the floor—when you exert a force on it by pushing it. If the box is initially at rest, it begins to move and gains velocity. When the box goes from not moving to moving, its velocity changes. When any object goes from not moving to moving, physicists say it accelerates. In other words, the object's velocity *changes*; it goes from having no velocity to having some velocity. Therefore, it can be said that *acceleration* is the *change* in velocity.

QUESTION

What is velocity?
Velocity is a measurement of both the speed of an object and the direction it is moving in. A moving object has velocity. A nonmoving object has no velocity. When a car is moving at 60 mph, that number is referring to how fast the car is moving, or the car's speed. However, when you say the car is moving at 60 mph heading north, you are reporting both how *fast* as well as the *direction* the car is moving. You are reporting velocity.

Sometimes people confuse the concept of velocity with the concept of momentum. Velocity of an object has to do with how fast it's moving. *Momentum* is related not only to how fast the object is moving, but also to how massive the object is. A truck moving at 60 mph has a lot more momentum than a car moving at 60 mph because the truck has a greater mass. Just be aware that velocity and momentum are not the same concepts.

What caused the box, or the pencil, to accelerate? According to Newton's second law, the force of the push (on the box), or the force of gravity (on the pencil) causes the object to change its velocity, or to accelerate.

ESSENTIAL

Newton's second law states that when a force acts on an object, it causes the object to accelerate. When you push on a box, you exert a force on it. If the box is initially not moving, it begins to move. The force of the push causes the object to accelerate, or change its velocity.

A simple experiment will shed light on the reason feathers sway or seem to float as they fall toward the ground, while objects like pencils don't. Instead of using feathers, you can use something easier to find around the house.

Try This Experiment

MATERIALS NEEDED:
- 2 sheets of paper 8.5" × 11"

PROCEDURE:
1. Give your child one of the sheets of paper. Have him hold it horizontally about 4 feet above the ground, then let go. Observe how the flat sheet of paper sways, or appears to float, as it falls toward the ground.
2. Now take the other sheet of paper, have him crumple it to the tiniest ball he can, hold it about 4 feet above the ground, and let go. What did you both observe?

Did the crumpled sheet of paper fall to the ground in the same manner as the flat sheet? Why do you suppose they behaved differently, even though they're made of the same material (paper)?

Here's a hint: Ask your child what the difference is between the flat sheet and the crumpled sheet of paper. Remind him that they were identical to start with, and they're both made of the same material. Do you think it matters that the flat sheet has a larger surface than the crumpled one?

If he answered yes to that last question, he is absolutely right. It does indeed matter that the flat sheet has a larger surface than the crumpled sheet. The crumpled sheet of paper falls straight to the ground—no sway whatsoever. The flat sheet, with its larger surface area, sways or "floats" as it's falling to the ground.

Take a few moments to consider and discuss the forces influencing the flat sheet as it falls. It's already been established that the force of gravity pulls the sheet down. However, while the sheet is falling through the air, another force comes into play. This other force is the force of the air that pushes upward against every part of the paper's surface. It's the very same force that pushes up on a skydiver's parachute. If the surface of the flat sheet is larger, the air can push up more. This force that involves the air pushing upwardly is called *air resistance*.

If you look at the two forces acting on the sheet of paper (shown in the following diagram), you'll notice that the two forces are acting in opposite directions.

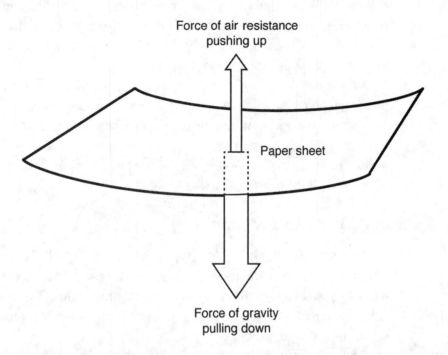

Force of air resistance
pushing up

Paper sheet

Force of gravity
pulling down

QUESTION

How does Newton's second law work if there is more than one force? In tug of war, the object getting pulled is the rope. It's being pulled to the right and to the left at the same time, so it is experiencing two opposite forces. If the rope is pulled with equal forces from both sides, it doesn't move. But if one team—say the team on the right— pulls slightly harder, then there is a difference between the two pulls. The difference between the two opposing forces is small and points in the favor of the direction of the bigger force (to the right). That difference is what causes the team on the right to begin accelerating—to change their velocity from not moving to moving. The bigger the difference between the two opposing forces, the bigger the acceleration and the faster the change in velocity.

When you're playing tug of war, if one team pulls *slightly* harder than the other, that team will make everyone begin to move in their direction *slowly*. It's exactly the same with the two opposite forces of gravity and air resistance. When the force of gravity is *slightly* bigger than the force of air resistance, the object's velocity changes in the direction of the bigger force *slowly*—that is, the flat sheet sways, or seems to float, as it falls to the ground. The same principle applies to a falling feather.

When you crumple the sheet of paper, the surface area the air can push against becomes smaller, reducing the force of air resistance. With the crumpled sheet, the force of gravity is *much* bigger than the force of air resistance, and it will pull harder, making the crumpled paper fall to the ground *faster*. This is also why a pencil falls straight to the ground when it's dropped instead of swaying or floating like a feather.

Falling Objects in a Vacuum

What do you think would happen if you tried the flat paper/crumpled paper experiment in vacuum? A *vacuum* is a space that has no air or other gases in it, so in a vacuum there wouldn't be any air pushing upward against the sheet of flat paper. What would happen to the force of air resistance? Do you think it would disappear?

The force of air resistance would indeed disappear. Both the flat and the crumpled paper would fall only due to the pull of gravity, which is the same for both. This means that both the flat and the crumpled paper would reach the floor at the same time.

You can easily find a coin-and-feather clear plastic vacuum tube on the Internet to demonstrate to your child how both a feather (light object) and a coin (heavy metal object) reach the bottom together when the air is evacuated from the tube. When air resistance is removed, there is nothing left to make the motion of a falling object slower.

Follow the Bouncing Ball

You've probably enjoyed playing with a super bouncing ball at some point in your life—maybe your child has a few of them around the house. They're those small rubber balls that fit in your fist and bounce high when you throw them onto the floor. Do all balls made of rubber have a bounce? Can anything else come out of the bounce besides a whole lot of fun? To answer these questions, all you need to do is follow the bouncing ball.

Try This Experiment

For this experiment you'll need some material from the hardware store and a pair of rubber balls commonly known as the "happy" and "unhappy" balls (you can easily find them by searching the web). Once you purchase a pair of these rubber balls, you're ready to explore the power of the bounce.

MATERIALS NEEDED:
- Pair of happy and unhappy rubber balls
- 2 wooden blocks 2" × 4" × 12"
- 2 small eye screw hooks
- 2-yard length of string
- Adjustable spring-tension curtain rod (approximately 24" to 36")
- Red fingernail polish

First, check for the bounce in the happy and unhappy rubber balls. Ask your child to stand on a wooden or vinyl floor, and place a ball in each hand. Have her hold both hands at the same height, then release both balls at the same time. Notice what happens to each ball. Do they both bounce back up once they hit the floor?

By now you've figured out that not all rubber balls behave the same way. One of these balls has bounce, while the other doesn't. Using the red fingernail polish, have your child paint a smiley face on the happy ball that bounces, and let it dry. Then try the following procedure with her, which demonstrates what that bounce can do.

PROCEDURE:
1. Hang the curtain rod tightly in a doorway above a wooden or vinyl floor, about 45" from the floor.
2. Help your child screw the small eye screw hook into each of the balls.
3. Cut the string into two 1-yard lengths, and tie each string to the screw hook on each ball.

4. Tie the loose ends of the strings onto the curtain rod, leaving 8" of space between the hanging strings. Make sure both balls hang at the same height from the rod, so that the final lengths of the hanging strings are the same.
5. Place the wooden blocks on the wooden or vinyl floor in front of each ball. Stand the blocks vertically upright on the smallest base. Make sure the height of each ball is such that it faces the upper segment of the wooden block in front of it.
6. Pull back both balls, keeping their strings stretched straight, until the strings are parallel to the ground.
7. Release both balls at the same time so that they swing together forward and strike the blocks in front of them simultaneously.

Which ball tips its block forward: the happy one with the smiley face or the unhappy one? Which ball bounces back? Do you think the bounce has something to do with tipping the block?

As your child will discover, the bouncing ball is the one that tips the block forward. And yes, the secret of the happy ball's tipping ability lies in its bounce. The happy ball bounces because it's slightly squished when it strikes the block. This is much like a tennis ball when it strikes a surface. You can easily find a video on the web of a bouncing tennis ball filmed in slow motion, which allows your child to see the squishing effect.

VOCAB

When a rubber ball or a tennis ball gets squished and bounces back, the ball is said to be elastic. Another way of stating it is to say that the ball has *elasticity*.

When the ball is squished, it acts much like a spring when you compress it. If you compress a spring then let go of it, it bounces straight back. When the squished, happy ball bounces back, it pushes harder on the block than the unhappy one that doesn't get squished and doesn't bounce. So the happy ball tips the block as a result of the crash, while the unhappy ball absorbs the crash.

The happy and unhappy balls are clearly both made of rubber, but they're made of different types of rubber. The bouncing happy ball is made of a synthetic rubber known as neoprene. This type of rubber acts like a spring that quickly returns to its original shape once it's compressed. Neoprene is used to make divers' wetsuits. The nonbouncing unhappy ball is made of another type of synthetic rubber known as Norsorex. This type of rubber doesn't quickly return to its original shape once it's compressed. It's used as crash-absorbing material, often worn by motorcyclists.

The *law of conservation of energy* states that energy cannot be created out of nothing and energy cannot vanish into nothing. Energy can only transform from one form to another.

QUESTION

What are some examples of conservation of energy?
When you turn on a light bulb, the electrical energy in the wires transforms into light and heat that warm up the bulb. When you eat breakfast, the chemical energy in the food is transformed into heat to keep your body warm at the average temperature of 98.6°F.

Both the happy and unhappy balls have kinetic energy when they strike the wooden blocks. *Kinetic energy* is moving energy. The word "kinetic" indicates that the energy results from movement. The energy of the squishy happy ball tips the block as the ball bounces back. In terms of the law of conservation of energy, the ball's kinetic energy is transformed into energy that's stored momentarily in the "squish," then released to tip the block. In contrast, the kinetic energy of the unhappy ball is converted into heat that dissipates into the air, which is why the nonsquishy ball comes to a full stop.

QUESTION

What is dissipated energy?
When energy is dissipated, it transforms into a form that can't be gathered again for further use. Energy typically dissipates as heat. For example, when you rub your hands together, all the energy you put into rubbing your hands turns into heat that dissipates. You can't gather all the heat from rubbing your hands and reuse it for some other purpose.

The Inertia of Ice Cubes

Your child has probably played with toy cars at some time in his life, but has he ever played with ice cubes? Some toy cars come with a remote control to help you steer the car and make it curve. But can you control the motion of an ice cube? Can you make it move along a curve?

Try the following activity to teach your child about the concept of *inertia* using ice cubes and other common household items.

VOCAB

Inertia is an inherent property of matter (the "stuff" objects are made of) that makes matter *resist changing* its state of motion or rest. In other words, if an object is moving, it doesn't want to change the way it is moving. If an object is not moving, then it wants to stay still.

Try This Experiment

MATERIALS NEEDED:
- Long smooth metal tray
- Dark juice, such as grape or pomegranate juice
- Ice cube tray
- Paper towels

PROCEDURE:
1. Fill the ice cube tray with grape or pomegranate juice and allow it to freeze overnight. Get one of the juice ice cubes out of the freezer and let it sit for 10 minutes; the cube should be slightly thawed for the experiment. (Make sure to use a bowl to thaw the ice cube because the juice could possibly stain the countertop, depending on its concentration.)
2. Have your child place the metal tray on a flat surface, and place the ice cube on it. Does the ice cube move?
3. Now, have him give the ice cube a push with his hand and let go of it. Note how the ice cube moves.
4. Examine the juicy track the ice cube left along its path. What is the shape of that track? Is it a straight line? Is there a way he can make the motion

of the ice cube trace a curve rather than a straight line by giving it a different push?

5. Wipe the tray clean and place it flat on a flat surface again.

6. Have your child give the ice cube a curved push and let go. Examine the trace of juice from the point where his hand left the ice cube. Is the trace straight or curved?

7. Repeat the experiment ten times after wiping the tray clean every time. How many times was the juice trace straight from the point after which his hand stopped touching the ice cube?

Newton's first law states that when an object is in motion, it stays in motion along the same line of motion when there are no unbalanced forces acting on it. When your child lets go of the ice cube, there are no unbalanced forces acting on it, and it can slide freely. The ice cube continues moving in the same direction it was moving when he released it. The *inertia* of the ice cube is what makes it resist changing that direction.

This is the same experience a car has when driven on icy roads the instant its wheels lock and it begins to slide. Once the car starts sliding, it will continue to move in the direction it started sliding, regardless of how the driver moves the steering wheel, just like the motion of the ice cube!

The Velocity of Bowling Balls

Bowling balls are the heaviest balls used in any sport. If you're a small person, you might wonder why there aren't small bowling balls to match your tiny physique. But the truth is that you can't play the game with a small, light ball.

To begin to understand the physics involved in a game of bowling, you must first know something about forces. There are two forces that act on a bowling ball when it's placed on a level wooden floor (such as a bowling lane). There is the force of gravity pulling the ball down, but there's also the force of the floor pushing the ball up to support it.

If the floor weren't hard—if it were made of Jell-O, say—it wouldn't be able to push the ball up hard enough. The force of gravity and the force of the wooden floor are equal in strength, but opposite in direction (one is up and the other is down), so they balance each other and the ball just sits there. If the floor were pushing up harder than the force of gravity pulling down, the ball would float up. Or if the force of gravity were stronger than the force of the floor, the ball would sink into the floor.

What forces affect the bowling ball after you throw it down the bowling lane? Believe it or not, they're exactly the same forces that affect the ball when it's just sitting on the floor or lane. Once the ball leaves your hand and is rolling down the lane, there's the force of gravity pulling it down, the force of the floor pushing it up, and they're exactly equal but opposite in direction. Note that there's very little friction from the floor because the bowling lane is so smooth. The friction is so small, like a penny to a hundred-dollar bill, that it's negligible.

You may be thinking that when you roll the bowling ball, your hand gives the ball a force. But there's no way you can "send" a force with the ball. Once it leaves your hand, you have no power over the ball, and definitely no force on it. When you set the bowling ball into motion, what you give it is *velocity*.

So what is it about the bowling ball that keeps it moving once it starts rolling? You don't necessarily have to visit a bowling alley to find out.

Try This Experiment

MATERIALS NEEDED:
- Bowling ball
- 50 sheets of newspaper (or any other paper)
- Flat, smooth wooden surface 3 yards in length (such as hardwood floor or a wooden table)

Note that if you don't have a bowling ball available, you can try the experiment with a billiard ball.

PROCEDURE:
1. Have your child place the bowling ball on the flat, smooth wooden surface, and give it a tap to make it start rolling. (If you are using a table, make sure you catch the bowling ball before it falls off the edge of the table.)
2. Ask her to crumple the newspapers into a big ball the size of the bowling ball. (If you're using a billiard ball, crumple the newspaper into the size of the billiard ball.)
3. Place the paper ball on the wooden surface, and give it the same tap as you gave the bowling ball.

Did you observe how the bowling ball wanted to keep rolling beyond the 3-yard length of the wooden surface? Did you notice that the paper ball didn't, that it stopped shortly after you tapped it? But they are the same in size. Why didn't they act the same?

Newton's first law (called the Law of Inertia) states that when an object is in motion it stays in motion when all the forces acting on it are balanced. But why does the object stay in motion? The more "stuff" packed into an object, the more it wants to stay in motion. The "stuff" in any object is called *mass*. The bowling ball has more "stuff" in it than the paper ball, so the bowling ball has a bigger mass than the paper ball. That's also why a bowling ball is heavier than the paper ball, because it has more mass in it.

QUESTION

Why is the steep-road sign depicted with a truck rather than a car?
Road signs warn drivers of a steep road ahead. The sign often shows a truck, not a small car or bicycle. The truck, having more mass, would have a harder time slowing down than something with smaller mass. That's just the nature of big masses. It is Newton's first law written all over that road sign, but in "sign" language.

Once an object with a mass is moving, and as long as the forces on it are balanced, it doesn't want to slow down. It wants to keep moving. That's simply how mass behaves. This property of mass is known as inertia.

CHAPTER 4

Electricity

More than ever, we depend on electricity in our everyday life. In fact, it is near impossible for a modern human being to go one full day without the use of electricity. Most people wake up to an alarm clock that's either plugged to the wall or battery powered. You might own an electric toothbrush, hence using more electricity when getting ready in the morning. By the end of your day, you've used electricity more than you can imagine. Electric parts and electric circuits vary in complexity, but some are simple and right at your fingertips. This chapter explores some ideas behind electric circuits as well as a few basic concepts related to electricity.

Static Electricity

You've probably reached for a doorknob in the winter after rubbing your feet on carpet, only to be zapped. You may have also been shocked attempting to close your car door after you've slipped out of your car seat. You've perhaps noticed warning signs at gas stations regarding static electricity. What is this thing called static electricity, and why can it be dangerous enough at gas stations such that it demands a warning sign?

VOCAB

Static Electricity: Static electricity is an accumulation of excess electrical charges on an insulated object. The word static means "stationary" or "not moving."

In order to understand static electricity, it is helpful to learn about atoms and what they consist of. The classical model of an atom includes two types of particles with electrical charge: *protons* and *electrons*. The protons reside in the center of the atom inside the nucleus. Protons have positive electrical charge. The electrons are negatively charged, and move around the nucleus in orbits like the planets move around the sun. Opposite charges attract, so the electrons (–) are attracted to the protons (+), and the atom stays intact. There is one other type of particle inside the nucleus that is electrically neutral. Such neutral particles are called *neutrons*.

A carbon atom, for example, has 6 positively charged protons (p+) and 6 negatively charged electrons (e–), making it electrically neutral. The carbon atom also has 6 neutrons (n) that do not affect its electrical charge.

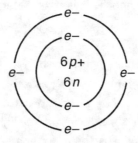

A carbon atom

All objects are made of matter, and matter is made of atoms. When there is an equal number of protons and electrons, there is no excess electrical charge in the object. However, when the object acquires extra charges for some reason, there is an imbalance between the positive and negative charges. This imbalance causes the object to be "charged."

ESSENTIAL

Atoms are the smallest building block in nature. Everything is made up of atoms. Examples of atoms are helium, calcium, iron, gold, silver, etc. When atoms bond together they form molecules. Examples of molecules are oxygen gas, hydrogen gas, carbon dioxide gas, water molecules, etc.

How can an object become "charged"? Only insulated objects can be charged. For example, plastic, Styrofoam, acrylic, and rubber are all insulated objects that can easily be charged. So if you're wearing shoes with rubber soles, any extra charge your body acquires will stay on you. One way you can get extra charges on your body in the winter (when the air is so dry) is by rubbing your feet against carpet while wearing rubber-soled shoes.

How about an object made of metal; can it be insulated? A metal can be insulated if it is not touching the ground or any non-insulated body. If a metal can be insulated, then it can also be charged. An interesting thing about charged metals is that they make the extra charges sit on the most outside surface of themselves, so they can be as far apart as possible from each other. This is because charges of the same kind repel each other. For example, if one stands on the inside of a charged metal cage and touches the inside of the metal, the extra charges on the outside wall will be out of reach. This means the person won't be zapped when touching the inside wall of an insulated metal cage. This is often referred to as the Faraday Cage example.

QUESTION

What is Faraday's Cage?
It is an insulated metal object, like the metal body of a car. At the moment lightning strikes, if a person is only touching the inside of the cage (car), the charges that are discharged by lightning will not transfer to the person and will not cause harm to the person within the cage (car).

Chapter 4: Electricity

Charges that are not paired with opposite ones always strive to find a partner of the opposite kind. When your body has extra electrons in the dry winter from rubbing your feet on the carpet, these electrons need a way to go find other protons to pair with. Since most people don't walk around totally barefoot in the winter with their skin touching the floor, their bodies are insulated by what they wear on their feet. The only opportunity the extra electrons have to escape being trapped on your body is when you touch a metal doorknob. At that instant, all the excess electrons escape your body in a mass exit, and that's when you feel "zapped"!

Similarly, your body can also acquire extra electrons in the dry winter when you brush against your car seat as you slide out of your car. When you have excess electrons on your body, you will feel the spark the instant you touch the car door. But can you experience static electricity in a way that is less shocking?

Try This Experiment

MATERIALS NEEDED:
- Fine-tooth comb
- 1 sheet of paper
- Person who has hair that's more than 5" in length
- Access to a water faucet

PROCEDURE:
1. Do this experiment in the dry winter season. Tell your child to rip the sheet of paper into tiny pieces about ¼" in length and width each, making a small pile of them on the table.
2. Using the comb, ask your child to comb the hair of the designated person who has hair longer than 5".
3. Now have your child bring the comb close to the paper pieces, hovering over them without touching them with the comb. What do you both observe? Does the comb pick up some of the torn pieces of paper?
4. Have your child try something else. Ask her to open the water faucet just enough to have a slender continuous stream of water.
5. Tell your child to comb that same hair again, then bring the comb close to the water stream at the top without touching the water. What does she observe?

61

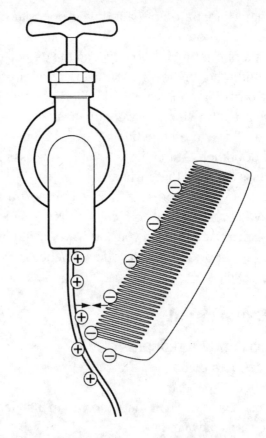

If your child was amazed by the water stream bending due to the comb's presence, explain that it is the effect of the static electricity that causes this trick. The extra electrons that the comb picked up from the hair attracted some of the protons in the water molecules, bending their path.

Static Electricity Cautions

There was obviously no danger in the simple static electricity experiments you and your child did. So why is there a warning against static electricity spark in gas stations?

Your body gets charged with a lot of extra electrons in the dry winter when rubbing your clothes on the car seat while exiting the car. By the time you stand up outside your car, you are very highly charged. When these charges escape your body at the instant of discharging, they do so very quickly, creating a spark. If there is flammable material connected in some form to your body, for example via the metal handle of the gas nozzle, it could spell disaster.

Here is how you can safely handle yourself. Touch your car door every time you exit your car seat before you touch anything else at the gas station. This will allow you to remove any excess electrical charge on you. Also, once you do so, do not get back into your car until you are done fueling. This will prevent you from building static electricity back up again while at the gas station.

Building a Circuit

Electric circuits are everywhere in our lives. When you turn on your desk lamp, it lights up because it is connected to an electric circuit. For the same reason, the burner on your electric stove gets hot and turns red when you switch it on. Your cell phone flashlight comes on, and the phone's other normal functions are possible because of the massive electrical circuitry housed within it.

These examples may make it sound like electric circuits are very complicated, but does it always have to be this way? How can you and your child experience a simple electric circuit made with simple stuff?

Try This Experiment

MATERIALS NEEDED:
- 5 miniature light bulbs rated 2.5V 0.3A
- 5 miniature bulb holders with circular plastic bases
- 3 size-D batteries
- Electrical tape
- 6 alligator clip wires

PROCEDURE:
1. Using the electrical tape, assist your child in securing the 3 D batteries in a row, end to end. Make sure the positive end (labeled +) of one battery is snuggled tightly against the negative end (labeled −) of the next battery before you secure them with the electrical tape. Now the battery pack is ready.
2. Assist your child in taping one end of an alligator clip wire to one end of the battery pack. Then help her tape another alligator clip wire to the other end of the battery pack.

3. Ask your child to screw each light bulb into the bulb holders so they can be ready for use. Assist her in noticing how each bulb holder has two metal ears (as shown in the following figure) where alligator clip wires can be attached.

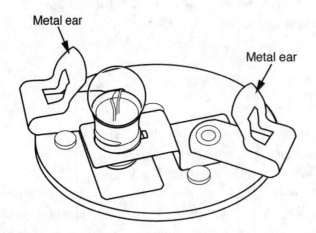

4. Using the wire attached to the positive side of the battery pack, clip the loose end of that wire onto a metal ear of the bulb holder.
5. Now tell your child to use another alligator clip wire to connect the other metal ear of the bulb holder to a second bulb holder, as shown in the next diagram.
6. Next, tell your child to connect the loose wire on the negative side of the battery pack to the second bulb holder. What do you both observe? Do both light bulbs light up?

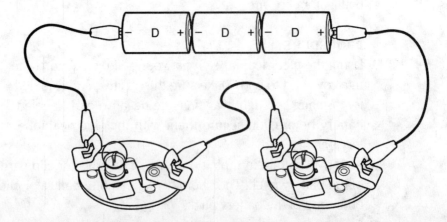

7. Tell your child to disconnect the wire between the two bulb holders.

8. Ask your child to connect a third light bulb with its holder in between the other two, as shown in the diagram. Ask her to notice what happens to the brightness of all bulbs compared to when there were two bulbs.

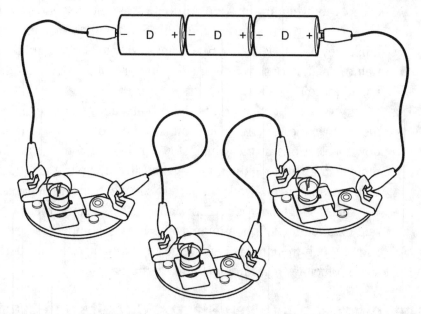

9. Suggest to your child to add yet a fourth bulb in the same fashion she added the third one. What do you both observe regarding the brightness of all bulbs compared to when there were three bulbs?

10. Finally, make one last suggestion to your child to add a fifth bulb. What do you both observe regarding the brightness of all bulbs compared to when there were four bulbs?

QUESTION

What is the definition of an electric circuit in its simplest form?
An *electric circuit* must be a closed loop. In a simple circuit there must be a power source like a battery, different conducting circuit elements like the light bulbs, and connecting wires. All these elements must be connected in one loop.

Did you both observe the bulbs getting dimmer and dimmer as you added more bulbs into the circuit?

A connected electric circuit allows electric charges (like electrons) to move inside the wires in a fashion similar to traffic. Notice how the bulbs allowed you both to "see" that traffic in motion. This traffic of electric charges is known as electric current. In a way it is like the current in a river, except the river current is moving water. Electric current is moving charges.

What do you think the light bulbs do to that traffic (or current)? Do you think they help the traffic move faster or slower? Do you think they help that traffic speed up or slow down? (Remember that the bulbs got dimmer as you added more.)

If your child concluded that the bulbs act as obstacles to the electron traffic flow, then she was right on. The light bulbs create resistance to the flow of electrons in the wires, slowing them down. It is similar to having more accidents along the highway that slow down traffic. The previous light bulb experiment allowed you both to see electricity in action.

The flashlight in your cell phone works in a similar fashion. This is only one example of infinitely many other, more complicated electric circuits. Even though the circuits can get more complex, they all operate under the same principles regarding moving electrons.

The Difference Between Electric Circuits and Static Electricity

There are several differences between electric circuits and static electricity. One difference is that electrons *move* inside the wires in electric circuits, but they stay stationary—*not moving*—when static electricity builds up. Also, all parts of an electric circuit must be connected and able to allow electrons to move through, so they must be made of conductors like metal, while static electricity can only stay put on insulated material, like plastic. Another important difference is that a power source, like a battery, is needed for an electric circuit, but is not needed to build up static electricity on an object.

The next time you turn on a burner in your stove and watch it get bright red, remember that you are watching electrons in motion inside the stove electric circuits as those electrons "light up" the burner.

Insulator versus Conductor

There are always warnings against letting a small child stick his finger in an electric socket. The danger of an electric shock is definitely not a joke. But what is it about the human body that allows one to be electrically shocked? What is that property called? Is there a way to prevent one from being shocked when touching a live electrical wire?

The property that allows an object to let electricity move through it is called *conductivity*. This is a category of objects known as conductors. A *conductor* allows electricity to move through it. It conducts electricity. As you might guess, the human body is one such example. There is another category of objects that do not allow electricity to move through. Those objects are known as *insulators*. One such example that may come to mind is rubber.

But is there a safe way to test which materials are conductors and which are insulators without the fear of being electrically shocked? Absolutely.

Try This Experiment

MATERIALS NEEDED:

- 2 miniature light bulbs rated 2.5V 0.3A
- 2 miniature bulb holders with plastic circular bases
- 3 size-D batteries
- Electrical tape
- 4 alligator clip wires
- Sewing needle
- Plastic lid
- Styrofoam peanut
- Pencil lead
- Human fingernail (after cutting your nails)
- Human hair
- Stainless steel pot
- Drinking glass
- Ceramic plate
- Wooden toothpick
- Tap water
- Salt

PROCEDURE:

1. Using the electrical tape, assist your child in securing the 3 D batteries in a row, end to end. Make sure the positive end (labeled +) of one battery is snuggled against the negative end (labeled –) of the next battery.
2. Assist your child in taping one end of an alligator clip wire to one end of the battery pack. Then help her tape another alligator clip wire to the other end of the battery pack.
3. Ask your child to screw each light bulb into the bulb holders so they can be ready for use. Assist her in noticing how each bulb holder has two metal ears (as shown in the following figure) where alligator clip wires can be attached.

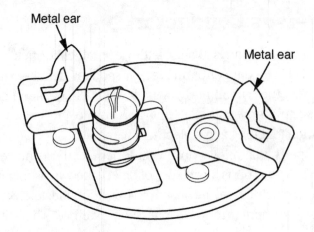

Metal ear

Metal ear

4. Using the wire attached to the positive side of the battery pack, clip the loose end of that wire onto a metal ear of the bulb holder.

5. Next, tell your child to connect the loose wire on the negative side of the battery pack to the second bulb holder.

6. Now tell your child to use another alligator clip wire to connect to the other metal ear of the bulb holder, leaving that wire loose. Do so for both bulbs, as shown in the following diagram.

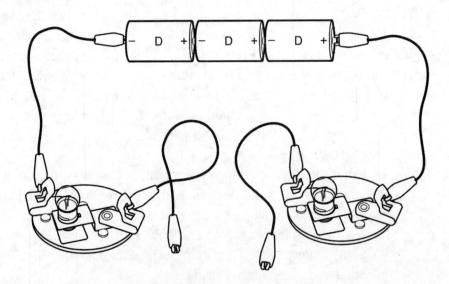

7. Tell your child to connect the two loose wire ends to either side of the sewing needle by clipping them. What does she observe happens to the light bulbs? Do the bulbs light up or stay off?

8. Assist your child in organizing the results of her observations by recording them in the second column in the following table.
9. Ask your child to remove the sewing needle, and connect the plastic lid between the two loose wire ends. What does she observe? Did the bulbs light up? Tell her to record her observation in the table.
10. Ask your child to test each of the materials in the list and record her observation of the light bulbs for each item in the table.
11. If your child wants to test other materials that come to mind, she can add those to the table.

Material Used	Bulbs Light Up (Yes/No)	Insulator	Conductor
Sewing needle			
Plastic lid			
Styrofoam peanut			
Pencil lead			
Human fingernail			
Human hair			
Stainless steel pot			
Drinking glass			
Ceramic plate			
Wooden toothpick			
Salted water			

Help her recognize the two categories of materials she used: those that allowed the light bulbs to light up, and those that didn't. Now ask her to think about which of those materials she used in the circuit would count as conductors. In other words, which are the *conductors*, and which are the *insulators*? As she goes through the list, tell her to put a check mark in the conductor column by the ones she thinks are conductors. Tell her to do the same in the insulator column for the materials she thinks are insulators.

The electric circuit is closed when you connect a conducting object between the two loose wires. In such a closed circuit, the light bulbs light up when *every* part of the circuit is made of a conductor. If there is one insulator along the path, the bulbs will not light up.

Conductors allow electric charges to flow through them like traffic flows on the highway. This flow of charges is known as an electric current. When an *insulator* is present, it is like reaching a road that's not finished: No cars could go down such a road. The electric charges cannot move along such a path, and there is no electric current in the circuit.

QUESTION

What makes charges move in an electric circuit?
A power source is what makes charges flow in a circuit. A battery is an example of a power source. The battery "kicks" the charges and moves them through it, like a soccer player kicks a ball as he passes it on. The charges maintain this current flow in the circuit as long as the battery is not dead.

Your daughter might have thought of testing human skin in the circuit, and may have found out that the bulbs didn't light up. Even though the human body is a conductor (because it is made of mostly water that has electrolytes), it is a poor conductor when using a power source like a battery. This is why it is safe to include one's finger in this circuit. However, using a power source like an electric outlet is not advised.

VOCAB

Electrolyte: An electrolyte is a substance that has an electric charge because it has ions. For example, when dissolving table salt in water, the sodium and chlorine atoms (which were sharing an electron) dissociate from each other, creating a positively charged sodium ion and a negatively charged chlorine ion. Such a solution is called an electrolyte.

The reason why a 4.5V battery pack doesn't cause a shock but a 110V electric outlet does lies in the strength of the electric current generated by these power sources. When connecting to the battery pack that's connected to the two light bulbs, the batteries generate a very small current that is harmless. When connecting to the electric outlet, the current generated is much, much larger and could be lethal.

So how can people be absolutely safe when working with electrical wiring? Well, as long as they keep an insulator on their feet, such as rubber-soled shoes, and work with tools that have insulated handles (like rubber coatings or plastic grips) they can have little fear of being connected to the circuit or getting shocked.

What's Inside a Light Bulb?

You're surrounded by light bulbs everywhere you go. You probably have at least a dozen light bulbs in your house. There are many different kinds of light bulbs today, but the most classic one that has endured the test of time is the incandescent light bulb.

VOCAB

Incandescent: An incandescent object emits light, or it glows, every time it is heated.

We take light bulbs for granted today, but a couple of hundred years ago that would not have been the case. Thomas Edison definitely didn't take the light bulb for granted; in fact, it was a very serious matter to Edison in the nineteenth century. He knew all the ins and outs of a light bulb, like any true inventor would.

QUESTION

Who exactly was Thomas Edison?
Thomas Edison was an American inventor and businessman. He is credited for having invented the incandescent light bulb that is powered by a direct electric current, such as the one a battery would generate. His first public demonstration of the light bulb took place in 1879 at Menlo Park in what is now known as Edison, New Jersey.

Have you seriously ever looked inside a light bulb to see all its parts? It might be too bright to stare at this hot, glaring object, but what if you strip it naked and take a really close look? You might be fascinated by its simplicity.

Try This Experiment

MATERIALS NEEDED:

- 2 incandescent 40-watt light bulbs (one as a spare)
- Packing tape
- Hammer
- Small trash bag

PROCEDURE:

1. Ask your child to use the packing tape to cover the entire glass surface of the incandescent light bulb (tell him to be careful to only cover the glass, and not the bottom metal part). Check to see that he has covered the entire glass surface with tape, and that no glass is exposed to the air.

2. Now, hold the spiral metal base of the light bulb in one of your hands, and the hammer in the other. You will need to tap lightly on the tape-covered glass of the light bulb until the glass breaks. Note that the shattered glass will be completely stuck onto the packing tape, and none of it will scatter. Once the glass breaks, the glass bulb will come undone from the metal base.

3. Dispose of the tape-covered glass bulb safely inside the small trash bag.

4. Now your child has a totally naked light bulb he can gaze into and examine. Ask your child what he can see in the bulb. Does he see the thin wire that is wound like a spiral? Ask him if he can trace the sides of the two metal wires of that spiral wire to their ends down in the metal base.

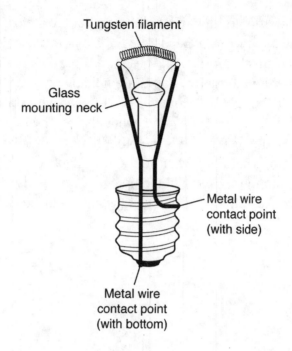

Tungsten filament

Glass
mounting neck

Metal wire
contact point
(with side)

Metal wire
contact point
(with bottom)

If your child pointed at the spiral wire, tell him this is called the tungsten filament. Tungsten is a metal that glows quickly when it gets hot. When the light bulb is connected in a circuit, and electricity flows through the tungsten wire, it gets hot and glows.

ESSENTIAL

Tungsten is the seventy-fourth element in the periodic table of all elements known to us. It is a metal, which means it conducts electricity, allowing electrical charges to move through it. Examples of other metals you might be familiar with are iron, nickel, copper, gold, and silver.

Most likely your child was able to trace the two side wires connecting the tungsten filament with the metal base. On one side, the metal wire comes down from the tungsten filament all the way down to the bottommost point of the base. This wire is illustrated as the left wire in the diagram. On the other side of the tungsten filament, there is another wire that comes down into the metal base. This wire connects to the side wall of the metal base.

In order for the light bulb to be part of a closed circuit, the two wires going into the metal base from the filament must each be connected in the loop of an electric circuit. These two wires are like the two hands of the light bulb. When these two hands are holding on to a wire on either side in the circuit, the light bulb can light up. The one wire connecting through the bottom of the bulb is one hand, while the other wire that connects to the side wall of the metal base is the other hand. This is illustrated in the following diagram. That's why when you screw a light bulb in, you must screw it all the way into the socket until the tip of the metal base touches the back end of the socket (otherwise, that hand would be loose and not touching a wire).

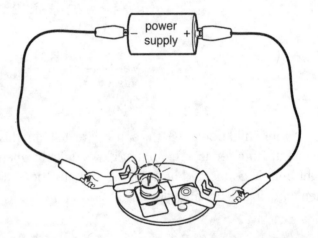

The glass bulb that you broke and removed serves as a protecting cover for the filament. It is also there to trap a gas placed inside the bulb. The gas used is an inert gas, like argon, which does not chemically interact with anything. The gas serves to surround the tungsten filament and help prevent it from being exposed to oxygen. Otherwise, if the tungsten filament came into contact with oxygen, it would burn (oxidize) quickly.

ESSENTIAL

Argon is the eighteenth element in the periodic table of elements known to us. It is one of the gases known as *inert gases,* that do not chemically interact with anything. An example of an inert gas that might be familiar to you is helium. It is a light gas used to inflate floating party balloons.

These are the most important parts of an incandescent light bulb. The other parts are there to support the structure. For example, there is an insulating layer close to the bottom of the base that separates the metal casing from the very bottom metal tip so that the two hands do not touch each other. The glass neck in the center of the bulb is there to help mount the tungsten filament.

Another Kind of Electric Circuit

Do you remember decorating your Christmas tree as a child, and how when one light bulb burned out all the other bulbs went off? Your parents would spend what seemed like an eternity trying to find out which light bulb was the burnt-out one so they could replace it. They did this by testing the light bulbs one at a time. These were the "older" Christmas lights. This problem has been remedied in the more recent Christmas lights, where if one burns out, only that one is off, and it is easy to spot and replace.

What's changed in the circuitry of Christmas lights so that the recent ones don't send you on a hunt? It's all in the wiring of the circuit.

Try This Experiment

MATERIALS NEEDED:
- 2 miniature light bulbs rated 2.5V 0.3A
- 2 miniature bulb holders with plastic circular bases
- 3 size-D batteries
- Electrical tape
- 3 alligator clip wires

PROCEDURE:
1. Using the electrical tape, assist your child in securing the 3 D batteries in a row end to end. Make sure the positive end (labeled +) of each battery is snuggled tightly against the negative end (labeled −) of the next battery. Now the battery pack is ready.
2. Assist your child in taping one end of an alligator clip wire to one end of the battery pack. Then help her tape another alligator clip wire to the other end of the battery pack.
3. Ask your child to screw each light bulb into the bulb holders so they can be ready for use. Assist her in noticing how each bulb holder has two

metal ears (as shown in the following figure) where alligator clip wires can be attached.

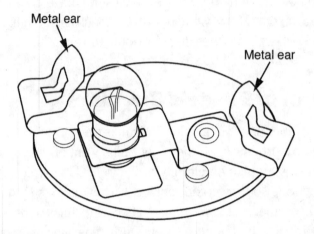

4. Using the wire attached to the positive side of the battery pack, clip the loose end of that wire onto the metal ear of the bulb holder.

5. Now tell your child to use another alligator clip wire to connect the other metal ear of the bulb holder to the second bulb holder as shown in the next diagram.

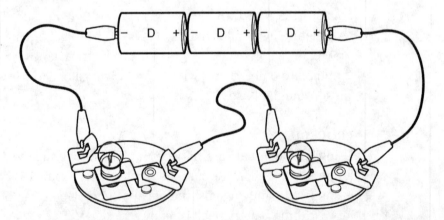

6. Next, tell your child to connect the loose wire on the negative side of the battery pack to the second bulb holder. What do you both observe? Do both light bulbs light up?

7. Now tell your child to loosen up one light bulb completely until it almost comes off. What does she observe? Does the other light bulb stay lit?

This one-loop circuit is known as a *series* electric circuit. This is because the light bulbs are connected in series, one next to each other, in one loop. In a series circuit, if one light bulb is taken out (or burned), all other light bulbs go out. Imagine if you had a hundred of those light bulbs connected in series and one of them burns out. You would need to test each one of those hundred bulbs until you find the one that caused all the others to go out! This is how the older Christmas lights used to be connected.

Now Try This Experiment

MATERIALS NEEDED:

- 4 miniature light bulbs rated 2.5V 0.3A
- 4 miniature bulb holders with plastic circular bases

- 1 size-D battery
- Electrical tape
- 8 alligator clip wires

PROCEDURE:

1. Assist your child in taping one end of an alligator clip wire to one end of the battery. Then help her tape another alligator clip wire to the other end of the battery.
2. Ask your child to screw each light bulb into the bulb holders so they can be ready for use.
3. Using the wire attached to the positive side of the battery, clip the loose end of that wire onto the metal ear of the bulb holder.
4. Next, tell your child to connect the loose wire on the negative side of the battery to the other metal ear of the bulb holder. What do you both observe?

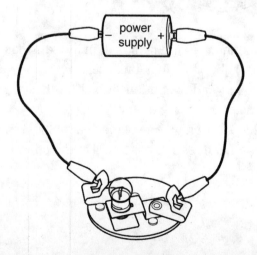

5. Next, tell your child to connect another loose wire to one of metal ears of the bulb holder, and do the same to the other metal ear of the buloh holder.

6. Ask your child to connect another bulb with its holder between the two ends of the loose wires as shown in the diagram. What do you both observe? Do both light bulbs light up?

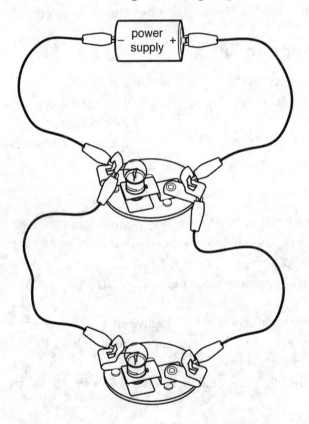

7. Ask your child to connect a third light bulb in the same fashion she connected the second bulb. Do all light bulbs light up?

8. Suggest to your child to add yet a fourth bulb in the same fashion she added the third one.

9. Now tell your child to loosen up one of the light bulbs completely until it almost comes off. What does she observe? Do the other light bulbs stay lit?

It was probably exciting for your child to see that taking out one bulb did not turn off all the others. This way of connecting light bulbs is known as a *parallel* electric circuit. This is because the light bulbs are sitting parallel to each other and parallel to the battery. They are really each connected to the battery directly through a long chain of wires on each side.

QUESTION

What is the definition of a parallel electric circuit in its simplest form?
A *parallel circuit* must have at least two closed loops. In a simple parallel circuit there must be a power source like a battery, two different conducting elements like light bulbs, and connecting wires. All these elements must be connected parallel to each other, like the steps of a ladder.

As electric charges (like electrons) move inside the wires, they do so in a fashion similar to traffic. When the traffic of electric charges moves from the positive terminal of the battery (for instance), they arrive at a junction. They can go through the first bulb, or travel further down to the next one. It's like traffic on the highway where some cars take one exit, but other cars take another exit. The more exits, the more options the cars have. If one exit is closed, it does not shut down the whole highway.

In a parallel circuit, if one light bulb is taken out (or burns out), none of the other light bulbs go out. Imagine if you had a hundred of those light bulbs connected in parallel. If one of them burns out, ask your child if it would be easy to spot the burned one. She is absolutely right; she could, and very easily so! This is how Christmas lights are designed today.

The next time you put up holiday lights, you can offer your child this fun quiz question: Are these lights connected to each other in series, or in parallel?

CHAPTER 5

Magnetism

Magnets are fun toys to play with. Their mesmerizing effect on a compass needle is something many kids around the world have been attracted to. They are also common household items found on many refrigerator doors across America. But magnets are more than fun toys and decorative objects. They have many important uses, such as electromagnets, induction stoves, and many others. Magnets are found inside all electronic equipment today, including your cell phone. This chapter explores some basic ideas about magnets and magnetism.

Magnetizing (and Demagnetizing) a Sewing Needle

Magnets are found everywhere in daily life. You probably have some of them on your refrigerator door glued to the back of a picture or an advertisement. If you or someone in your family has a sewing kit, then they may have a magnet for pins to cling to. It is perhaps what clips the door of your medicine cabinet shut. And if you use tools all the time, you might prefer magnetized screwdrivers that make it easy to hold screws while placing them where you want them.

VOCAB

Magnetize: To magnetize a metal object means to give it a magnetic property, so that it can pick up some metal objects via attraction.

Perhaps you have played with magnets at some point in your life to see what kinds of metal objects a magnet can pick up. But what is more fun than playing with a magnet is making one. If you think this is a sophisticated task that requires some serious equipment, you might be surprised to find out that it is easy and uncomplicated to create a simple magnet.

Try This Experiment

MATERIALS NEEDED:
- 1 sewing needle
- 4 flat metal-head straight sewing pins
- Strong bar magnet
- Compass

PROCEDURE:
1. If the bar magnet sides are not labeled N (for North) and S (for South), then have your child use the compass needle to identify N and S. Have him bring one side of the bar magnet near the side of the compass needle that's labeled N (it is usually the side that's colored in red). If the N side of the compass needle is attracted to the side of the magnet he brought near it, then that side of the magnet is S (South). Tell your child to make a note of which side of the magnet is S.

2. Ask your child to scatter the straight pins on a table, just a few inches apart so they are not touching.
3. Tell your child to hold the head of the needle in one hand.

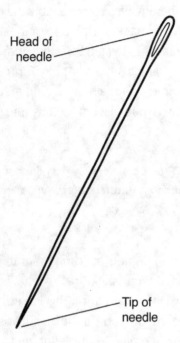

Head of needle

Tip of needle

4. Now have him hold the bar magnet in the other hand.

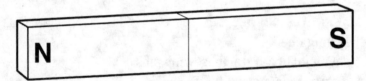

N   S

5. Ask your child to stroke the needle, from head to tip, with one side of the bar magnet (say with the north side). Have him do this repeatedly in the same direction at a steady, medium speed, about 5–10 times.
6. Now tell your child to touch the tip of the needle in his hand to one of the straight pins on the table. Ask him to lift up his hand holding the needle. Does the needle pick up the pin?
7. Tell your child to see if his needle can pick up more than one of the pins on the table. Ask him to test whether his needle can pick up all four pins at the same time.

By now your child has figured out that he has just made a tiny magnet out of his needle. How exciting! By stroking a metal object like a needle (which is made of steel) with one side of the bar magnet, a permanent magnet is created out of a sewing needle. However, such a magnet is small and weak, so it can only pick up tiny objects like pins and needles.

But is there a way to demagnetize the needle? There is a quick way to demagnetize objects.

VOCAB

Demagnetize: To demagnetize a metal object means to make it lose its magnetic property.

Now Try This Experiment

MATERIALS NEEDED:
- 1 magnetized sewing needle
- Wand lighter (like a BBQ lighter)
- Pliers

PROCEDURE:
1. Assist your child in holding the head of the needle with a pair of pliers.
2. Lighting the wand lighter, hold the hand of your child that is holding the pliers in your hand, and bring the needle inside the flame. Keeping the needle in the flame will make it glow. Let the needle glow for about 10 seconds, then set it aside on a piece of paper for a few seconds to cool.
3. Now ask your child to touch the tip of the needle to one of the straight pins on the table. Ask him to lift up his hand holding the needle. Does the needle pick up the pin?

ESSENTIAL

The *Curie temperature* was discovered by a French physicist named Pierre Curie in the late nineteenth century. He worked with his Polish/French wife, Marie Curie, who was also a physicist, working on experiments related to radioactivity. They were both honored for their extraordinary scientific contributions by being awarded the Nobel Prize in Physics in 1903.

If most of the needle glowed hot inside the lighter flame, then the needle would have become demagnetized. This means the needle would no longer pick up the pins. Its magnetic effect has been removed by heating it. When the metal of a permanent magnet is heated above what is known as the Curie temperature, the metal loses its magnetization.

North versus South Pole

Words like north and south poles usually make people think of the geographic regions known as the North Pole and the South Pole that explorers once set out to explore. There are, however, two other kinds of north and south poles. Those are the north magnetic and the south magnetic poles. And when referring to our planet, we should be specific about whether we are referring to the north *geographic* or the north *magnetic* pole.

QUESTION

What are the geographic north and south poles?
The north geographic pole lies in the Arctic and is the most northern point on earth. The south geographic pole lies in the Antarctic and is earth's most southern point. Planet Earth rotates about itself once every day. It spins about an imaginary axis that connects the north and south geographic poles.

How do magnetic poles behave near each other? When you use a compass needle to find north, does the magnetized compass needle point in the direction of Earth's north magnetic or the south magnetic pole? And how are the earth's *magnetic* poles related to the earth's *geographic* poles?

Try This Experiment

MATERIALS NEEDED:

- 1 sewing needle
- 2 flat metal-head straight sewing pins
- Strong bar magnet
- Compass

PROCEDURE:

1. If the bar magnet sides are not labeled N (for North) and S (for South), then have your child use the compass needle to identify N and S. Have her bring one side of the bar magnet near the side of the compass needle that's labeled N (it is usually the side that's colored in red). If the N side of the compass needle is attracted to the side of the magnet she brought near it, then that side of the magnet is S (South). Tell your child to make a note of which side of the magnet is S.

2. Ask your child to sit at a table, and to place one of the straight pins to her left and the other one to her right.

3. Tell your child to hold the head of the needle in one hand.

4. Now have her hold the bar magnet in the other hand.

5. Ask your child to stroke the needle, from head to tip, with the *north* side of the bar magnet. Have her do this repeatedly in the same direction at a steady, medium speed about 5–10 times, then set the needle somewhere in front of her, away from the two pins.

6. While holding the head of the pin to her left, ask your child to stroke the pin, from head to tip, in the same fashion with the *north* side of the magnet, then place the pin back on the table to her left.

7. Now tell your child to pick up the needle by its head, and bring its *tip* very close to the *left pin's tip* (that's lying on the table). What does she observe happening? Does the tip of the needle repel or attract the tip of the left pin? If your child observed that the needle's tip and the left pin's tip repelled each other as illustrated in the following diagram, then she's absolutely correct. This is because both needle and left pin were magnetized from head to tip by the same *north* magnetic pole. This makes the needle and left pin magnetized identically. In other words, if the tip of the needle became magnetized north, the tip of the left pin was also magnetized north.

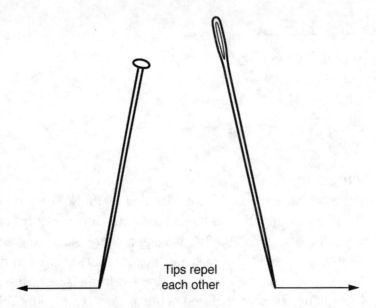

Tips repel
each other

8. Now have your child do the following. While holding its head, ask your child to now stroke the right pin, from head to tip, with the *south* side of the magnet in the same fashion as before. Have her place the pin back on the table to her right.

9. Now tell your child to pick up the needle by its head, and this time to bring its *tip* very close to the *head of the right pin* (that's lying on the table). What does she observe happening? Does the tip of the needle repel or attract the head of the right pin?

If your child observed that the needle's tip and the right pin's head repelled each other as illustrated in the following diagram, then she's right on track. This is because the needle was magnetized by the *north* magnetic pole (making its tip magnetized *north*) while the right pin was magnetized by the *south* magnetic pole (making its tip magnetized *south*). Note that when one side of the needle becomes magnetized *north* (for example its tip), then its head automatically becomes magnetized *south*. The same is true for the pin: When its tip is magnetized *north*, then its head is automatically magnetized *south* and vice versa. That's just how nature works!

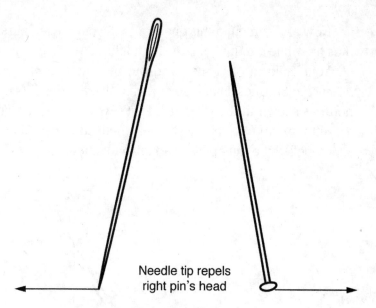

Needle tip repels
right pin's head

Ask your child what was different between the left and right pins. Remind your child that the left pin's tip was magnetized north. What was different about the way she magnetized the right pin?

Your child probably remembered that when magnetizing the right pin, the magnet was flipped, and therefore the left and right pins were magnetized by opposite magnetic poles. This would make the poles on the right needle be the reverse of the poles on the left needle as illustrated in the following diagram.

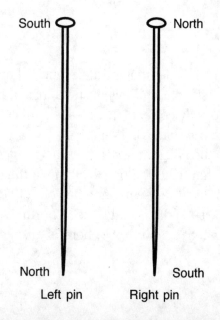

South   North

North   South

Left pin   Right pin

Now ask your child this question: Why did the left pin's tip repel the needle's tip, while the right pin's head did the repelling?

Your child most likely found out by now that *magnetic poles that are alike repel*. She most likely remembered that the needle's tip was magnetized north as shown in the diagram. That's why the needle's north tip repelled the left pin's tip (which was also magnetized north). The same needle's tip later repelled the right pin's head (also magnetized north).

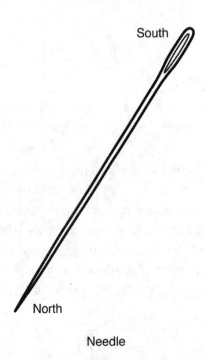

South

North

Needle

If magnetic poles that are alike repel, what about magnetic poles that are opposite? Ask your child what she thinks. If her answer is that they *attract*, she's completely correct. This means a magnetic north pole attracts a magnetic south pole, and vice versa.

People use a compass to find the geographic north direction. It is an especially handy tool if one is hiking in the country. A compass needle is very much like the sewing needle your child magnetized. The red side of the compass needle is magnetized north, while the other side of the needle is magnetized south. So, here is an interesting question to ask your child: in which geographic direction would earth's south *magnetic* pole be? Is it in the direction of the *geographic* north pole, or the *geographic* south pole? Remind her that a magnetic north is attracted to a magnetic south.

Since the magnetic north pole of the compass needle points toward the geographic north, then it must have been attracted by a magnetic south pole, therefore the *geographic north* pole must be the *magnetic south* pole.

ESSENTIAL

Earth's north and south magnetic poles are not permanent, as the geographic poles are. The north-south magnetic poles on planet Earth flip every few hundred thousand years, making the north magnetic pole a south one, and vice versa. Scientists discovered this when studying the ocean floor of the Mid-Atlantic Ridge, which has stored this pattern over millions of years.

So the next time you find yourself talking about earth's north and south poles, you might want to clarify whether you are referring to earth's *geographic* or *magnetic* poles.

What Are Magnets Made Of?

Magnets come in different sizes, shapes, even colors. Some are plated with a silver color, some black, and some even gold, among other colors. But what do they all have in common? Are there common materials magnets must have in them in order for them to become permanent magnets?

As a rule of thumb, if a magnet cannot strongly attract a particular substance to the point where it will stick to the magnet, then it can never be made out of that substance. For example, if a magnet cannot attract plastic, then a magnet cannot be made out of plastic alone. There are magnets coated with plastic, but the plastic has nothing to do with the magnet being a magnet. So what material is needed to make a permanent magnet?

Try This Experiment

MATERIALS NEEDED:

- Cylindrical neodymium magnet (½" diameter, 2" length)
- Iron nail
- Penny
- Piece of copper pipe of any size that's available
- Sewing needle
- Pure gold ring
- Pure silver ring
- Small aluminum pan
- Screwdriver
- 2 sheets of paper
- Pencil

Ask your child to make a prediction as to which items may be attracted by the magnet. It is always fun to compare the results of an experiment to a prior prediction.

PROCEDURE:

1. Ask your child to use the two sheets of paper to record her results. Tell her to write at the top of one page the word ATTRACTED, and at the top of the other page the words NOT ATTRACTED.
2. Tell your child to place the objects in the materials list on a table so they are available for her to test them. Ask her to hold the magnet in one hand.
3. Now tell her to touch the magnet to each object, one at a time. Ask her to write the name of each object that sticks to the magnet on the sheet with the ATTRACTED label. Tell her to remove that object from the magnet so she can be ready to test the next object. All objects not attracted by the magnet should be listed on the other sheet.
4. Have your child test the objects that are not attracted by the magnet twice, so that she can be certain they weren't. If she wants to add other objects to the list of things to test, encourage her to do so, and ask her to record them on one of the two data sheets.

Ask your child if she was surprised by some of the results of this experiment. Did she expect the penny or the copper pipe to stick to the magnet? What about the gold and silver rings, and the aluminum pan?

All these items just named are metals, and it is easy to assume that all metals would be attracted to a magnet. The penny is copper plated, but is really made out of zinc, which is another metal. By now your child has figured out that some metals aren't attracted to a magnet. Some of the metals she tested that ended up on her NOT ATTRACTED list were zinc, copper, gold, silver, and aluminum. These are metals that cannot alone be made into a permanent magnet.

Now have her examine the ATTRACTED list. She should find there the iron nail, the sewing needle, and the screwdriver. What material do they all have in common? Ask your child what she thinks.

If your child guessed iron, as the "iron nail" suggests, then she guessed right. The nail is indeed made of iron, which is known as *ferromagnetic*. The sewing needle and the screwdriver are made of steel, which has iron in it. The sewing needle is also plated with another metal called nickel, which is also ferromagnetic.

VOCAB

Ferromagnetic: Ferromagnetic refers to elements that can either become permanently magnetized, or that are strongly attracted by a permanent magnet. There are three metals that are ferromagnetic: iron, nickel, and cobalt. Other ferromagnetic materials include some rare earth elements, such as neodymium.

A magnet has a magnetic field. The magnetic field is invisible, but can be felt when bringing the two north sides of two different magnets close to each other. The repulsive effect between the two close north poles that refuse to touch indicates the presence of a magnetic field that is "sensed" by them at a distance.

When a magnet is brought close to an item that contains ferromagnetic material, the ferromagnetic material "senses" the presence of the magnetic field. The ferromagnetic material reacts to the presence of the magnetic field by becoming strongly attracted by it. In other words, once the magnet is at a certain distance from the item, the item starts to move toward the magnet as it is guided by the magnetic field of that magnet.

What is a permanent magnet?
A *permanent magnet* is made out of ferromagnetic material. Once it becomes magnetized, a ferromagnetic material does not lose its magnetic property easily unless heated above a certain high temperature.

Since the items that contained ferromagnetic material were strongly attracted to the magnet, then the material those items are made of can be used to make a permanent magnet. Most magnets nowadays are not made of one element alone, like iron. Magnets today are made of an alloy (which is a combination of different elements) that must contain ferromagnetic material. For example, a permanent magnet can include other non-ferromagnetic material like aluminum, but *must* have one or more of the ferromagnetic ones. A neodymium magnet is made of iron, neodymium, and boron. An Alnico magnet, which is the oldest permanent magnet, includes aluminum, nickel, and cobalt among other metals.

Electricity and Magnetism: The Two Sisters

Some phenomena in nature cannot occur without something else happening at the same time as an associated effect. For example, every time the sun comes up over the eastern horizon at sunrise, it is automatic that there will be light everywhere. The sunrise and the lighting effect are associated together. This happens because of the nature of the sun, which is to illuminate.

Electricity and magnetism are another such example. When we have electricity moving in wires, magnetic effects show up immediately. The two are like sisters that cannot be separated. So how can such a phenomenon be seen and observed, and is it something that can be useful in some everyday life application?

Try This Experiment

MATERIALS NEEDED:

- 2 miniature light bulbs rated 2.5V 0.3A
- 2 miniature bulb holders with plastic circular bases

- 3 size-D batteries
- Electrical tape
- 3 alligator clip wires
- Liquid-filled compass
- Clear tape

PROCEDURE:

1. Using the electrical tape, assist your child in securing the 3 D batteries in a row end to end. Make sure the positive end (labeled +) of one battery is snuggled tightly against the negative end (labeled –) of the next battery. Now the battery pack is ready.

2. Assist your child in taping one end of an alligator clip wire to one end of the battery pack. Then help her tape another alligator clip wire to the other end of the battery pack.

3. Ask your child to screw each light bulb into the bulb holders so they can be ready for use. Assist her in noticing how each bulb holder has two metal ears (as shown in the following figure) where alligator clip wires can be attached.

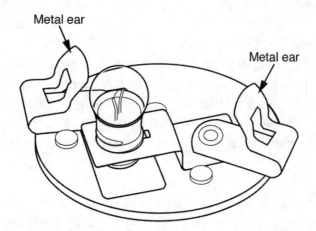

Metal ear

Metal ear

4. Using the wire attached to the positive side of the battery pack, clip the loose end of that wire onto the metal ear of one of the bulb holders.

5. Next, tell your child to connect the loose wire on the negative side of the battery pack to the metal ear of the other bulb holder.
6. Now tell your child to use the third alligator clip wire and connect it to the other metal ear of the bulb holder on the right. Tell her to leave the other side of this wire loose for a minute.
7. Now it is time for your child to use the compass. Ask her to place the compass flat on the table next to the bulbs. Tell her to place the loose wire on top of the compass. Assist her in lining up the loose wire exactly parallel to the compass needle, as shown in the following diagram. Once the loose wire and the compass needle are in alignment, have her use the clear tape to tape the wire onto the compass needle. Ask her to also tape both wire and compass onto the table so they don't move.

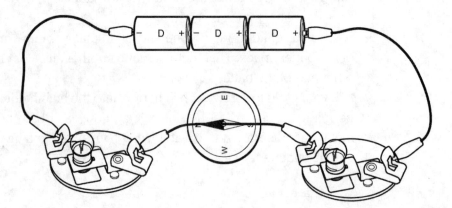

8. Tell your child that she is now ready to connect the loose end of the wire to the left bulb holder's empty ear that is not connected to the battery. Before she does that, tell her to focus on the compass. Once she connects that wire, both light bulbs should light up. What do you both observe happening to the compass needle the instant she connects the wire?

The light bulbs light up, showing that electricity is indeed moving through the wires. But there is another effect associated with the moving electricity. This other effect shows up in the compass needle that moves (or deflects)!

But isn't a compass used to detect a magnetic field? After all, people carry compasses so they can find the direction they need to travel in, especially if they are out in the wilderness. The compass responds to the presence of the earth's magnetic field, aligning its needle with the direction north. Some people even like to play with the compass needle by bringing a magnet nearby and watching the needle be attracted to the magnet. So what does a battery and a bunch of wires and bulbs have anything to do with magnetism? After all, your child didn't bring any magnet near the compass.

QUESTION

What is a magnetic field?

When a magnet is present, it alters the space around it. This altering of the surrounding space that some nearby objects can sense is called a *magnetic field*. For example, if you bring two south poles of two magnets near each other, they "sense" the magnetic field of the other magnet and refuse to come closer to touch.

Every time there is electricity moving in the wires, there is automatically a magnetic field that shows up at the same time. Electricity and magnetism cannot be separated. The magnetic field shows up right around the wires. That's why the wire had to be laid right on top of the compass. Since the compass responds to the presence of a magnetic field (as it does to earth's magnetic field), it can actually detect the magnetic field close by in the wires.

Can this phenomenon be put to good use? Can a magnetic field that is generated by electricity be made into something useful? One very important, and very useful, tool built this way is called an electromagnet (as in electric magnet). All one needs in order to make an electromagnet is to wrap the wire many times around something made of iron, like an iron nail, and connect the two ends of the wire to a battery. It's as simple as that!

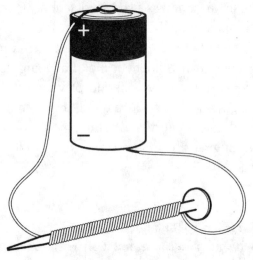

Simple electromagnet

QUESTION

Who discovered electromagnets?
Danish physicist Hans Christian Oersted discovered electromagnets. In 1820, Oersted was doing a demonstration in one of his lectures on electricity, connecting wires to a battery, when he noticed a nearby compass needle deflect. It was by accident that electromagnetism was discovered, as so many other discoveries in science have been.

Electromagnets

Electromagnets are used in many places. For example, if one needs to have a magnet they can turn on or off when needed, they use an electromagnet. Electromagnets are used in junkyards when heavy objects like cars need to be lifted and moved around. The electromagnet is turned on when the car is ready to be lifted. When the electromagnet is turned off, the car drops into the location it needs to sit. If a permanent magnet were used, it would be near impossible to "peel" the car off that giant permanent magnet once it was stuck to it.

CHAPTER 6

Building Stuff

In the modern world, you are surrounded by all kinds of structures built by engineers and architects. Some of those structures are stationary, like buildings, bridges, towers, stadiums, etc. Other structures are not stationary in the sense that some parts can move and/or rotate, such as mechanical structures that use motors. In this chapter, you and your child will explore some of the design ideas behind many engineering projects. These explorations will assist your child in not only understanding some of the essential basics, but will demonstrate how engineers think when building stuff, and why they have so much fun doing what they do.

Building a Motor

A motor is a machine that can make objects rotate. For example, the blades of a fan or a helicopter are made to rotate—or spin—with the use of an electric motor. Electric motors are machines that need electricity in order for them to rotate an object. In other words, the motor's input is electricity, and its output is mechanical movement in the form of rotation.

Sounds complicated? You're about to find out how simple it is to make your very own electric motor using simple ingredients you can easily obtain. We will focus on building a direct-current (or DC) motor that uses batteries you can buy at your local hardware store. You can purchase most of the material you need to build your motor from a hardware store, and some of the others from a crafts store.

Try This Experiment

MATERIALS NEEDED:
- 20" length of enameled copper wire, 26 gauge (AWG)
- 2 connecting wires with alligator-clip ends
- 6-volt battery
- Cylindrical neodymium magnet ½" in diameter and ½" in height
- 2 large safety pins
- Smooth Styrofoam disk
- Dowel with 0.5" diameter and 4" in length
- Sandpaper
- Pliers

PROCEDURE:
1. Assist your child in taking the stretch of copper wire and winding it around the dowel 4–5 times. Once he has 4–5 turns of wire, tell him to remove the dowel, and wrap the loose end of the wire around the looped wires twice to make a knot and tighten the loops together, as shown in the following picture. Have him do the same at the other loose end of the copper wire. Assist him in making sure the excess straight wire on either end is along a straight line to make a shaft about which the motor will rotate.

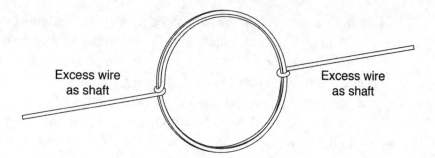

Excess wire as shaft

Excess wire as shaft

2. Use sandpaper to entirely remove the enamel from one end of the straight copper wire. Lay the loop flat on a surface, and use the sandpaper to remove the enamel only from the top face of the other straight wire that's not yet sanded off (see the following illustration).

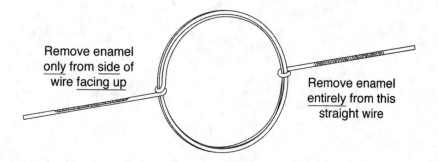

Remove enamel only from side of wire facing up

Remove enamel entirely from this straight wire

3. Use a pair of pliers to clip off the fastening end of two safety pins (see the following illustration).

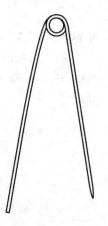

4. Now have your child push the neodymium magnet halfway into the Styrofoam disk so that it sticks slightly above the Styrofoam surface level. Place the safety pins down on either side of the magnet so that each forms a triangle that points up. Place the looped copper wire in such a way that its shaft rests inside the holes of the safety pins (see the following illustration). Note: You might need to push the safety pins further into the Styrofoam in order to bring the looped copper wire very close to the magnet, but without touching it.

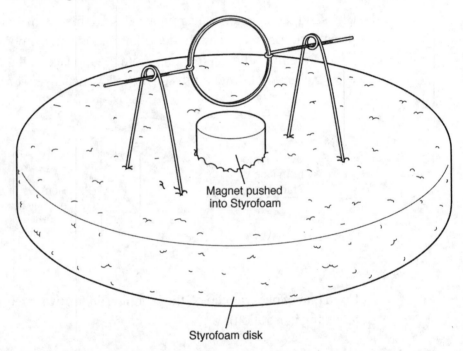

Magnet pushed
into Styrofoam

Styrofoam disk

5. Next, ask your child to use an alligator clip wire to connect the base of one safety pin to the positive terminal of the battery, and another alligator clip wire to connect the base of the other safety pin to the negative terminal of the battery (see the following illustration).

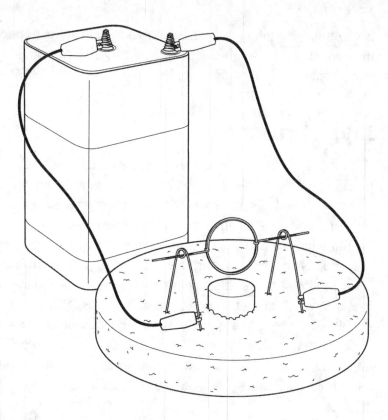

Use your forefinger to give the copper loop a little spin and watch it spin around on its own afterward!

Who invented the first rotating electric motor?
In 1834, the German-speaking Prussian, Moritz Jacobi, successfully built the first real electric motor whose mechanical output power was amazingly strong. However, the first device that was built to rotate, using electromagnetism, was invented by the Englishman Peter Barlow (known as Barlow's wheel) in 1822.

So next time you turn on a fan and watch it rotate, or use a food processor to prepare a dish, or perhaps grab a power tool to fix something, ask your child whether he thinks there is a motor inside any of these devices that is causing the rotation. It is fun when your child starts to become aware of the connection between electrical objects that have rotation and the presence of an electric motor within them.

Building a Truss

Trusses are found in virtually every modern building. They are used to provide support for the structure so it can withstand heavy loads. Trusses can be seen in buildings, the roofs of houses and large stores, bridges, football stadiums, and airports among countless other places.

But what is a truss? What is the simplest way to construct a truss? Who uses trusses and for what purpose? What materials are trusses made of?

A *truss* is a two-dimensional structure (a plane) made of straight segments of wood or metal connected together to form triangles. In terms of stability and strength, a triangle can keep its shape under a heavy load, as opposed to a square. In the following diagram, you can see how a load on the triangle is distributed through its sides such that the structure of the triangle holds its shape firmly and does not collapse.

LOAD

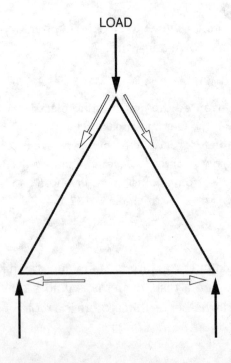

In contrast, when a square structure is loaded, the square will change its shape into a rhombus where its angles are no longer right angles, as shown in the next diagram. Such a structure does not hold its shape; or in other words, it collapses when loaded.

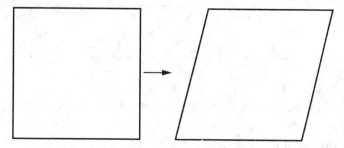

One way a square can be supported so that it does not lose its structure is to connect the two opposite corners with a diagonal line, turning the square into two triangles, as shown in the following diagram. This demonstrates how essential the shape of a triangle is in building stable structures.

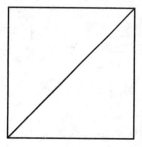

A truss is built out of connecting triangles. The simplest such truss can be constructed of two adjacent triangles that have a connecting line on top, as shown here.

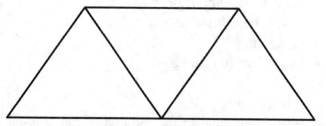

Such a truss is historically known as a Warren truss. The shape of this truss was patented by the British engineer James Warren in the late eighteenth century. When connecting more of these triangles to form a longer truss, they can be used in building a bridge, as shown in the following diagram. Show your child the Warren truss diagram so she knows what it looks like.

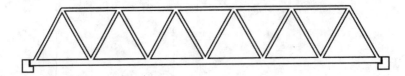

You can see another example of using triangles in supporting the wings of old propeller biplanes. The wings of many of those planes were stacked on top of one another, supported by trusses.

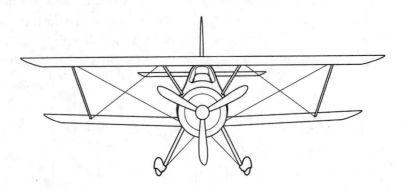

Is there an easy way to construct a truss at home? Indeed there is, and it's a lot of fun.

Try This Experiment

MATERIALS NEEDED:
- 15–19 Popsicle sticks
- Glue gun
- Glue sticks (for glue gun)

PROCEDURE:
1. Assist your child in using the glue gun. Ask her to form a triangle by gluing together the ends of 3 Popsicle sticks, as shown in the following diagram.

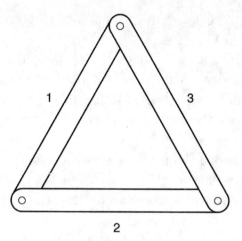

2. Using the glue gun, have your child attach a fourth Popsicle stick horizontally at the top corner of the triangle, as shown in the next diagram.

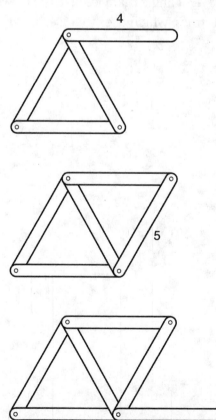

3. Next, have your child glue a fifth Popsicle stick diagonally to form the second (upside-down) triangle.
4. Have your child glue a sixth Popsicle stick horizontally on the bottom. Ask her to continue to repeat the steps of adding a diagonal, then a horizontal stick each time, until she uses all 15 sticks. If she is excited about making a longer truss, she can use all 19 sticks.

When your child is done gluing all the sticks according to the diagram, ask her what kind of truss she now has. Does it look like a famous truss that is named after someone? If your child answered that she has made a Warren truss, compliment her on her sharp memory.

There are other types of trusses besides the Warren truss. Other known trusses are shown in this next diagram. Ask your child if she can spot all the triangles in each truss. Some trusses use equilateral triangles, like the Warren truss. Other trusses use right angle triangles, like the Howe and the Pratt trusses. There is also the K truss, which uses triangles making the shape of the letter K.

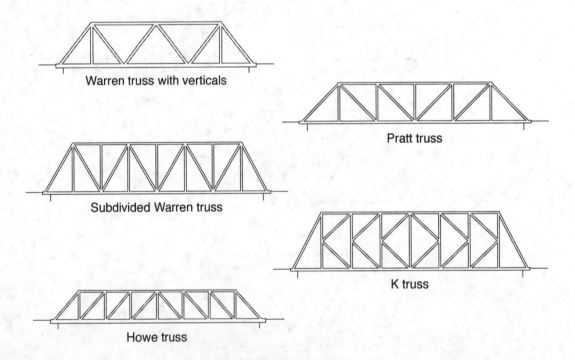

Warren truss with verticals

Pratt truss

Subdivided Warren truss

K truss

Howe truss

QUESTION

Who is the Howe truss named after?
The Howe truss is named after the American inventor William Howe who was from Massachusetts. He was one of the pioneers in developing bridge trusses in the United States. He patented the famous Howe truss in 1840.

There are many other types of trusses. If your child is interested in them, you can do a simple Internet search together to look at the multitudes of other types.

Architectural and civil engineers rely heavily on the use of trusses in constructing buildings, bridges, towers, etc. They know the sturdiness of triangles well when it comes to construction.

QUESTION

Who is the Pratt truss named after?
The Pratt truss gets its name after both Thomas and Caleb Pratt. They were railroad engineers who lived in the 1800s in Boston. Thomas designed the truss with his father, Caleb, and patented the design in 1844.

Architects who design houses use trusses for the roofs. One of the most common roof trusses is called the Fink truss, shown in the following illustration. Almost all house trusses are made of timber in the United States, owing to the abundance of timber in this country. Assist your child in identifying the equilateral triangle in the center, and the other right angle triangles off to the sides.

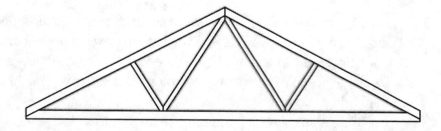

The idea of strengthening a structural design by using triangles is seen in other structures designed by architects. One such fine example is the Spaceship Earth feature at Disney World's Epcot Center. It is a giant sphere of triangles in both its inner shell and the outside cladding. The triangles strongly support the structure and keep it rigid. Every triangle in the inner shell is further divided into four smaller triangles in the outer shell. When you gaze at the Spaceship Earth from the outside, you see the outer shell with its more than 11,000 small triangles.

How old is the use of trusses in construction?
The ancient Egyptians built rope trusses to support the central beam of their ships. It is hard to discern whether it was the ancient Greeks or the ancient Romans who invented the truss. However, the Romans definitely put the truss to use when they constructed wooden roof trusses.

But you don't have to travel to Disney World to see an elaborate structural design that uses triangles. You can begin to point out triangles used in different trusses used with tall roofs inside airports, large hardware stores, bridges, towers, roller coasters in amusement parks, and many other places. Point out the next transmission (or electrical power line) tower you happen to pass by. Draw your child's attention to how these towers' triangles are made of steel, not timber, because they transmit electricity. It's fun to start engaging your child in noticing all the places around her where triangles are put into use to support a structure.

Building a Bridge

Seeing a bridge is a common, everyday occurrence for most people. When crossing a river or any waterway, you have to drive on or walk along a bridge. You might even walk along a people bridge constructed between buildings in a large hospital or company complex. Sometimes you might see a pedestrian bridge along a nature trail that crosses over a stream.

Bridges are often supported by trusses. A truss is a structure formed of connected segments of triangles made of a material like steel or timber. The triangular shape can easily distribute a load better than any other geometric shape. A truss is most commonly two-dimensional. In order to construct a bridge—which is three-dimensional—many trusses are incorporated into the bridge design.

Regardless of the kind of bridge—its style, purpose, whether it supports people or vehicles or freight trains, carried by pillars or suspended—all truss bridges rely on trusses to support their load-carrying structures.

The simplest design for a truss is the Warren truss, which you saw earlier in this chapter. Even though the design of such a bridge is simple, it still can hold a large load. You can build a simple bridge by constructing two Warren trusses and a walkway. In order to find out how strong your bridge is, you will need a luggage scale to test how much force your bridge can support.

Try This Experiment

MATERIALS NEEDED:
- Bag of Popsicle sticks
- Glue gun
- Glue sticks (for glue gun)
- Bag of cable ties
- Scissors
- Digital luggage scale
- 2' length of twisted nylon rope ½" in diameter

PROCEDURE:
1. Assist your child in using the glue gun. Ask him to form a triangle by gluing together the ends of three Popsicle sticks, as shown in the diagram.

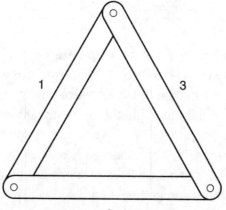

2. Using the glue gun, have your child attach other Popsicle sticks, one at a time, in the order of the numbering shown in the diagram. Tell him to add the sticks with care, making sure the top horizontal sticks and the bottom horizontal sticks line up along as straight a line as possible.

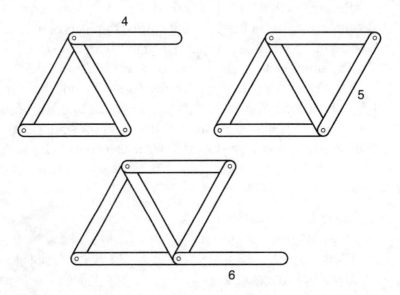

3. Ask your child to glue together as many as 19 sticks following the pattern described, until his truss looks like the one in the next diagram.

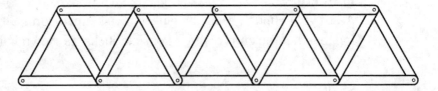

4. Tell your child to assemble the same shape truss again, using the same number of sticks. He should have two such Warren trusses that will form the sides of his bridge when he finally assembles it.

5. Now it's time for your child to make the bottom walkway of the bridge. Ask him to glue together 4 Popsicle sticks in one long straight line. Have him make two such long lines of sticks.

6. Tell your child to set the two long lines of sticks on the table parallel to each other, so that the distance between the two lines is the length of one Popsicle stick.

7. Ask your child to place more Popsicle sticks perpendicular to the two long lines in such a way that they look like a ladder, and to secure them in place with glue. Lay the perpendicular sticks very close to each other, so that they are about ¼" apart.

8. Now have your child reinforce the bottom walkway with diagonal Popsicle sticks, as shown in the diagram. Remind him to secure the additional Popsicle sticks in place with glue.

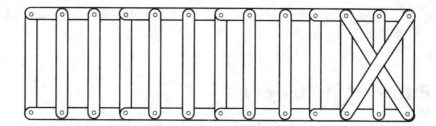

9. Tell your child to place diagonal Popsicle sticks along the entire length of the bottom walkway.

10. It is now time to assemble the bridge. Tell your child to place the Warren trusses he built earlier along either side of the bottom walkway. Let the top lengths of the two trusses touch, like the two sides of a house roof meet to form a triangular shape.

11. Using the cable ties, ask your child to tie the side of the bottom walkway to the bottom of one truss. Do the same for the other truss. Finally, tie the two top lengths of the trusses together.

12. Now it's time for your child to test the strength of his truss. He will need to place the ends of his truss on the edges of two tables placed side by side so that there is only air underneath the truss. Using the nylon rope, tell him to make a vertical loop around the truss, then hang the luggage scale from it.

13. Using his own strength, have your child pull the luggage scale down and note the reading on the scale. How much downward force can his bridge support?

If your child's bridge can support 50 or 60 pounds of force, then he's constructed a pretty sturdy bridge out of Popsicle sticks, using trusses and triangles. This illustrates the power of a triangular shape.

There have been famous truss bridges built to last. Some are supported by pillars on the bottom of the bridge, like the Forth Bridge in the east of Scotland, just a little west of Edinburgh City. Some bridges are suspension bridges, like the San Francisco Golden Gate Bridge. But whether it is a suspension bridge or not, such bridges cannot be strongly supported without the essential use of trusses.

The next time you go on a road trip in an area with one or more bridges, engage your child in identifying whether the bridges have trusses. If so, ask your child whether he can identify if the bridge uses a Warren truss or some other kind of truss.

Building a Tower

Towers are built in different shapes and sizes to serve different purposes. Some carry high-voltage power lines, in which case they are called transmission towers. There are also radio towers, cell phone towers, clock towers, and so on. There are also ancient tower-like structures, such as the obelisks the ancient Egyptians were famous for. There are other famous towers around the world: the Eiffel Tower in Paris, France; the CN Tower in Toronto, Canada; Burj Khalifa in Dubai, UAE; the Azadi Tower in Tehran, Iran; and of course the leaning Tower of Pisa in Italy.

QUESTION

Why is the Tower of Pisa leaning?
The Tower of Pisa is leaning because the soil underneath it (which is made of clay, sand, and mud) began to settle in an uneven way. This happened shortly after construction began. Since its building was completed in 1372, the tower has continued to lean further every year. Galileo is said to have conducted his famous experiment of dropping the musket and cannonball from the top of Pisa Tower in the sixteenth century.

Just as the name implies, a tower is a tall structure. Typically a tower is taller than it is wide. The width of a tower often tapers off with height. But why is that most often an important design feature?

Try This Experiment

MATERIALS NEEDED:
- 100 empty soda cans
- Bag of thick rubber bands

PROCEDURE:
1. Tell your child to construct the tallest tower she can from stacking empty soda cans one on top of the other.
2. Testing the sturdiness of her tower, have your child blow hard on the singly stacked cans. If they tumble easily, have her remove one can from the top, then repeat.
3. Have your child make her tower shorter until it does not tumble when she blows on it. Ask her how many stacked cans she has left.
4. Now tell her to build a different kind of tower, one that is wide on the bottom and gradually gets narrower on top.
5. Using 36 cans, tell her to construct the base of the tower with all 36 cans. Have her use the rubber bands to group every two cans together. Once she groups the cans in pairs, tell her to stand three pairs along one side, then place another row of three pairs, then another, until she has made 6 rows with 6 cans in each row.
6. Ask her to place a rubber band around every two adjacent soda cans that are not already tied together. Tell her to do this with all the loose cans until they are all connected together as one body.
7. Next, ask your child to construct a similar array of soda cans using 25 cans, arranged in a square shape, with 5 rows of 5 cans each. Tell her to secure all the cans to each other using rubber bands.
8. Now tell your child to stack the smaller square of soda cans on top of the bigger square. Make sure the two squares are centered.
9. Next, ask your child to construct a similar array of soda cans using 16 cans, arranged in a square shape, with 4 rows of 4 cans each. Tell her to secure all the cans to each other using rubber bands. Tell her to place this set on top of the last set.
10. Now ask your child to construct a similar array of soda cans using 9 cans, arranged in a square shape, with 3 rows of 3 cans each. Tell her to secure all the cans to each other using rubber bands. Tell her to place this set on top of the last set.

11. Tell your child to construct a similar array of soda cans using 4 cans, arranged in a square shape, with 2 rows of 2 cans each. Tell her to secure all the cans to each other using rubber bands. Tell her to place this set on top of the last set.

12. Finally, have your child place one can in the center on top of the entire pile. She has now completed the construction of a powerful tower.

Ask your child to blow hard on her tower from the side. Does this new tower easily collapse like the singly stacked soda cans? Ask her if this is a sturdier tower. How much taller is it (by soda can units) compared to the singly stacked one that remained intact when blowing on it?

Ask your child what is different about the two towers. Why is the second one more sturdy than the first? Is it possible that is because it has a wider base to stand on? If your child tells you that the wider base provides more support, then she intuitively understands an essential design criterion for most towers.

CHAPTER 7

Making It Go

Things that move capture the imagination of children and adults alike. You can probably recall times when you've seen a car on the road that made you look twice, gazed up into the sky to see a hot-air balloon crossing overhead, watched a water-skier seemingly glide on the surface of the water, or followed the motion of a sailboat as it sailed into the horizon. There are many different factors that make things move, such as fuel, hot air, a difference in water surface tension, or wind. In this chapter, you and your child will explore some building projects that make different objects move. Perhaps one, or more, will capture your child's imagination.

Balloon-Powered Car

Vehicles today are powered in so many different ways. There are gasoline-fueled automobiles, and ones that run on diesel. Solar cars exist, even if they are currently mostly students' projects in engineering departments. Electric cars have been making their way onto the scene, and hydrogen fuel cell cars are becoming a reality.

Since the invention of the wheel, earlier people have relied on animals for "horsepower" to supply the power for movement. But today, technology is being designed to take people places, some of which they have never been.

Are there other ways to power a car that is simpler than all this technology, without having to rely on an animal to pull it? The answer is yes, you can use your own breath; but the vehicle would have to be a toy car in order for it to move. The idea behind this experiment is that you and your child can build a car from scratch and use an "alternative source of energy" to power it.

Try This Experiment

MATERIALS NEEDED:

- Balloon
- 1 regular drinking straw
- 2 acrylic straws
- Tape
- 3" wide double-sided tape
- 4 blank CDs
- 8 identical plastic caps or lids (from juice bottles or milk containers)
- Wooden skewers
- Rectangular balsa wood sheet ($\frac{1}{4}$" thick) 10" × 4"
- Awl, or other hole-poking tool
- Ruler or tape measure
- Utility knife
- Glue gun
- Glue sticks (for glue gun)

PROCEDURE:

1. If the balsa wood sheet is longer than 10", use the utility knife to cut a 10" length of that 4"-wide sheet. This is the body of the car.
2. Using the glue gun, demonstrate to your child how to attach the first acrylic straw to the front edge of the balsa wood sheet. Make sure to center the straw along that edge. Assist your child as he attaches the other thick-walled straw to the back edge of the balsa wood sheet.

3. Assist your child in poking holes through the centers of the plastic caps.

4. Using the hot-glue gun, help your child glue a plastic cap (with the open side of the cap facing the CD) onto the center of the CD. Make sure the hole in the center of the cap is lined up with the center of the CD. The plastic cap is like a hubcap. Ask your child to place another plastic cap on the other side of the same CD, so that the CD has a hubcap on each side.

5. Tell your child to place the remaining 6 plastic caps on the other 3 CDs in the same fashion. The wheels of his car are ready.

6. Using the skewers, tell your child to push one skewer through the holes of the "hubcaps" of one of the wheels he made. The holes poked into the plastic lids should be just big enough to allow the skewer to go through snugly.

7. Tell your child to slide the skewer through the straw mounted along the front of the body of his car (the front edge of the balsa wood sheet).

8. Next, ask your child to push the other end of the skewer into the holes of another one of the wheels, so that he has both front wheels mounted. The skewer should fit snugly onto the second hubcap. Tell your child to push the two wheels close to the straw ends, but to leave just enough wiggle room for the skewer to rotate freely inside the straw.

9. Ask your child to follow the same steps to mount the rear wheels onto the body of his car.

10. Next, tell your child to slide the regular straw slightly into the balloon, then tape the balloon securely onto the straw.

11. Using the double-sided tape, ask your child to wrap the tape once all the way around the width of the balsa wood (the body of the car) and fasten the two ends of the tape on the back side.

12. To perform the experiment, find a long, smooth floor surface (such as a wooden or smooth concrete floor). Have your child place the car on the floor at one end of the long surface.

13. It is testing time! Tell your child to blow into the balloon through the straw until it is fully inflated. Tell him to place his thumb at the end of the straw to cover it until he is ready to launch the car. Have him place the balloon with the attached straw onto the sticky tape on the car, with the straw lined up along the length of the car. When he's ready, tell him to let go of the straw, and observe what happens to the car.

How far does the car go? Is the room long enough to allow for the balloon to deflate fully?

This type of car is obviously not meant to keep going very long like the ones that use batteries, but hopefully your child will have more fun with this car that he created than a store-bought car.

Powering a Boat with Soap

Boats can be powered by a person rowing tirelessly until he gets to his destination. Boats can also be powered by the wind and fuel. Some boats used to be powered by coal, like steamboats.

A simple boat can be powered by something else, like soap, and it is all related to the surface tension of water. When an object is placed in water, the surface tension of the water surrounding the object is all the same, so the object does not move. But if something can make the surface tension in the rear of a boat smaller than in the front of it, the greater surface tension in the water in the front can pull the boat forward.

QUESTION

What is surface tension?
A liquid like water has *surface tension* when it is in contact with the air. The molecules in the water are much more attracted to each other (they stick together) than to the air around them. The water molecules pull so strongly toward each other that they act as if there is an elastic sheet stretched around them.

This idea was demonstrated by scientists using soap. Soap lowers the surface tension of water. That's why soap feels slippery on the skin, and spreads more easily. If there is a reservoir in the rear of a light boat that releases soap into the water behind the boat, the spreading soap lowers the surface tension behind the boat, allowing the water in front of the boat (with higher tension) to pull the boat forward.

Try This Experiment

MATERIALS NEEDED:

- ⅛" polystyrene foam sheet
- Scissors or a craft knife
- Dishwasher soap
- Small glass
- Teaspoon
- Liquid dropper
- Long basin filled with water (about 25"–30" in length)'
- Rubbing alcohol

PROCEDURE:

1. Using the following drawing as a template, assist your child in cutting a piece of the polystyrene foam in the exact shape and size of the diagram (you might suggest to your child to trace the exact shape onto a piece of paper, then use that paper to draw the shape onto the polystyrene foam). This is the small boat that will be powered by soap. The boat should be about 1.5" in length and 1" in width at the base.

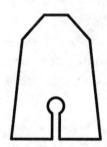

2. Fill the basin with water. Ask your child to place her polystyrene mini boat on the surface of the water.
3. Tell your child to pour some of the dishwasher soap into the small glass and add some water, then stir with the spoon. This will create a liquid soap that she can add to the boat with the dropper.
4. Using the dropper, ask your child to draw some of the liquid soap into it and then squeeze the liquid soap into the hole in the back of the boat. The hole acts like the soap reservoir for the boat. What does the boat do? Does it move forward for a short spurt? Does the boat then stop afterward?

Your child just witnessed how the difference in surface tension between the water in front and behind the boat propelled it forward. This difference in surface tension was created by the soap. Unfortunately, the soap acts like a surfactant, spreading over the water and lowering the water's surface tension all around the boat. That's why the boat stops. In order to make the boat move forward again, she would have to replace the water in the basin with new water that has no soap in it.

That's not fun! Is there another way to make the boat move forward constantly? The answer is yes. In 2013, Charles Renney, Ashley Brewer, and Tiddo Jonathan Mooibroek in the United Kingdom demonstrated that there can be better liquids, other than soap, to lower the surface tension of water behind the boat. They used rubbing alcohol!

Have your child repeat the experiment again. This time, tell her to use a clean dropper to add a couple of drops of rubbing alcohol into the hole in the rear end of the boat. Does the boat move forward? If so, tell her to add another couple of drops into the boat's reservoir (the hole). Is the boat propelled forward again? Tell her to keep adding more drops of alcohol, and notice that she does not need to replace the water in the basin like she did when she used soap.

The reason alcohol works better than soap is because the alcohol lowers the surface tension behind the boat, but—unlike the soap—alcohol does not spread over the surface of the water all around the boat; rather, it mixes with the water. This way the water can keep its higher surface tension.

QUESTION

What are visible signs of water surface tension?
A water droplet is spherical in shape. This is due to the strong attraction between water molecules. The molecules in a water drop pull inwardly toward each other with an equal amount of force, creating a spherical shape to the water drop, and tension on its surface. So the fact that a water droplet is a sphere *is* a visible sign of water surface tension.

It's true the boat is a miniature boat, but it serves the purpose of demonstrating yet another scientific principle. Surface tension of a liquid like water is an important phenomenon behind why water droplets are spherical in shape. It is also the reason why some bugs like water striders are able to "glide" on the surface of water.

Mousetrap Car Race

Things that are powered by something normally have some form of stored energy that can be converted into motion (and often heat). For example, when you push a heavy object in order to move it, you are able to do so only because you gave your body food earlier that day. This means the source of the energy (behind the work you did) was stored in the food you ate earlier. In other words, energy is constantly transforming from one form into another.

The gasoline you put into your car's tank has stored energy in it. Once that gasoline is ignited inside the engine, the stored energy in the gasoline transforms into work that eventually turns the car's axles. There are other ways energy can be stored to power vehicles. One such way is the energy stored in the wound torsion spring of a mousetrap. Yes, it's true that you can only power a small vehicle, but the principle is the same. To power the car, you are transforming the stored energy in the wound spring into motion.

Try This Experiment

MATERIALS NEEDED:

- Old-fashioned spring-loaded mousetrap
- 4 blank CDs
- 8 identical plastic caps or lids (from juice bottles or milk containers)
- 2 jumbo-sized safety pins
- 1 acrylic straw
- Wooden skewers (⅛" diameter)
- Rectangular balsa wood sheet (¼" thick) 14" × 4"
- 2 plastic clothes hangers
- Fishing line
- Cable ties
- Awl, or other hole-poking tool
- Ruler or tape measure
- Utility knife
- Wire cutter
- Scissors
- Athletic tape
- Glue gun
- Glue sticks (for glue gun)

PROCEDURE:

1. If the balsa wood sheet is longer than 14", then use the utility knife to cut a 14" length of that 4"-wide sheet. This is the body of the car.
2. Using the utility knife, cut out a rectangular notch from the rear end of the balsa wood frame. The notch should be 1" deep and 2" wide, as shown in the following diagram.

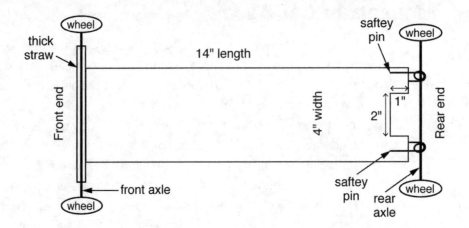

3. Using the glue gun, assist your child in securing the thick-walled straw to the front edge of the balsa wood sheet. Make sure to center the straw along that edge.

4. Using the wire cutter, cut off the fastening ends of the jumbo safety pins. This will need some force, so you might want to do that task yourself.

5. Now use the hot-glue gun to securely fasten the long ends of each safety pin on the top and the bottom of the rear end of the car frame. **IMPORTANT: Make sure the holes of the pins line up perfectly face-to-face. The rear axle will slide through those two holes.**

6. Now it's time to make the wheels of the car. Assist your child in poking holes through the centers of the plastic caps.

7. Using the hot-glue gun, help your child glue a plastic cap (with the open side of the cap facing the CD) onto the center of the CD. Make sure the center of the cap is lined up with the center of the CD. The plastic cap is like a hubcap. Ask your child to place another plastic cap on the other side of the same CD, so that the CD has a hubcap on each side.

8. Tell your child to place the remaining 6 plastic caps on the other 3 CDs in the same fashion. The wheels of his car are ready.

9. Using one of the skewers, tell your child to push the end of that skewer through the hole in the hubcap of one of the wheels he already made. The hole poked into the plastic caps should be just big enough to allow the skewer to go through **snugly**.

10. Tell your child to slide the free end of the skewer through the straw mounted on the front end of his car.

11. Next, ask your child to push the other end of that skewer into the hole of another one of the wheels, so that he has both front wheels mounted. The skewer should fit **snugly** onto the second hubcap. Tell your child to push the two wheels toward the straw ends, but to leave just enough wiggle room for the skewer rotate freely inside the straw.

12. Ask your child to slide the second skewer through the mounted safety pins in the rear of the car, and center it. Inform your child that this skewer will serve as the rear axle that will be powered by the mousetrap. NOTE: Do *not* mount the rear wheels *yet*.

13. Using the athletic tape, cut a foot-length of the tape and wind it around the center of the rear axle until the tape makes a thick padding that's ¼" in thickness.

14. Secure a cable tie strongly over the center of the athletic tape, then cut the excess cable with scissors. The tie will serve as a notch to loop the fishing line around. Use the glue gun to further secure the cable tie over the tape so that the tie does not move, wiggle, slide, or rotate. Make sure to *not* cover the tie notch with any glue, so that the notch sticks out.

15. Now tell your child to place the rear wheels onto the rear axle as he did with the front wheels.

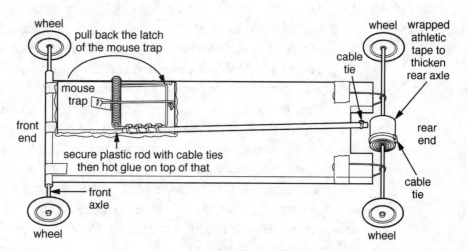

16. Now it's time to make a few adjustments to the mousetrap. Using the utility knife, cut out the bottom horizontal part of the plastic hanger. You need about a 12" length plastic rod. This is something you might want to do yourself, since it will need a lot of effort.

17. It is now critical to figure out where to attach the plastic rod onto the mousetrap. After loading the mousetrap, hold it so that the metal latch is close to you, and the side the latch will snap onto is on the far side. The plastic rod will need to be attached to the left arm of the latch, as shown in the diagram. Assist your child in tying the plastic rod onto the left metal arm of the mousetrap using cable ties. Cut off the excess cables, and secure the cable ties onto the mousetrap arm using hot glue.

18. Next, fasten a cable tie about an inch from the tip of the plastic rod. Cut off the excess cable and hot glue the cable tie onto the rod securely.

19. Now it's time to secure the mousetrap to the frame of the car. Using the hot glue gun, tell your child to place the loaded mousetrap plus plastic rod at the front right corner of his car frame, as shown in the diagram.

20. Carefully release the load from the mousetrap so the plastic rod faces forward, toward the front of the car. This will help your child assess how much fishing line to use. Tell him to tie one end of the fishing line around the plastic rod below the cable tie. Tell him to tie the fishing line a couple of times, then secure it to the rod with hot glue.

21. Ask your child to extend the fishing line all the way to the rear axle where the cable tie is. Tell him to cut his line a little longer than where it reaches the axle so that he has enough excess line to make a loop. Assist your child in making a loop at the end of his fishing line.

22. Now it's time for your child to power his car with the mousetrap. With the plastic rod facing the front of the car, tell your child to put the fishing line loop around the cable-tie notch in the rear axle. Assist him in turning the rear wheels so that the fishing line starts winding around the wrapped athletic tape on the rear axle. This should start lifting the plastic rod that's extended from the mousetrap arm. Tell him to keep winding the fishing line around the rear axle until the plastic rod moves all the way back and it is lying down along the frame of the car, as shown in the diagram. Tell him to hold the rear wheels so that he prevents them from rotating. His car is now ready to be tested.

23. Tell your child to stand at one end of a long hallway with a smooth surface (such as a wooden or smooth concrete floor). Have your child place the car on the floor.

24. It is testing time! Tell your child to let go of the rear wheels.

How far does his car travel before it stops? Measure that distance and record it.

Ask your child to make another mousetrap car, but use a shorter plastic rod (perhaps 8" long). Have him race both cars side by side. Do they both travel just as far? Which one travels the furthest? He probably found out that the car with the longer rod travels further.

These investigations can become the entry point into the world of design that has intrigued engineers for centuries. The mousetrap car can be the first of many design projects that engage your child for the rest of his life.

Water Rocket Launch

Rockets are a fascination for many. Some people's interest in rockets starts rather early in childhood, and they never lose the fascination. Some of them end up studying rockets, even building them to send to space. Those are rocket scientists, like the ones who work at NASA.

QUESTION

What does NASA stand for?
NASA is the National Aeronautics and Space Agency. It was founded in 1958 by the U.S. government. NASA builds satellites that orbit our planet so they can learn more about Earth and space. NASA builds probes and spacecrafts that help to inform scientists about distant worlds such as other planets and moons, asteroids, comets, stars, and galaxies.

Is there an easy way to make a rocket that is safe to launch in your own neighborhood park? Absolutely. The best such rocket is a water-air rocket. When air is compressed inside a partially filled water bottle, the built-up pressure inside the bottle becomes too large at some point, and the bottle launches into the air like a rocket.

Try this experiment outside on a warm day and where there is plenty of open space around you.

Try This Experiment

MATERIALS NEEDED:
- Empty 1-liter soda bottle
- Bicycle pump with hose (one that can stand upright)
- Electrical tape
- 6"-long PVC pipe (3" in diameter)
- Hacksaw

PROCEDURE:

1. Assist your child in covering the outside edge of the loose end of the bicycle pump hose with electrical tape so that it can fit tightly into the mouth of the soda bottle.
2. Using the hacksaw, help your child cut out a small square window at one end of the PVC pipe right at the edge, so only three cuts need to be made. The PVC pipe will serve as a vertical launcher for the bottle rocket. The window will allow your child to insert the hose of the bicycle pump into the PVC pipe.
3. Tell your child to fill ⅓ of the bottle with water.
4. Ask your child to thread the bicycle pump hose into the PVC pipe through the little cut-out window and out the other end. Tell her to set the PVC pipe standing on the ground so that the window is resting on the ground. The PVC pipe should be standing upright on its end.
5. Assist your child in tightly fitting the bicycle hose into the mouth of the bottle without spilling any of its water content. Make sure the hose fits really tightly, so you and your child can pump enough air into the bottle to build up plenty of pressure for the launch.
6. Now have your child place the bottle (hose attached) onto the PVC pipe such that the bottle is standing vertically with the mouth of the bottle inserted into the PVC pipe. Make sure the bicycle pump stands on the ground about a foot from where the PVC pipe is standing.
7. Tell your child to start pumping air into the rocket. She will start to see bubbles form in the water inside the rocket. Make sure she is standing off to the side of the bottle and *not* looking directly down at it. You might want to assist her in pumping air into the bottle. How many pumps does it take before the rocket launches? Can she estimate how high it flew?

Your child will want to repeat the launch of her rocket. See if you can wind a couple more turns of electrical tape around the end of the pump hose so that you can fit the hose even more tightly into the bottle. The tighter the connection between hose and bottle, the higher the air pressure builds inside the bottle, and the higher the rocket goes. This is a fun activity that may launch your child into rocket science!

CHAPTER 8

Naked Eye Astronomy

Celestial objects have intrigued human beings since the dawn of mankind. For most of human existence, relying on those heavenly objects was the way to navigate through space, and also to identify the seasons. The continued interest in looking up at the heavens may be one of the last activities that connect today's humans with their ancestors. This chapter will explore some basic ideas in observing the skies. It will focus on the moon, the sun, and the constellations. Even though the presented concepts are basic, they have persisted throughout history in their relevance to the lives of human beings around the globe. They continue to play a significant role today for many people in many places on our planet.

Keeping a Moon-Phase Journal

When the moon is visible at night, it is the brightest object in the night sky. People in ancient cultures were constantly aware of the cycle of the moon as it changed its phase, and this information was significant to their daily lives. Some calendars today still follow the moon's cycle, such as the Jewish and Islamic calendars. There are still indigenous people around the globe today who use the moon as a method to count elapsed time in number of lunar cycles. The moon's cycle was not only important for religious purposes, but also for telling time and for navigational purposes. Thousands of years ago, some ancient cultures in central Africa used the moon to predict if their crops would grow. They learned how to predict whether the season would be rainy or dry based on observing the orientation of the horns of the crescent moon.

Today, there are so many distractions in everyday life that people rarely look up at the sky, let alone take note of the presence of the moon. It is very simple to learn to become aware of the moon's phases, and to learn to tell time, and directions, simply from the moon. It all starts with keeping a moon journal for one full cycle of the moon.

VOCAB

Lunar: Lunar means pertaining to the moon. For example, a lunar cycle is one full cycle (revolution) of the moon around earth. A lunar month has days spanning the length of one full moon cycle. A lunar calendar includes a set number of months that follow the moon's cycle, like the Islamic calendar that is made of twelve lunar months.

Try This Experiment

MATERIALS NEEDED:
- 4 sheets of paper
- Pencil
- Internet access (for cloudy days)

PROCEDURE:
1. Using a search engine on the Internet, find out when the next new moon will be. (A moon cycle is generally considered to begin with the new moon.) Have your child start his observations of the moon on that day.

2. Help your child create a table with four columns on his paper sheets. Ask him to make 30 rows in the table, one for every day of observation. (He will most likely need to use more than one sheet of paper for the entire table.) The provided table can serve as an example to illustrate what his table would look like. He will need to expand this table into 30 rows to accommodate every day of the lunar cycle.

3. Tell your child he does not need to stay up late or wake up very early on the days when the moon rises and/or sets at times outside his normal waking hours. Assist him in finding the rising and setting times with an Internet search for those days. He can simply search for "data for moon on" and type the date, including the year as well as the city where you live.

4. On days or evenings that are clear, walk outside with your child and observe the moon's shape if it is visible that day or night.

5. Have your child record the moon's data for each day in his table. Assist him in making it a daily habit to either step outside to look for the moon, or (in case of cloudy days or days when the moon is not visible during his waking hours) find moon information for that day on the Internet. Encourage him to do his data entry every day.

Use this sample table to help your child make an expanded version for all the days in the moon's cycle. In the column that lists the shape of the moon, have your child draw the shape of the moon for that day.

SAMPLE MOON PHASES RECORD

Day Number	Shape of Moon	Moonrise Time	Moonset Time
1			
2			
3			

Once an entire lunar cycle is recorded (from one new moon to the next new moon), you can sit down with your child to look at his record and see what he can learn from it.

Ask your child first to examine the Shape of Moon column in his table. What does he notice about the shape of the visible moon day after day? Quiz him on whether he notices more of the moon's disk becoming illuminated with each subsequent day until full moon. Prompt him to notice what happens to the moon's illumination in the second half of the cycle following the full moon phase. Does he observe that the disk of the moon becomes less and less illuminated as the moon goes through the second half of its cycle?

Next, have your child examine the Moonrise Time column. What does he notice about the rising time of the moon day after day? Ask him if he observes that the moon rises later every day. Ask him to calculate the number of minutes the moon rises later every day. Using a separate sheet of paper, tell your child to start at the top of his table, subtract the moonrise time in the first row from that in the second row and write the difference on a new sheet of paper. Ask him next to subtract the moonrise time in the second row from that in the third row and record it underneath the first difference he calculated. Tell him to do the same calculation for all subsequent numbers in the Moonrise Time column until he reaches the end of the table in his moon phases record. If he took all the numbers he calculated and wrote on the separate sheet of paper, then found their average, he would find that the moon rises (on average) about fifty minutes later every day.

QUESTION

How do you calculate an average of many numbers?
To calculate the average of many numbers you would first add up all those numbers to find their *total sum*. Next you would count *how many* of those numbers you have. Finally, you would divide the *total sum* by *how many*, and that would give you the average.

Next, have your child examine the Moonset Time column. What does he notice about the setting time of the moon day after day? Ask him if he observes that the moon sets later every day just like it rose later every day. Ask him to calculate the number of minutes the moon sets later every day, and write down that number on another separate sheet of paper. Tell him to make the same calculation for the entire fourth column in his moon phases record. If he took all those number of minutes and found their average, he would find that the moon sets (on average) about fifty minutes later every day.

The reason the moon rises (and sets) about fifty minutes later every day, is due to the moon's rotation about planet Earth. If the moon didn't rotate around planet Earth, then it would always rise and set at a precisely fixed time day after day. Also, if the moon didn't constantly rotate around planet Earth, it would always keep the same apparent shape relative to someone observing it from earth. In other words, the shape of the illuminated surface of the moon would never change at all from the perspective of humans.

Moon Navigation

Before the advent of modern times a skilled navigator was a prized person in society. Navigation was done using objects in the sky like the sun, moon, planets, and stars. Notable to those fine navigators were the movement of those heavenly objects in the sky above. The canopy overhead that we call the sky was like a map that assisted those in earlier times to find their orientation in space, and also as a clock to tell time.

So how can one use the moon to navigate through space and time? How can the phase of the moon and its location in the sky on a particular day be helpful to figure out the cardinal directions, as well as time? It all boils down to understanding the phases of the moon as the moon moves around earth.

Everything in the sky rises in the east and sets in the west. It is a result of the earth's rotation. This includes the sun, moon, planets, and stars.

The moon is the closest celestial object to earth, and it moves around the earth. It takes the moon about 29–30 days to complete one cycle about the earth. Because of this gradual rotation of the moon around earth, the moonrise time (and moonset time) occurs later every day for each moon cycle.

New Moon Phase

At the beginning of a moon cycle the moon is lined up in the same direction as the sun relative to an observer on earth. In other words, if an observer on earth faces the direction where the sun is, then the moon will be in that same direction as well. The moon is said to be in a new moon phase when it is in the same direction as the sun relative to earth. In this phase, both the moon and sun rise above the horizon at the same time. They also set below the horizon at the same time. This means that a new moon *rises in the east at sunrise*, and *sets in the west at sunset.* Also, because the moon and sun in this phase are in the same direction relative to someone on earth, the side of the moon that is lit by the sun is facing away from earth. This makes the new moon not visible on that day because the side of it that is lit is facing away from earth.

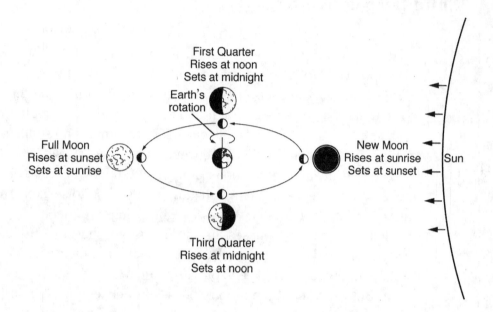

First Quarter Phase

At a quarter of the way through the moon's cycle, the moon is said to be in a first quarter phase. For an observer on earth, this is when the *right* half of the moon's disk appears lit. A first quarter moon *rises in the east at noon*, and *sets in the west at midnight.* The first quarter moon is exactly halfway between a new moon and a full moon. Note that its rising time at noon is halfway between sunrise and sunset, and its setting time at midnight is halfway between sunset and sunrise.

Full Moon Phase

Half a moon cycle later, when the moon is on the opposite side of the sun (relative to an observer on earth), the moon is said to be in a full moon phase. In this phase, when the sun sets the moon rises, and vice versa. This means that a full moon *rises in the east at sunset*, and *sets in the west at sunrise.* Because the lit face of the full moon that's facing the sun is also facing the earth, the entire disk of the moon is fully illuminated on that day.

Third Quarter Phase

At three-quarters of the way through the moon's cycle, the moon is said to be in a third quarter phase. This is when the *left* half of the moon's disk appears lit for an observer on earth. A third quarter moon *rises in the east at midnight*, and *sets in the west at noon*. The third quarter moon is exactly halfway between a full moon and the next new moon. Note that its rising time at midnight is halfway between sunset and sunrise, and its setting time at noon is halfway between sunrise and sunset. Note that reference to rising and setting times at noon and midnight are approximate, not exact. Those times change slightly from season to season. They also move forward by one hour when daylight savings is added.

The previous four phases are the main four phases of the moon on its cycle around earth. If you place them on the perimeter of a circle they would be separated from each other by a quarter of the circle's circumference. But what about the moon's phases in between these four primary phases? Do those have names as well? The answer is yes. The following two paragraphs introduce the "in-between" phases.

The Waxing Journey

When the moon is in the first week of its cycle, a crescent moon is visible in the sky with its horns facing the left side of an observer. This crescent moon appears thicker night after night, and is known as a *waxing crescent moon*. In its second week, the moon no longer has a crescent shape; it starts to gradually become more and more rounded on the left side. In this second week of the moon's cycle (after the first quarter) it is known as a *waxing gibbous moon*.

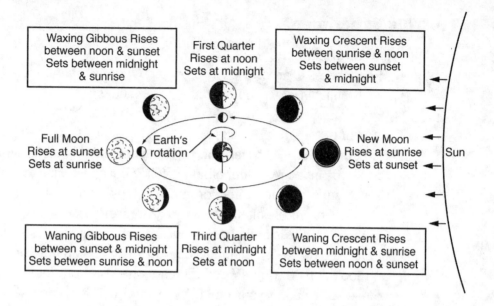

The Waning Journey

Once the moon is past its full moon phase, it is at the beginning of the third week of its cycle (before the third quarter). The moon is still rounded on both sides, but now the illuminated right side seems to get less and less rounded day after day. This is known as a *waning gibbous moon*. In the last week of its cycle, the moon's lit face becomes a crescent shape, but its horns are facing the right side of an observer. This crescent moon appears thinner night after night, and is known as a *waning crescent moon*.

The moon's motion in the sky is like a clock that's always been there. With this knowledge of the phases of the moon, and their rising and setting times, you and your child can now learn how to navigate using it. Make sure to study the phases of the moon with your child before you start using the moon to navigate.

Try This Experiment

MATERIALS NEEDED:
- Moon phases chart previously provided (with the main four phases)
- Red flashlight (for use during night observations)

PROCEDURE:
1. On a ***full moon*** night, step outside with your child right after sunset and look at the moon. Ask your child the following question: If the full moon rises at sunset, which direction are you looking at? Ask her if the full moon will be visible all night (since it just rose)?
2. On the day of a ***third quarter moon***, when the moon's disk is half-illuminated on the left, step outside with your child an hour before noon and look at the moon. Which direction are you both looking at when you see it? Remind your child that a third quarter moon sets around noon. Ask your child if this third quarter moon will be visible for the rest of the day into the evening.
3. A day ***after a new moon***, when there is a thin crescent moon in the sky, step outside with your child right after sunset and look at the moon. Which direction do you both have to look at in order to see the crescent moon? Is it in the direction the sun is setting? Ask your child if this crescent moon will be visible all night.
4. On the day of a ***first quarter moon***, when the moon's disk is half-illuminated on the right, step outside with your child an hour after noon and look at the first quarter moon. In which direction are you both looking when you see it? Remind your child that a first quarter moon rises around noon. Ask your child if this first quarter moon will be visible for the rest of the day into the evening.

Why does the full moon appear bigger near the horizon?
This phenomenon is called the Moon Illusion. Its been known since ancient times. In the early eleventh century, Ibn al-Haytham from Iraq provided an explanation for the Moon Illusion. He explained that the apparent change in the moon is a psychological illusion because the mind perceives the moon as a closer object when it is near the horizon and "interprets" the moon as seemingly bigger. When the moon is higher in the sky, there are no objects around it (like buildings, trees) to compare it to, and so it feels more distant making it seem smaller.

If your child's answer pertaining to the first question about the *full moon* was that she would look east because the full moon rises in the east (as everything else does), then she is perfectly correct. And if she said the full moon will be visible all night because it just rose at sunset, then she nailed it.

Examine both your answers to the questions related to observing the *third quarter moon*. If you both said you found the third quarter moon in the west because it was about to set at noon, then you are both correct. And if your child figured out that this moon will not be visible for the rest of the day and into the evening because once it sets it disappears from the sky, then she is really beginning to tune in to the moon phases.

Both of you guessed right if you said you're looking west when observing a thin crescent moon, right after sunset, the *day after a new moon*. And yes, that moon was found in the same direction in which the sun was setting. And if your child said that the crescent moon will not be visible all night because it would shortly set in the west, then she's got it.

Finally, examine your answers to the questions related to observing the *first quarter moon*. If you both said you found the first quarter moon in the east because it just rose at noon, then you are both on target. Your child has most likely figured out by now that this moon will be visible for the rest of the day and into the evening, because it has just risen and will be visible for the next twelve hours.

These are the main phases to remember about the moon in order to navigate. Once you and your child get accustomed to using these four main phases, you can start observing the moon in its waxing and waning crescent and gibbous phases, using the second diagram in this lesson.

So if you're lost on a hike in the middle of the day, and you look up at the sky and see a moon with its right half lit (meaning a first quarter moon), and it is roughly 2 P.M., then you know you are facing east.

Or if you're on an overnight family trip and you're bored in the car, try to look for the moon, and guess the direction you're traveling in. If you look out the window and see a moon with its left half lit (meaning a third quarter moon), and it is late morning, then you know you are looking westward. And if you're on the passenger side of the car, and you are gazing west as you look out the window, then the car must be traveling south. It's a fun way to keep your mind engaged and entertained as you gradually improve your navigation skills.

Does the Sun Always Rise in the East?

Everyone takes for granted that the sun rises in the east and sets in the west. When people get in their cars, they pay no attention to the position of the sun in the sky for navigational purposes. But if everyone needed to rely on the sun to find out which direction was east, for instance, they would look carefully every morning.

If people's everyday life depended on confirming the cardinal directions by reading the position of the sun in the sky, such a significant inquiry would require great accuracy. Does the sun always rise exactly in the east every day of the year? It turns out the answer to this question is *no*!

Try This Experiment

MATERIALS NEEDED:
- Window in your house exactly facing east (or a street you frequent that is lined up along the east-west directions)
- Sheet of paper for recording observations

PROCEDURE:
1. Prepare your child mentally by telling him this observation will take place over the span of a year.
2. Start your observations around March 21. Stand with your child in the room an hour after sunrise and face the middle of the window that's

facing east. Make sure the sun has risen high enough so that you can see it through the window. Mark the spot where you are standing so you can come back to the same spot every time. Where do you both see the sun? Is it right along the middle of the window (neither to the left nor the right)? You should see the sun along the middle of that window if the window faces exactly east. Have your child record this morning's observation, along with the date (March 21) on the paper sheet. Save the paper.

3. If you are instead using a street facing east, then take a walk with your child an hour after sunrise. Cross that street while looking at the sun's location relative to the middle of the road. Where do you both spot the sun? Is it right over the middle of the road? Have your child record this morning's observation, along with the date (March 21) on the paper sheet. Save the paper.

4. Now repeat the previous observation three months later, on June 21. Where do you both spot the sun? Is it right along the middle of the window? Is the sun right over the middle of the road? Or has the sun shifted its location to the left (north of east)? Have your child record this morning's observation, along with the date (June 21) on the paper sheet. Save the paper.

5. Now repeat the observation three months later, on September 21. Where do you both spot the sun? Is it back along the middle of the window? Is the sun back over the middle of the road? Have your child record this morning's observation, along with the date (September 21) on the paper sheet. Save the paper.

6. Finally, repeat the observation one last time three months later, on December 21. Where do you both spot the sun? Is it right along the middle of the window? Is the sun right over the middle of the road? Or has the sun shifted its location to the right (south of east)? Have your child record this morning's observation, along with the date (December 21) on the paper sheet.

If you and your child observed the sun rising exactly in the east (along the middle of the window, or above the middle of the road that's facing east) on March 21 and September 21, then you have both observed the sunrise during the equinoxes. There are two equinoxes: the vernal (spring) equinox, and the autumnal (fall) equinox. On the equinoxes, the sun rises exactly in the east and sets exactly in the west.

QUESTION

Were there ancient cultures that took notice of the equinoxes?
The Aztecs were among many ancient cultures who observed the equinoxes. The architectural design of their capital city, Tenochtitlan, showed an intentional alignment of structures with the direction of the rising sun on the equinoxes. The sun would rise exactly between the twin temples of the Great Temple (called Templo Mayor) on the morning of the fall and spring equinoxes.

On June 21, you have both probably seen the sun rising to the left of the window frame (or over the left side of the road that's facing east). In other words, you both saw the sun rise north of east (NE). This day is known as summer solstice. On this day, the sun rises the most north of east (NE), and sets the most north of west (NW). On December 21, you have both observed the sun rising to the right of the window frame (or over the right side of the road that's facing east). In other words, you both saw the sun rise south of east (SE). This day is known as winter solstice. On this day, the sun rises the most south of east (SE), and sets the most south of west (SW).

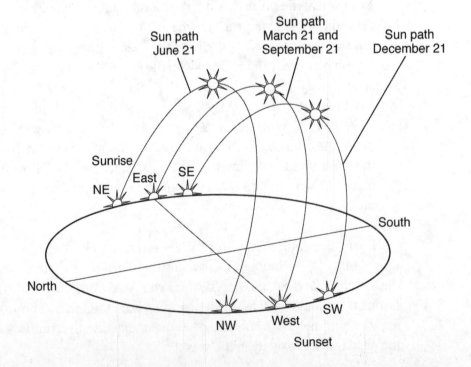

The previous illustration shows the path of the sun in the sky on the different dates you observed the sun after it had risen.

The reason the sun shifts its rising (and setting) locations throughout the year is because of the tilt of Earth's axis. If the axis of Earth were not tilted, there would never be changes in the locations of sunrise and sunset.

Stonehenge

Many ancient cultures were very tuned to the motion of the sun throughout the year. In fact, that's how they could tell which season it was. One such example is the structure built in Stonehenge in England between 3000 and 2000 B.C.

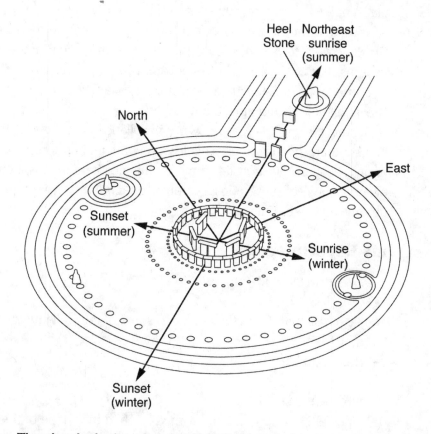

The sketch depicts the stones built at Stonehenge to mark sunrise on the summer solstice. If one were standing right in the middle of the central round structure, the sun would rise exactly over the Heel Stone (facing NE) on the morning of the summer solstice.

If you frequently travel the highways that run along an east-west axis in the country, you and your child will start to notice where the sun sets throughout the seasons. It is never always exactly in the west. It is a wonderful feeling to know the sun's motion so intimately.

The Easiest Constellations to Recognize

It is fun to look up at the sky and take notice of stars and the patterns they make. It is something that people have done throughout the world, through time, regardless of culture, age, gender, or race.

Observed star patterns have not changed their shape throughout millennia. When the ancient Greeks looked up at the sky, they perceived the patterns, as did the Babylonians and the Egyptians before them. The ancient Greeks gave a few names, based on their mythological figures, to the star patterns that were visible in the northern hemisphere. These star patterns, also known as constellations, still hold the names of many of the ancient Greek mythological figures today.

There are eighty-eight known constellations throughout the northern and southern hemispheres. This lesson will focus on four well-known and easily recognizable constellations in the northern hemisphere. You can observe some of these constellations throughout the year, but others only during certain seasons.

Try This Experiment

MATERIALS NEEDED:
- Compass
- Sky chart that shows the outline of some of the well-known constellations
- Red flashlight

PROCEDURE:
1. On your sky chart, identify with your child the shape of the star pattern known as the Big Dipper (which is part of the constellation Ursa Major). The Big Dipper has the shape of a ladle that's easy to spot. Also, its stars are bright enough to see even with a little bit of light pollution.

2. Step outside in early August, around 9–10 P.M. Help your child find the direction north, using the compass. Looking over the northwestern horizon, gaze up gradually until you both find the Big Dipper.

3. The next constellation to help your child locate on the sky chart is Orion. Orion is easy to identify, starting with the three stars that are lined up diagonally close together. These three stars make up what is known as the belt of Orion (a legendary hunter from Greek mythology). The best time to observe Orion is in the winter. In fact, Orion is visible all winter long. To easily find Orion, have your child look for it above the east-southeast horizon around 9 P.M. sometime in early December.

4. The next constellation to help your child locate on the sky chart is Cygnus. Cygnus is easy to identify because its stars make the shape of a cross. In fact, Cygnus is known as the Northern Cross. The best time to observe Cygnus is in late summer, in late August or early September. Have your child look high in the sky, almost overhead, around 9–10 P.M. in late summer, and try to identify the stars that make a cross pattern.

5. The last constellation to help your child locate on the sky map is Cassiopeia. Cassiopeia is easy to identify because it looks like a *W* or *M*. Cassiopeia never sets; the constellation is always above the horizon all year round. Such a constellation is called a *circumpolar constellation*. Pick a time to observe Cassiopeia, say in late October. Have your child look above the northeastern horizon at around 8–9 P.M. in late October, until he identifies the stars that make a *W* pattern.

QUESTION

What's the meaning of these constellations' names?
Some of the constellations were named after characters in ancient Greek mythological stories. For example, Ursa Major was the big bear, Orion was a giant hunter, Cygnus meant "swan," and Cassiopeia referred to a queen, the wife of king Cepheus. Each one of these names was part of an elaborate mythological story that left its imprint on the night sky.

Once your child learns to identify these constellations, have him trace how they change their position in the sky night after night. For example, by late April, Orion would have drifted westward far enough that it would have gone out of view below the horizon. Most of the Big Dipper is visible year round, and so is Cassiopeia. However, Cygnus would be totally out of view by winter, as it also would have drifted westward and disappeared below the horizon.

Identifying constellations is always a fun activity, especially when taking a walk or traveling by car at night. So the next time you are on a night trip in the car, you can help make the time pass by asking your child which constellations he can identify.

CHAPTER 9

Household Chemistry

Chemical reactions happen inside your body all the time. For example, that's how foods are broken down inside your stomach in order to digest them, and how your body makes heat to stay alive. But chemistry is also everywhere around you. An appetizing brownie would not be so delicious without a whole lot of chemistry that must take place within the ingredients. It is certain chemicals in foods that make things taste sour, sweet, salty, and so on. Chemistry is also what provides energy for the batteries that power the electronic devices you use. This chapter will explore some basic ideas in chemistry that will help you and your child gain a glimpse of how chemistry is such an integral part of daily life.

How Batteries Work

You use batteries in many things every single day of your life. You charge the battery of your phone every day; your alarm clock may have backup batteries in case the electricity goes out; your rechargeable laptop and tablet are convenient because you can carry them around. The watch on your wrist and even your car require battery power to run.

How does a basic battery work? What happens inside a battery so that it can provide power? What is necessary to make the battery work? Why does it eventually stop working, so that you have to buy a new one? Luckily, there is a simple way to investigate and learn how to make a battery at home.

Try This Experiment

MATERIALS NEEDED:

- 5 zinc washers, size #10
- 5 pennies
- Freshly squeezed lemon juice
- Thick paper towel
- Scissors
- Plate
- 2 electric wires with alligator clips at their ends
- Piece of aluminum foil (3–4" in width)
- 1 LED light bulb

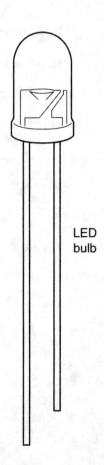

LED bulb

PROCEDURE:

1. Assist your child in cutting the paper towel into square pieces that are 2" × 2". Tell him to cut up about 10 such pieces.

2. Now ask your child to fold each paper towel piece in half 4 times. In other words, fold the 2" × 2" square in half, making a 2" × 1" rectangle. Then fold that rectangle in half, making a 1" × 1" square. Repeat the last two steps again until the final folded piece would be a thick square with sides that are ½" × ½" that are slightly smaller than the penny's diameter. Have your child fold all the 2" × 2" paper towel pieces in this fashion before moving on to the next step.

3. Have your child dip the folded pieces of paper towel into the freshly squeezed lemon juice), without squeezing out the juice. Ask him to place those pieces on the plate.

4. Tell your child to clip 1 alligator clip wire to 1 arm of the LED bulb, and another wire to the other arm.

5. Next, ask your child to place one of the zinc washers on the aluminum foil. On top of the washer, have him place one of the folded paper towels soaked in lemon juice, then a penny on top. Have him place another folded paper towel that's soaked in lemon juice on the penny, then a zinc washer on top of that. Basically, tell him to alternate washer and penny (with folded paper towels soaked in lemon juice in between penny and washer) until the last piece on top is the fifth penny. Tell him he doesn't need a paper towel over the last penny. Now he's got a battery.

6. It's time for your child to test his battery. Tell him to touch the loose end of one of the alligator clip wires to the aluminum foil. Assist him in touching the other alligator clip wire's loose end to the top penny. What do you both observe? Does the LED bulb light up?

When the LED bulb lights up, tell your child it is totally powered by pennies, zinc washers, and the lemon juice!

VOCAB

Electrode: An electrode is a metal used in an electric circuit that comes in contact with some other nonmetal part of the circuit (like an electrolyte, for example).

A battery requires three ingredients: a zinc electrode, a copper electrode, and a liquid containing electrolytes like lemon juice. Copper has a stronger electronegativity than zinc does. This means copper has a stronger ability to attract electrons than zinc does. In this case, zinc gives away electrons that flow toward the copper (via the wires), and the bulb lights up.

QUESTION

What is an electrolyte?
An *electrolyte* is a substance that, when added to a solvent, it becomes ionized (dissociates into its parts, with each part having an electric charge). An example of an electrolyte is salt. When salt is added to a solvent like water, each salt molecule breaks into its constituent atoms with each carrying an electric charge. Because salt behaves in this fashion, meaning it acts like an electrolyte, it can dissolve in water.

Because the zinc gives up electrons to copper, the zinc electrode is the negative terminal of the battery (also known as the *anode*). And because the copper is eager to receive electrons from the zinc, the copper electrode is the positive terminal of the battery (also known as the *cathode*).

But what role does the electrolyte play inside the battery? It is specifically the acid inside the lemon juice that acts as an electrolyte and dissociates into positive and negative ions. A simple example of an electrolyte is table salt. It consists of one sodium atom and one chlorine atom that are combined. When table salt is dissolved in water, the sodium and chlorine atoms dissociate, becoming positive and negative ions. The negative ions from the electrolyte allow the zinc atoms that just lost electrons (and became positive as a result of that) to move away from the zinc electrode. The positive ions in the electrolyte move toward the copper electrode, because they like the newly arriving electrons the copper took from the zinc, and they will snatch those electrons.

An animated picture looks like this: When the zinc gives away electrons, the electrons fly away along the path of the wire toward the copper that's electron-thirsty. The wire connecting zinc to copper acts like a superhighway for the electrons. The ions inside the electrolyte are heavy, and don't move around as easily as the lighter electrons can along the superhighway. However, the negative ions can sweep away (neutralize) the zinc that lost its electrons. If the negative ions didn't do that, then there would be too many zinc atoms that lost electrons congregating around the zinc electrode, and the flow of electrons would stop. The positive ions are bribed by the newly arriving electrons on the copper electrode, and move toward the copper.

QUESTION

What is electronegativity?
Metal atoms, like zinc and copper, have a tendency to either lose some of their electrons or attract other electrons. When a metal atom has a strong tendency to attract electrons from other atoms, it is said that is has a strong *electronegativity*. Copper has a stronger electronegativity than zinc.

So the zinc and copper electrodes on their own cannot make up a battery; neither does the electrolyte on its own. In other words, the lemon juice alone, or the lemon itself, is not a battery. To turn a lemon into a battery, you need the zinc and copper electrodes. In place of a lemon you can use a lime, a potato, or anything that contains acid, like vinegar.

Eventually, all the zinc gets used up. Also, when all the negative and positive ions in the electrolyte find partners on either electrode, then the electrolyte no longer exists. Whichever one happens first brings the power of the battery to an end.

Alkaline or Acidic?

One of the many ways food can be categorized is by whether it is alkaline or acidic. Whether a particular food is considered alkaline or acidic depends on a measurement of certain ions in that food.

In order to understand the nature of ions, we must start with a discussion on atoms. An atom is the smallest building block in nature. The smallest atom found in nature is the hydrogen atom. A hydrogen atom (its symbol is H) is made up of one proton (a positive charge in the center—or nucleus—of the atom) and one electron (a negative charge that moves around the nucleus). One positive charge attracts one negative charge; therefore, if the hydrogen atom has one positive charge and one negative charge, it is electrically neutral. Most atoms can easily share electrons with other atoms; when they do, so that all the combined atoms are electrically neutral, they form what is known as a *compound*.

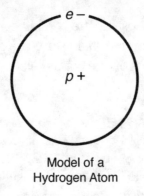

Model of a
Hydrogen Atom

Atoms can lose or gain electrons. When a neutral hydrogen atom, H, loses an electron, it is left with only one positive charge (or proton), but no electrons; it is then called a hydrogen ion (its symbol is H^+). An ion is not electrically neutral. Remember that atoms can combine together; they do so by sharing electrons. A hydrogen atom, H, can share one electron, while an oxygen atom, O, can share two electrons. If a neutral oxygen atom, O, shares one electron with a neutral hydrogen atom, H, there is still another electron the oxygen atom can share in that union. Such a union between one hydrogen atom and one oxygen atom produces an ion known as a hydroxide ion, OH^-.

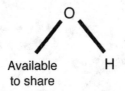

Available
to share

So what do ions have to do with a food substance being acidic or alkaline? If the substance has a high concentration of hydrogen ions, H^+, it is considered acidic; however if the substance has a high concentration of hydroxide ions, OH^-, the substance is considered alkaline. The measurement of acidity or alkalinity is called a *pH measurement*. To measure the pH of a substance is to measure the concentration of hydrogen ions in it. In fact, the letters pH refer to the "power of Hydrogen."

The numerical measurement of pH ranges from 0 to 14. At pH=0, the substance is strongly acidic, and at pH=14, the substance is strongly alkaline. Pure water has pH=7 (neutral pH). Therefore, any substance that has a pH less than 7 is considered acidic, and if its pH is higher than 7 it is alkaline.

For example, white vinegar has a pH range between 2–2.4, making it acidic. Milk has a pH of about 6.6, making it closer to neutral. Baking soda has a pH that is slightly higher than 8, making it alkaline.

What about other foods you have in your kitchen? Are they acidic or alkaline? You can easily measure the pH of any liquid food using litmus paper. There are also digital pH testers; however, some of them require calibration.

Obtain some litmus paper and test the pH of the following foods. (Consult the chart that comes with your litmus paper to establish what color changes indicate acids and alkalines.) It is best to test these foods in a liquid form, so **make sure to juice a fruit or vegetable before you test it**. Record your results in the following table so you can categorize your findings. Also, feel free to add more food items to the list of things you would like to test. For example, you can find out what happens to the pH of your milk once you add a sugar-rich cereal to it.

NOTE: Make sure you use freshly squeezed fruits and vegetables.

RECORD OF FOOD pH:

Food (in liquid form)	pH value	Acid, Alkaline, or Neutral
Club soda		
Cow's milk		
Coconut milk		
White vinegar		
Apple cider vinegar		
Sugar in spring water		
Salt in spring water		
Carrot		
Cucumber		
Tomato		
Lemon		
Orange		
Pineapple		
Bell pepper		
Sweet potato		
Eggplant		
Buttermilk		
Sugar-sweetened fruit juice		

Different foods have an acidifying or an alkalizing effect once in the human body. If you would like to find out how different foods affect the body in terms of pH, read the next section, "More Food Chemistry."

More Food Chemistry

Most people move through their everyday lives without thinking about whether the food they eat is alkaline or acidic. In fact, most people think of the measure of acidity, or the pH test, as something that belongs in a chemistry lab. You might be among the few who do test the pH of the food you eat. But another important question to ask is the following: Does the pH of food change when it's in your body? In other words, does the pH of food assimilated in the body test differently than if you test the pH of that food outside the body?

You might recall that the numerical measurement of pH ranges from 0 to 14. A strongly acidic substance has pH=0, while a strongly alkaline substance has pH=14. Pure water sits right in the middle at pH=7 (neutral pH). If a substance has a pH less than 7, it is acidic. If its pH is higher than 7, it is alkaline. For example, our stomach acids have a pH range between 1 and 3. That number can increase to 4–5 when there is food in the stomach. The small intestines, however, have a pH that is equal to 8, making the environment in the small intestines alkaline. It is very important for your blood to have a pH range from 7.35 to 7.45, otherwise, it can be fatal.

VOCAB

Acid: An acid is a chemical compound that turns litmus paper red (its pH is low). It usually tastes sour. Acids have the ability to react with some metal compounds. For example, the acetic acid found in vinegar can react with calcium carbonate (found in eggshells), forming bubbles of carbon dioxide gas.

In order to test the pH effect of food once you ingest it, use pH strips that have a pH range from 4.5–9.0 to test your saliva. Such strips come in small increments (smaller than one, usually increments of a half) allowing for more accuracy in readings. Also, those strips usually come with a color chart you can use to read the pH based on the color. (There are also digital pH testers; however, some of them require calibration.)

Make sure to juice a fruit or vegetable before using it. Record your results in the table on the next page. Feel free to add more food items to the list of things you would like to test.

Try This Experiment

MATERIALS NEEDED:

- pH testing strips ranging from 4.5 to 9.0
- Cow's milk
- Coconut milk
- Vinegar
- Sugar in spring water (2 tablespoons of sugar in an 8-ounce glass of water)
- Spring water
- Carrot
- Cucumber
- Tomato
- Lemon
- Orange
- Sugar-sweetened fruit juice

NOTE: Make sure you use the fruit and vegetable items when they are freshly squeezed.

PROCEDURE:

1. Prepare your child by telling her that she can only test one item on the list at a time. No food or drink (other than water) should be taken at least 2 hours before testing the pH of the saliva. Otherwise, tell her that her readings would not be accurate. Perhaps it is best to test a couple of items every day.
2. Tell your child to do this experiment first thing in the morning, before eating anything, even before brushing her teeth (as the toothpaste can affect the measurement). Have her prepare the pH strip and the food she wants to test (in liquid form).
3. Ask her to swish some plain spring water around in her mouth a few times, then spit it out.
4. Next, tell her to touch one of the pH strips on her tongue, and immediately match her strip colors to the chart in order to identify her base pH value before putting any food in her mouth. Have her record that pH value on the table on the next page.

5. Immediately after the previous step, ask your child to swish about 1 ounce of the liquid food she plans on testing that day in its pure form, then swallow it.

6. Have your child wait 2 minutes before testing her saliva. Tell her that she needs to use a new pH strip to test her saliva after the liquid food she just ingested. Ask her to touch a new pH strip to her tongue, and immediately match the new strip colors to the chart. Once she identifies the pH value of her saliva after ingesting this food, have her record that value in the third column on the following table.

7. Ask your child the following questions: Did this food make her saliva more acidic or more alkaline? In other words, did her pH shift slightly toward becoming a little more acidic, or more alkaline? Was this food acidifying or alkalizing? Tell her to record her answer in the last column of the table.

8. Your child can test other items in the list; make sure she has not eaten or drunk anything but water for 2 hours prior to the pH test.

RECORD OF FOOD pH:

Food (in liquid form)	pH before ingesting the food	pH after ingesting the food	Acidifying or Alkalizing?
Cow's milk			
Coconut milk			
Vinegar			
Sugar in spring water			
Carrot			
Cucumber			
Tomato			
Lemon			
Orange			
Sugar-sweetened fruit juice			

Did some food have an alkalizing effect on the body and others an acidifying effect? If your child answers yes, then she now has an insight into how foods can change the chemistry of her body. It is often surprising to find out that lemons have an alkalizing effect on the body once ingested, even though lemons test as an acid when they are outside the body. It all depends on how the food is chemically assimilated in the body.

Chapter 9: Household Chemistry

Separating Salt from Water

Table salt is a common presence in most people's diets. Food without a proper amount of salt just doesn't taste the same. A steak would not taste the same without some salt, and imagine pizza or spaghetti sauce with absolutely no salt whatsoever! Salted crackers without salt would be . . . well, saltless and tasteless.

Before electricity was invented, when people did not have refrigerators, meat was cured with salt in order to preserve it over a long period of time. An example of salt-cured meat that still survives today is jerky.

But where does table salt come from? Is it grown on trees? Is it mined from the depths of the oceans? The answer is that table salt does come from the oceans and the salty seas, but it doesn't have to come from deep within the ocean. It is fairly easy to remove salt from ocean- and seawater.

The ancient Phoenicians, who controlled the trade of salt in the Mediterranean Sea, knew how to extract salt from seawater. Some Mediterranean countries, like Cyprus, still do that today. Salt has long been an important natural resource for many countries, like India.

But how is salt extracted from seawater? If ancient people did so thousands of years ago before the modern era, then it must be a process that does not require much technology.

Try This Experiment

MATERIALS NEEDED:
- Salt (unless you live near an ocean and have access to saltwater from the ocean)
- Water
- Large Teflon pan
- Teakettle, or cooking pot

PROCEDURE:
1. If you are using ocean water, have your child pour half a gallon of ocean water into the Teflon pan. It is best to do this experiment in the summer when it's hot, otherwise the salt will take a long time to be extracted. (If you are using ocean water, skip the next two steps.)
2. If you do not have access to ocean water, then warm up half a gallon (8 cups) of water in the teakettle or pot, and pour it into the Teflon pan.

3. Ask your child to add ½ cup of table salt into the warm water, and stir it until all the salt has dissolved.
4. Tell your child to place the Teflon pan outside in a sunny place, where it can get sun for a good portion of the day. If she is doing this experiment indoors, tell her to place the pan in front of a window that gets a lot of sun. Inform your child that she will have to be very patient, as it may take days for the water to evaporate from the pan and leave the salt behind.
5. Remind your child to check on her pan at least once every day. This way, she can observe the changes that take place over time. What does she find after all the water has evaporated? Is it a somewhat white powder?

The powder left behind after the water evaporates is salt. Salt is a chemical compound that is composed of one sodium atom and one chlorine atom. The name of this compound is sodium chloride. In the periodic table of the elements, sodium has the symbol Na, and chlorine has the symbol Cl, so sodium chloride would be chemically expressed as NaCl. When salt is dissolved in water, the sodium dissociates from the chlorine, forming ions. The sodium becomes a positive ion, Na^+, while the chlorine becomes a negative ion, Cl^-. The reason salt dissolves in water is because the positive sodium ions (Na^+) are attracted to the negative side of the water molecules, while the negative chlorine ions (Cl^-) are attracted to the positive side of the water molecules.

QUESTION

What is the periodic table of the elements?
The *periodic table of the elements* organizes all 118 known atoms in a big grid. Starting at the top left corner of the table, hydrogen is listed as the lightest of all atoms. Moving from left to right along each row, each atom gets heavier by one proton than the one before it. The elements are arranged in certain locations, depending on specific characteristics of each. The modern periodic table traces its roots back to Russian chemist Dmitri Mendeleev. Mendeleev classified the 63 elements known by 1871 according to certain patterns he noticed. He used his table to predict properties of more elements that were discovered later.

If you and your child had to mix salt with water to make saltwater, then the white powder is the table salt you used, which is sodium chloride (NaCl). If you used ocean water, then that powder may have more than just sodium chloride. There may be other minerals present in the ocean water that are now part of your salt. If you obtained the ocean water from an area where the ocean is clean and not polluted, then you can use the salt you just made.

On average, 1 gallon of ocean water would give you a little more than ½ cup of salt. So if you live near an ocean and you want to have locally made salt, you cannot get more local than right in your own home.

Ice versus Dry Ice

You've probably heard people mention dry ice. It is said that dry ice can keep things much cooler than ice made from water. You might have even been to a Halloween party where someone used dry ice to make floating fog to help create an eerie atmosphere.

Now you'll get a chance to investigate the difference between regular ice and dry ice. What is "dry" about dry ice? Doesn't all ice get wet when it starts to melt?

Try This Experiment

MATERIALS NEEDED:

- 1 bag of dry ice
- Insulated gloves for handling dry ice
- Container to put the dry ice in
- 2 small bowls
- Spoon
- 2–3 ice cubes from the freezer
- 2 different color balloons

PROCEDURE:

1. Tell your child to put a few cubes of ice from your own freezer into one of the bowls.
2. Using the insulted gloves, assist your child in placing the dry ice into a container. *Caution*: always use insulated gloves when handling dry ice. Place a small chunk of dry ice into one of the small bowls.

You will probably have to wait a while until the ice from your freezer starts melting in the bowl. But check out the bowl of dry ice. What do you both notice?

If you wait long enough for the ice from your freezer to totally melt in the bowl (an hour or two). What's left in that bowl?

3. Use the insulated gloves again. Stretch open the neck of one of the balloons, and ask your child to use a spoon to scoop up some of the dry ice and drop it into the open mouth of the balloon. Tie the balloon shut and set it on your counter.
4. Have your child place a couple of ice cubes from your freezer into the other balloon, then tie it shut and set it on the counter close to the balloon with dry ice.
5. Wait a while until the ice from your freezer starts melting. When you both come back to check out the ice in each of the balloons, how do you find each balloon? Do you find both of them still at the same size as when you tied and left them on the counter?

When you came back to check the two bowls of ice, you probably found one with water from the melted ice cubes, while the other one was empty! Where did the dry ice go? Did it evaporate? That's exactly right, dry ice undergoes *sublimation* rather than evaporation.

VOCAB

Sublimation: Some substances go directly from being a solid to a gas, without passing through a liquid state. When this happens, it is said the substance has undergone sublimation. Frozen carbon dioxide (dry ice) is one such example.

But what about the two balloons? The one with regular ice just ended up having water in it once the ice melted. The one with dry ice ended up being inflated! Why is that? Well, when water is frozen, it occupies roughly a similar size as (or just slightly larger than) liquid water. That's why that balloon stays about the same size. However, the balloon with dry ice gets bigger because the dry ice underwent sublimation, turning from a solid into a gas. Dry ice is none other than frozen carbon dioxide gas, like the gas you expel from your lungs every time you exhale. Gases expand to take up a lot more space than solids do, because gases are much less compacted than solids are. Gases have a much lower density than solids do. That's why the balloon inflates.

QUESTION

What is the difference between evaporation and sublimation?
A substance like water can go from being a solid (ice) to a liquid (water) then to a gas (water vapor) when the water evaporates. When a substance goes through the intermediate liquid state as it transitions from a solid to a gas, then it is said that the liquid undergoes evaporation as it turns into gas. When a substance undergoes sublimation, it goes directly from a solid to a gas without ever becoming a liquid in between.

The temperature of water when it freezes is 32°F, while the temperature of dry ice is about −109°F! That's why you should use insulated gloves when handling dry ice. Otherwise, you can get a freeze burn.

Be grateful that temperatures don't drop to −109 degrees Fahrenheit in the winter, otherwise every time you exhaled, your breath might turn into dry ice and sprinkle over your feet!

CHAPTER 10

Biology Basics

Biology is the study of life and living organisms. This includes humans, animals, plants, and any other living organisms like fungi, bacteria, and algae. In particular, biology focuses on studying the growth of these living organisms, how they populate, and the way they function in order to survive, among many other things. In this chapter you will explore some basic concepts in the biology of plants, fungi, and humans; some of the functions that enable them to survive; and some characteristics they pass down from generation to generation. Through these explorations, biology will "come to life" in your living environment.

How Plants Make Food: Photosynthesis

Every living organism needs to eat. Some are picky eaters, others are not. Plants in general are among the least picky eaters. The presence of forests that are not maintained by anyone shows that those plants are not finicky about their nutritional needs.

Plants use a process called *photosynthesis* to make their own foods in the form of sugars. Plants make their own sugars using only sunlight, water, and carbon dioxide, which is present in the air humans and animals expel from their lungs when they exhale. Plants take human waste gas products (carbon dioxide) and use it to make their own food.

QUESTION

What is photosynthesis?
Photosynthesis is a chemical process that can only occur within the biological systems of living plants. In this chemical process, the plant stores the energy of sunlight inside sugar molecules it makes from water and carbon dioxide molecules. It takes six water molecules plus six carbon dioxide molecules (plus sunlight) to make one sugar molecule and six oxygen molecules.

The amount of sunlight a plant is exposed to has an effect on how much "food" it can make for its own growth. Is there an easy way to test this in a controlled fashion? In other words, is there a direct way to observe how controlling sunlight directly affects a plant's ability to make food for itself so it can grow? Absolutely.

Try This Experiment

MATERIALS NEEDED:
- Organic cotton wool
- Mustard seeds
- Spray bottle
- 2 deep glass or ceramic plates

PROCEDURE:

1. It is best to do this experiment during a warm season such as spring, summer, or early fall. Tell your child to make a thick layer of cotton wool in both plates, then slightly spray each with water to dampen the cotton.

2. Now ask your child to sprinkle some of the mustard seeds on each of the cotton surfaces. Tell her to spray the seeds with water again until the cotton wool is lightly soaked with water and the seeds are wet on top.

3. Tell your child to place one of the plates in a dark corner of the house that does not get sunlight at all, and the other plate near a window that gets plenty of sunlight throughout the day without being in direct sunlight.

4. Tell your child to check the moisture of the cotton wool in both plates every day. If she is doing this experiment in the summer, she might want to spray the plate in the lit spot once in the morning and once in the evening to make sure the seeds don't get dry.

5. Tell your child to check and see if her mustard seeds are sprouting in the first ten days. Once they do, have her observe how fast those sprouts grow in the plate that gets sunlight compared to the one that doesn't. Ask her if there is a difference in the sprouting speed in both plates.

6. Urge your child to look after her two plates and touch the cotton wool on each to check for dampness every day. In about thirty days there should be a full canopy of mustard greens on at least one of them. Which one has the full canopy of greens?

7. Tell your child to continue to spray both plates with water and to keep the cotton wool damp on each for another ten to fifteen days. Which plate has its mustard greens grow taller?

If you child reports back to you that the mustard greens in the plate near the window that gets sunlight experienced the fastest growth, then she now knows how critical sunlight is to the plants' growth.

Everything grows when it eats and gets nutrients. The way plants make food for themselves using sunlight, water, and carbon dioxide through the photosynthesis process involves something in their green leaves called *chlorophyll*. The molecules of chlorophyll are found in every green plant, and it is what makes plants look green. These molecules absorb sunlight and use the energy that reaches them from the sun to make (or synthesize) sugars from basic ingredients like water and carbon dioxide. This entire process the chlorophyll molecules perform is what is called photosynthesis. The chlorophyll molecules can synthesize sugars (basically food for the plant) by using sunlight. That's where the name *photo* (meaning light) and *synthesis* (indicating that it is making something) comes from.

VOCAB

Chlorophyll: Chlorophyll is the green pigment in plants. These pigments are green because they absorb all the red and blue light from the sun, but not the green light. This is why plants appear green; they reflect the green light. Chlorophyll is found in plants and algae.

All the energy in the sunlight absorbed by the plant is stored inside the sugar for later use. Just as people who take in food to use for energy that is released later on throughout the day do.

One interesting result from photosynthesis is that plants release the oxygen freed through the process back into the air. In other words, as the plant uses carbon dioxide and water coupled with sunlight, it makes not only sugar inside its own "body," but also releases oxygen as a result of that process. This is why there is a concern about losing more trees and forests on earth; because the plants "breathe out" oxygen for humans and animals to survive, a reduction in that oxygen source is cause for apprehension.

Deciduous versus Coniferous Trees

Depending on where you live, you may see trees that lose their leaves part of the year and become "naked," trees that keep their leaves yearlong, or a combination of both. This behavior in a tree is part of the tree's scheme to survive in the environment in which it lives.

In general, trees are categorized in two ways in terms of losing or keeping their leaves throughout the year: deciduous and coniferous trees. *Deciduous trees* lose all their leaves during certain parts of the year, while *coniferous trees* keep their leaf coverage year round.

QUESTION

Are there other deciduous plants besides trees?
Yes. Any plants that lose their leaves during certain parts of the year are called deciduous. This includes shrubs and herbaceous perennial plants that live for several years. Examples include mint and basil as herbaceous plants, while lavender and Russian sage are considered shrubby perennials.

A good inventory of the trees that live near you would be a great, educational opportunity for your child to help him become acquainted with the natural world in his immediate environment. With a few specific observational tools he might grow fond of studying trees and plants.

Try This Experiment

MATERIALS NEEDED:

- Time to walk in your neighborhood
- Time to walk in a nearby park
- Time to walk in a state park
- Small notebook to keep observations

PROCEDURE:

1. This is an activity that may span the length of two seasons starting with summer. Take a walk with your child with the intent to study the trees in your neighborhood. Tell him to become familiarized with the different shapes of the mature trees on the first walk. Tell him to notice if the shape of those trees is round, or some other shape, like a cone. Remind him to record his observations in his notebook at the end of the walk. You might want to encourage him to draw a sketch of each tree so he can remember them later.

2. The second time you go for a walk, ask him to notice the shape of the leaves on the different trees he identified the first time. Ask him to specifically notice if the surfaces of the leaves are wide and big, or narrow and small. You can prompt him to collect a leaf sample if the tree is close to the sidewalk. Remind him to record these additional observations in his notebook when he is done. Encourage him to sketch the

outline of each leaf. This will help him assess how large or small the leaf size is.

3. As the days progress, tell him to become aware of which trees lose their leaves and which ones stay green. Remind him to record those observations as well in his notebook.

4. Do the same activities when you have a chance to visit a nearby park. In a park environment, your child has opportunities to observe more trees, and to collect more leaf samples for his sketches.

5. If you have a chance to visit a state park, or even a national forest later on, your child would have an even larger pool of trees to examine and observe.

At the end of the fall season, you can have your child go through his notebook together with you to examine what information he has collected in it. You can help him organize his findings by asking him some of the following questions: How does the size of the leaves from trees that shed their leaves compare to those leaves from trees that didn't? In other words, was the leaf size of deciduous trees significantly different than the leaves of coniferous trees? Which ones were larger? Also, how did the shape of a deciduous tree compare to that of a coniferous tree? Encourage your child to look back through his notebook for answers to these questions.

If your child noticed that deciduous trees have leaves that are large in surface area compared to coniferous trees, then he's figured out one important clue to identifying which trees are deciduous or coniferous. Also, if he noticed that deciduous trees have a rounded shape on top, then he now has two clues. Here is where you can assist him in putting it all together so he can see the bigger picture.

Deciduous trees need to have more nutrients in order to grow and survive. They do so by first growing broad leaves that can get more sunlight and make food for the plant. That's why their leaves are relatively larger than those of coniferous trees. The large leaves increase their photosynthetic abilities. They also maximize the amount of sunlight each leaf receives by having a round canopy on top. The roundness of the canopy allows more leaves to be exposed to sunlight. When they eventually shed their leaves and the leaves fall on top of their roots, the leaves break down and compost over time, enriching the soil with nutrients for the next growing season. They basically make their own fertilizer.

Photosynthetic: Relating to photosynthesis, which is a plant's ability to synthesize or make sugar for itself (to serve as food) out of water, carbon dioxide, and sunlight.

This description of deciduous trees paints the image of workers that toil hard during the summer season when their leaves are on the branches in order to ensure they will have nutrients in the soil for the next growing season when spring comes around. Such trees cannot survive in an environment that is very harsh, where the soil is poor and water is scarce.

Are there other types of deciduous trees?
Yes. There are deciduous trees that are known as *drought deciduous*. This is because they lose their leaves when it gets very hot (rather than in the cold of winter). An example of that is the palo verde of Arizona. The branches of this tree are green; the tree relies on the branches for photosynthesis when it sheds its leaves.

Coniferous trees work differently. Their leaves are very small compared to the leaves of deciduous trees. Their leaves can look needle-like, and are not exposed to as much sunlight as the broader leaves of deciduous trees. This is not a problem for coniferous trees because they keep their leaves year round, and so photosynthesis happens throughout the year whenever the sun is shining. The needles on a coniferous tree don't all fall at one time because such trees don't need soils that are rich in nutrients. Remember that deciduous trees drop their leaves in order to compost and become a fertilizer that enriches their soils with nutrients. Coniferous trees don't require such a fertilizing effect, and settle for making just enough food from photosynthesis year round using their tiny leaves. This is why those trees have a conical shape. The cone shape helps minimize damage by wind, ice, and snow. Their narrow, slender leaves ensure that sunlight reaches every one of those needles to optimize the photosynthesis ability of the tree year round.

There are more deciduous trees and forests in the eastern half of the country, where water is abundant and the soil is richer with nutrients. In the western half of the country, more coniferous trees are seen, where they can survive harsher climates and poorer soils. Examples of deciduous trees are oak, maple, mulberry, black walnut, birch, and elm. Some examples of coniferous trees include pine, firs, spruce, and junipers.

Fermentation: Making Sourdough Starter

Bread has been an essential staple for human beings for thousands of years. The most commonly consumed bread today relies on a very important biological process called fermentation.

VOCAB

Fermentation: a chemical process that involves microorganisms like yeast or bacteria. The fermentation process converts sugars and carbohydrates into alcohol, releasing carbon dioxide gas.

Fermentation does not only occur during the process of making bread; other examples of fermentation happen during the process of making wine and beer. Fermentation is also present every time milk becomes yogurt.

Another example of fermentation—although it may be unpleasant—is flatulence. Gas in the lower intestines is a byproduct of fermentation that takes place in the colon by the bacteria residing there.

Whenever sugars or carbohydrates are present in a warm environment, these microorganisms (bacteria or yeast) get to work immediately and begin to consume ("eat") these sugars or microorganisms. At the end of the fermentation process there is a lot of carbon dioxide gas that makes the bread rise, the beer become gaseous, or the human belly expand and inflate.

But is it easy to closely observe this process of fermentation? After all, when the bread rises as the dough sits in a warm place, it seems hard to notice fermentation happening. There is the before and after effect, where the dough seems to have doubled in size. But is there a more direct way to "see" the fermentation process release carbon dioxide gas?

Try This Experiment

MATERIALS NEEDED:

- All-purpose, nonbleached wheat flour
- Spring water
- Wide-mouth 16-ounce glass jar
- Cotton cheesecloth
- Wide rubber band
- Spoon

PROCEDURE:

1. It is best to do this experiment in a warm season. Have your child place 5 tablespoons of all-purpose, nonbleached wheat flour in the glass jar.

2. Now tell her to stir just enough spring water into the flour to make it the same consistency as pancake batter. Ask her to add the water gradually, stirring it into the flour. Assist her in gauging whether the consistency is like pancake batter, or if more water is needed. If the mix turns out too watery, tell her she can add a little more flour to fix it.

3. Help your child to cut a piece of the cheesecloth to cover the top of the jar with some excess extending past the rim of the jar. You might want to tell your child that the cloth is used to cover the jar instead of a jar lid in order to allow the mix to "breathe."

4. Now have your child secure the cheesecloth around the rim of the jar with a wide rubber band. Tell your child to place the jar in a warm room, but not in direct sunlight.

5. Inform your child that she will need to stir the mixture with a spoon once a day for several days, in order to prevent mold from forming on the surface.

6. After about 2 days (depending on the temperature of the room in which the jar sits) have your child look closely at the contents of the jar. What does she observe? Does she see bubbles beginning to form?

7. Tell your child to check on her jar every day and observe the changes happening inside of it. Are there even more bubbles forming every day?

8. When the bubbles start to make the batter rise in the jar, let your child know that it is time to "feed" those microorganisms inside the mix with a

couple more tablespoons of flour. Remind your child to also add a little more spring water. Tell her to add just enough water to keep the mix at the consistency of pancake batter.

9. Now have your child observe the contents of the jar closely, perhaps two or three times a day, in order to see the changes that will happen more quickly. Tell her to look for more bubbles in the mix. Ask her if she observes how those bubbles make the mix rise inside the jar. When this happens, tell her the starter mix is now ready to be used to make bread. A mix like this is called a *sourdough starter.*

This fermentation process is the ancient process people used to make bread for thousands of years. The reason the flour starts to undergo fermentation is because yeast is everywhere. This is the naturally occurring yeast that is present in the flour, in the air, on the skins of grapes and other fruits, etc. When the conditions are right—meaning when there is moisture and a warm environment, as well as "food" for the yeast in the form of sugars or carbohydrates—the yeast microorganisms start to "eat" those sugars and carbs, converting them into alcohol and carbon dioxide. It is the carbon dioxide gas that shows up as bubbles in the starter mix, making it rise. It is the active life cycle of those microorganisms that gives bread the ability to rise in order to have just the right texture.

As long as you continue to "feed" the starter mix by adding more flour and water, it will survive. There are families who have kept their sourdough starter "alive" for hundreds of years, passing it down from generation to generation. If you need to give those microorganisms a break from "eating" and making gas, you can place them in a cool location like the refrigerator to slow down the fermentation process. They still need to be stirred once a day, though.

Every time you need to make sourdough bread, you can use part of the starter to make the bread rise, then "feed" what remains in the jar with 2–3 tablespoons of flour, and some water to bring it back to the same consistency as it was before. You can look up many recipes on the Internet for sourdough bread using the starter you and your child just made. This bread is more delicious than any store-bought bread.

Potato, Carrot, and Cell Osmosis

When you feel thirsty, you reach for a glass of fresh water. Because the human body is comprised of 70 percent water, this liquid is very important in many functions of the body, down to the level of the cells. But how do the cells "drink" water once the water is made available around the cells? The answer is all about osmosis.

Osmosis is a natural, biological process that happens whenever there are two water-based liquids with different concentrations present on either side of a surface that is semipermeable. For example, when there is water with low salt content on one side of a semipermeable surface and highly salted water on the other side, some of the water from the low-salt side migrates and moves through the semipermeable surface into the high-salt side, until the concentration of salt on both sides becomes equal. It is specifically and only the water molecules that move from the low-salt side to the high-salt side in order for both solutions to reach equilibrium in salt content.

VOCAB

Semipermeable: A semipermeable surface is one that allows certain substances to pass through but not others. For example, plastic wrap is not permeable at all, while a cotton cloth is totally permeable, letting all liquids pass through. A biological semipermeable surface is a cell wall or membrane. It allows water (but not anything dissolved in the water) to pass through its surface.

In general, whenever there is something dissolved in water, like salt or sugar, the dissolved substance is referred to as the *solute*, while the water is referred to as the *solvent*. Because water has a smaller molecule than the salt or sugar, the water molecules are the ones that move across the partially permeable (or semipermeable) surface.

But how does this work for cells of living things? Can the effects of osmosis be observed directly?

Try This Experiment

MATERIALS NEEDED:

- 1 potato
- Apple corer
- 1 large carrot
- Vegetable peeler
- Fresh water
- Salt
- 2 clear drinking glasses
- Tablespoon
- Two different color cotton strings, each 6" in length

PROCEDURE:

1. Assist your child in peeling the potato.
2. Use the apple corer to carve out a cylindrical piece of potato about 4" in length. This will take some effort, so you might want to assist your child in this process.
3. Tell your child to tie a piece of cotton string around the potato cylinder with a double knot, then slide it off the potato cylinder. Tell your child to save that loop of string to use for measuring the diameter of the potato cylinder later.
4. Tell your child to fill one of the glasses with plain water and place the potato cylinder in the glass. Let this piece sit in the glass for a few hours.
5. Now tell your child to use the other glass to prepare a very salty water solution. Ask her to fill the other glass with water, then have her add 2–3 tablespoons of salt to the water. Tell her to stir the salt until it is all dissolved in the water.
6. Have your child peel the carrot.
7. Tell your child to tie the other color cotton string around the widest part of the carrot with a double knot, then slide it off. Tell your child to save that loop of string to use for measuring the diameter of the carrot later.
8. Now tell your child to place the carrot inside the second, salty glass of water with the wide side of the carrot on the bottom (for stability). Let the carrot sit in the salty water for a few hours as well.

9. A few hours later, ask your child to check on the potato cylinder. What has changed about it? Has it become fatter or more slender? Remind your child that she can use the string she tied around the potato cylinder earlier to measure. Does that tied string still fit around the potato cylinder after it has soaked in water?

10. Have your child check on the carrot a few hours later as well. What has changed about the carrot? Is it still crisp and hard, or has it wilted and become somewhat soft? Has it become fatter or more slender? Remind your child that she can use the string she tied around the carrot earlier to measure. Does that tied string still fit snugly around the widest part of the carrot after it has soaked in salty water?

If your child found that the potato had increased in diameter, then she has visibly seen the effects of osmosis on the cells of that potato. Also, if she found out that the carrot became wilted and more slender and that the string now fits loosely, then it is also the result of osmosis. Osmosis in the potato allowed water to move into the cells of the potato, and the potato became fatter. In the carrot, however, water moved *out* of the carrot cells and the carrot became thinner.

Imagine the wall of each cell inside the potato and carrot as a semipermeable membrane. On either side of the cell wall there is water (*solvent*). There are also many different substances that are dissolved in the water (*solutes*) inside the cell.

When the concentration of the solutes inside the cell is high compared to the outside of the cell, then water molecules move across the cell wall into the cell until the concentration of solutes is the same on both sides of that wall. This is why the potato cells inflate as water crosses the semipermeable wall into each cell. There is a higher solute concentration inside the cells than outside, and water moves from the low to the high solute concentration until there is equal concentration on either side of the cell membrane. This is how the cell "drinks."

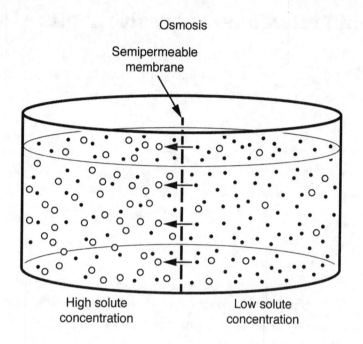

Osmosis

Semipermeable
membrane

High solute
concentration

Low solute
concentration

When the concentration of the solutes outside the cell is high compared to the inside of the cell, then water molecules move across the cell wall out of the cell until the concentration of solutes is the same on both sides of that wall. This is why the carrot cells deflate as water crosses the semipermeable wall out of each cell. There is a higher solute concentration outside the cells than inside, and water moves from the low to the high solute concentration until there is equal concentration on either side of the cell membrane. This is how cells lose water.

It is exactly this mechanism that takes place inside the human body. Osmosis allows water to move into the cells or out of them. So in order for cells to "drink" water, there has to be a lower concentration of solutes (or higher concentration of water) outside the cells in order for water to move into the cells. This is partially why water is so important for all living organisms. So the next time you drink water, remember that your cells are also drinking that water.

Dominant versus Recessive Traits

It is often easy to identify which children belong to which parents at a school or daycare center. There are certain characteristics the children have that they've inherited from their parents. The parents' genes determine the children's genetics.

Genetics: Genetics is the study of hereditary traits, the differences and resemblances that get passed down from generation to generation in all living beings, humans, animals, plants, etc.

Children carry their parents' genes. But what do genes mean? *Genes* are like a blueprint that carries instructions on how the child will look, among many other traits. Every child carries two sets of genes: one from the mother and one from the father.

Certain traits are determined by the set of genes one has inherited from both parents. One way traits can be categorized is by whether they are dominant or recessive (not dominant). Dominant traits have a higher probability of expressing themselves than recessive ones.

Dominant: Dominant means overpowering or influencing. For example, someone who is strong can overpower others; someone who has a dominant personality can easily influence others.

How can a recessive trait be understood experientially? Is there an easy way to see it in people around you? The answer is yes.

Recessive: Recessive means something that has the tendency to recede or move back. Recessive has often a connotation in relation to genes indicating that a certain trait is unable to express its characteristic.

Try This Experiment

MATERIALS NEEDED:
- Notebook to record observations
- Pen

PROCEDURE:
1. Have your child look at all his family members' eyes and record the colors of each person's eyes. Tell him to divide eye color into two categories: brown and blue (Green eyes can be placed in the same category as blue for simplicity).
2. If your own family members all have the same color eyes (all brown or all blue), then tell your child to look for a family that has mixed color eyes (perhaps the family of a school friend). Have him check the eye color of each member of that family and record his observations in his notebook.
3. Tell your child to record his observations for some other families that are known to him.

Now it's time for your child to examine his observations. Did your child find one family where one parent had brown eyes while the other had blue eyes, yet all the children had brown eyes? If so, then he found the mostly dominant trait for eye color. Brown is the mostly dominant color of eyes. If one parent has entirely brown eye genes, then most likely all the children of that parent will have brown eyes.

If the parent with brown eyes carried the genes for blue eyes, the blue eyes trait would not necessarily show up in that parent. But if that parent mates with another parent who has blue eyes, then the blue eye genes have a higher chance of showing up in the children. When blue eye genes from both parents show up together, then the child can have blue eyes. In other words, the parent with brown eyes can possibly carry the genes that can participate in the making of blue eyes in the children.

If the entire family has blue eyes in several generations, then most likely all members of the family have only blue eye genes. It would be very rare for anyone in that family to have brown eyes.

QUESTION

Who is the Father of genetics?
Gregor Johann Mendel lived in the nineteenth century, and is known as the father of genetics. He was from a region known today as the Czech Republic. His experiments on pea plants enabled him to understand how certain traits were inherited, establishing the rules of heredity. He coined the terms "dominant" and "recessive" to describe certain traits.

Here are some other dominant traits that express themselves in people: Curly hair is dominant, and dark hair is also dominant. It is fun to look for other traits that express themselves in people as dominant or recessive. You can engage your child in this activity when you are out and about, and observe families that pass by you in the park or the mall, or on the sidewalk.

CHAPTER 11

Making Math Matter

One of the best ways to make math concepts stick is to provide kids with fun activities that allow them to practice their math skills in low-stakes settings. The games and activities in this chapter will surely appeal to your child, even if math isn't his favorite subject. Most are math review activities designed to reinforce the concepts your child is already learning in school. Ideally, the material in this chapter will serve as a springboard, inspiring you and your child to brainstorm together and create your own fun math games and activities.

Designing Wallpaper Using Percentages

This simple activity is fun for artistic kids, especially those with a flair for design. It also offers them an easy way to visualize percentages.

MATERIALS NEEDED:
- 100-square grid
- A set of fine-tip colored markers

You can design your own 100-square grid on blank paper using a straight edge, or you can find a grid online to print out. Just do a search for "Blank 100 Grid." If you download a grid from an online source, be sure it actually has 100 blank squares (count 10 columns across the top and 10 rows across the side).

The Setup

For this activity, tell your child that her task is to create a design for some new wallpaper on the 100-square grid. She can use some artistic license in the design, but there are some requirements for the new wallpaper:

WALLPAPER DESIGN SPECS:
- 30 percent of the squares must contain stars
- 20 percent of the squares must contain half moons
- 25 percent of the squares must be shaded blue
- 15 percent of the squares must be shaded gray, silver, or purple
- 10 percent of the squares must be kept blank

Percentage Basics

After your child has completed her design, use it as a basis for discussing percentages. Percent simply means per hundred. Fifty percent, or half, of the squares in the wallpaper design have shapes inside them (i.e., stars or moons). Twenty-five percent (or a quarter) of the squares are shaded blue.

Decimals can easily be converted into percentages. Simply multiply the decimal number by 100 and place the % symbol after the resulting number. For example, 0.25 can be converted into a percentage by multiplying it by 100 and placing % after the number. So $0.25 \times 100 = 25\%$.

QUESTION

Does it matter whether you use decimals or percentages?
Decimals and percentages both represent parts of a whole. Technically speaking, since one can easily be converted into the other, it doesn't matter whether you use decimals or percentages. However, decimals make more sense in certain contexts, and percentages make more sense in others. For instance, survey results are usually given in percentage terms (e.g., 62% of American households include at least one pet). Decimals are more often used in measurements, especially when accuracy is important (e.g., measurements in a scientific lab).

To convert a percentage into a decimal number you simply reverse the procedure. Remove the % symbol and divide the number by 100. For instance, suppose you want to convert 49% into a decimal. After removing the percent sign, you simply divide 49 by 100. So 49% is equivalent to 0.49.

ESSENTIAL

Since fractions also represent parts of a whole, they can be converted into percentages. The easiest way to convert a fraction into a percentage is to first convert the fraction into a decimal number by dividing the fraction's numerator by its denominator. After that's done, multiply the resulting decimal number by 100 and place the % sign after it.

Tic-Tac-Toe Math Review

Tic-tac-toe is one of the fastest and easiest games to play. It's also an easy game to adapt into a math review activity. It can be used for any level of math and for any math concept. Of course, with the math review component, the game will take longer to complete.

MATERIALS NEEDED:
- Paper
- Pen or pencil
- A supply of math review questions

Game play for the Tic-Tac-Toe Math Review is similar to the way the game is typically played. The difference is that after drawing a three-by-three grid on your paper, you populate the nine squares with math review problems. For longer, more complex problems, you'll of course need a larger grid with larger squares.

When it's a player's turn, he doesn't just choose a box and fill it with an X or O, as with standard play. First he must successfully complete the math review problem in the box he wishes to claim. If the player finds the correct solution to the problem, he fills in his X or O. If he doesn't answer correctly, he can attempt another review question in a different box. On his next turn, he may reattempt the problem previously missed, if the other player hasn't already claimed that box.

Following are six sets of problems you can use to populate the squares in your tic-tac-toe game. The problems cover six different topic areas (for convenience, answers are provided in parentheses).

MULTIPLICATION:

- 10×9 (90)
- 7×11 (77)
- 5×15 (75)
- 6×12 (72)
- 8×14 (112)
- 7×30 (210)
- 3×22 (66)
- 2×18 (36)
- 10×20 (200)

DIVISION:

- $100 \div 10$ (10)
- $88 \div 11$ (8)
- $72 \div 9$ (8)
- $120 \div 40$ (3)
- $144 \div 12$ (12)
- $250 \div 5$ (50)
- $90 \div 15$ (6)
- $99 \div 33$ (3)
- $1,000 \div 200$ (5)

SIMPLIFYING FRACTIONS:

- $5/10$ ($1/2$)
- $4/12$ ($1/3$)
- $2/8$ ($1/4$)
- $10/25$ ($2/5$)
- $9/81$ ($1/9$)
- $20/30$ ($2/3$)
- $7/7$ (1)
- $6/8$ ($3/4$)
- $100/1000$ ($1/10$)

ADDING AND SUBTRACTING DECIMALS:

- 0.10 + 0.35 (0.45)
- 0.02 + 0.03 (0.05)
- 0.50–0.20 (0.30)
- 0.33–0.03 (0.30)
- 0.65–0.15 (0.50)

- 0.12 + 0.08 (0.20)
- 0.80 + 0.20 (1.00)
- 0.01 + 0.14 (0.15)
- 0.95–0.35 (0.60)

ESSENTIAL

Place value is important when interpreting a decimal number. The number to the immediate right of the decimal point is the tenths place. The number immediately right of that is the hundredths place, and the thousandths place is just right of that. As an example, the number 20.3 can be read as twenty and three tenths, which is the same as 20 and $\frac{3}{10}$.

EXPONENTS:

- 2^3 (8)
- 4^2 (16)
- 5^4 (625)
- 10^2 (100)
- 11^2 (121)

- 3^3 (27)
- 4^4 (256)
- 2^5 (32)
- 2^8 (256)

VOCAB

An *exponent* is shorthand notation for raising a number to a particular power. For example, 4^3 is 4 raised to the 3rd power, which is like writing 4 × 4 × 4. Note that in that example, the number 4 is known as the *base* and 3 is the *exponent* or the *power*.

SOLVING FOR AN UNKNOWN:

- 4 + X = 6 (2)
- 7 + X = 10 (3)
- 12–X = 6 (6)
- 2X = 8 (4)
- 3 / X = 3 (1)
- X–2 = 9 (11)

- X / 2 = 4 (8)
- 5X = 15 (3)
- X + 9 = 17 (8)

For some of the topics you'll want to keep plenty of scratch paper on hand. Also encourage your kid to create his own math review questions for use in the tic-tac-toe game. Encourage him to create some basic questions and some more challenging ones that he can't easily answer in his head.

Does the order of operations really matter?
Order of operations can matter a lot if you're solving a problem involving more than one mathematical operation. Consider the problem $5-4 \div 2$. Without a predetermined order of operations, you could solve the problem by subtracting 4 from 5 and dividing the result by 2, giving you an answer of ½. Alternatively you could solve the problem by dividing 2 into 4 and subtracting the result from 5, which gives you an answer of 3. Both ½ and 3 can't be correct. The rules of math say you should first perform any operations that are inside parentheses. Then you should take care of any exponents or roots. After that, perform any multiplication and division, working from left to right. Lastly, take care of all addition and subtraction, again moving from left to right. Based on the standard order of operations, 3 is the correct answer to the problem.

Bingo Math Review

Another fun way to review math principles is to turn the review into a bingo game. If your child already knows how to play the standard version of bingo, she should find this version intriguing. If your child has never played traditional bingo, that's no problem as the game is super easy to learn.

MATERIALS NEEDED:
- Standard bingo cards
- Bingo markers or pennies
- Bingo balls or a computer with Internet access
- A supply of math review questions

Note that you don't have to purchase bingo cards in order to do this activity; there are numerous websites that offer free downloadable bingo cards. Simply do a search for "Free Bingo Cards." Pennies work well as bingo markers, and while they're not exactly free, most households already have a supply of them at hand. You also don't have to purchase bingo balls; there are websites that will generate random bingo numbers.

Standard Bingo Game Play

A standard bingo game involves a card with five columns and five rows. The five columns, at the top, are labeled "B-I-N-G-O." The space in the middle of the card is marked as the free space. All of the other squares contain a number. A space on the bingo card is thus designated by a letter—B, I, N, G, or O—and a number. For example, suppose the upper left-hand space contains the number 12. That space would be designated as "B12."

Each player in the game begins with a blank card; no two players' cards can be identical with respect to the numbers in the squares. Someone must serve as the caller. The caller's job is to use some means to randomly select spaces on the bingo cards. Throughout the game's history, the most common means of randomly selecting spaces on the cards has been the use of bingo balls. Much like lottery balls, bingo balls are typically mixed up in a ball cage and then, one by one, randomly selected from the cage. When the letter-number combination is called out by the caller, any player with that letter-number combination covers that space on her card with a bingo marker or penny. The first player to cover five spaces in a row, in a column, or along a diagonal, is the winner.

Note that if you don't already own bingo equipment (i.e., bingo balls and a ball cage), you don't have to purchase it to try the bingo math review. There are online bingo number generators that will generate random bingo numbers for you. Simply do a search for "Bingo Number Generator."

Bingo with Math Review

Bingo Math Review is played just like standard bingo with one modification. Every time a letter-number combination is called, a math question is also given. A player with that letter-number combination doesn't simply cover the space with a marker—not yet. First the player must write down her answer to the given math question. After the caller checks the answer and finds that it's correct, the player may cover the space. Ultimately, in the math review version of the game, a player must answer at least five questions correctly to win the game (or four questions if utilizing the free space).

The earliest version of the game of bingo originated in Italy circa 1530 as a lottery called *Lo Giuoco del Lotto D'Italia*. In the nineteenth century, a version of bingo was used in Germany as a teaching game for children to help them learn spelling, history, and math.

Review Questions

The beauty of Bingo Math Review is that you can use it to review any math concept from any grade level. You can come up with questions for your child to answer, or you can easily find appropriate math review questions online. For example, if your child is in fourth grade you can search "4th Grade Math Review Questions."

A number raised to the 1st power is just the number itself, so 3^1 is just 3. A number raised to the 0th power is always 1, so 7^0 is 1.

You can mix and match the math review topics, or you can focus the review on a specific topic, such as fractions, decimals, long division, etc. The game can also be used with college-level math topics. Bingo is more fun with more than one player, so you can make the game more interesting for your child by playing along yourself.

Card Math Review

Mastering mathematics principles requires practice—just like any other skill. Some kids who are math lovers may enjoy practicing with standard math worksheets. For other kids, it's helpful to introduce creative alternatives to ordinary math drills. One approach is to use playing cards to create a game, or games, that reinforce specific concepts.

MATERIALS NEEDED:
- Standard deck of playing cards
- Timer
- Paper and a pencil
- Marker

The Multiplication Card Game

Before you begin play, you'll want to remove the face cards from the deck. Also, make a decision about whether you're going to keep the ace cards in the deck, or remove them. If you play with the aces, make sure your child understands that an ace has the value of "1." You can also create a game board, which simply consists of a blank sheet of paper with a multiplication symbol about 2" tall in the center of the page.

For the simplest version of this game, explain to your child that you're going to flip over two cards and place them side by side on the game board (one on either side of the multiplication symbol). Explain that he has a limited amount of time in which to multiply the two values together. Set the time limit based on your child's math ability. You want your child to succeed at the game, but you also want it to carry some challenge. For this simple version, in which the child is multiplying two values, the time limit should be relatively short. If your child comes up with the correct answer within the allotted time, he gets the points indicated on the faces of the two cards (e.g., an ace and an 8 will give him 9 points for the round).

The game is more fun if two or more kids can play together who are similar in terms of their math ability. With more than one player involved, you can leave out the timer. As soon as the cards are flipped, the race is on. The first kid at the table to shout out the correct answer wins the round and the points. The game is over when all the cards have been flipped.

When your child is ready, consider increasing the complexity of the game by flipping three cards. Of course, since he'll be performing two multiplication operations (the product of the first and second card values multiplied by the value of the third card), you'll want to increase the time limit. Keep scratch paper and a pencil handy if you elect to play the three-card version.

The Fraction Card Game

In addition to using the card deck to practice his multiplication, your child can use the cards to practice with fractions. The materials needed are the same as those required for the multiplication game. Again, before playing, remove the face cards from the deck and make a decision about whether or not to include the aces. The game board for the fraction card game is a blank sheet of paper with a thick marker line about 4" long drawn in the center of the page. This line is the fraction line.

ESSENTIAL

The top number in a fraction is known as the *numerator* and the bottom number is called the *denominator*. One way to think about the numerator and denominator is to imagine a perfectly round cookie that's cut into four equal pieces. If you pick up one piece, you're holding one out of four pieces of the whole cookie—that is, ¼ of the cookie. The numerator is the number of pieces of the cookie you're holding (which is 1), and the denominator is the total number of pieces that make up the cookie (which is 4).

There are a few ways you can play the fraction card game. In every version of the game a fraction is created by turning over one card and placing it above the line, then turning over a second card and placing it below the line.

One way to play the fraction card game is to create two game boards—or two places to stack cards on the same game board—and turn over four cards per round, creating two fractions side by side. In this version of the game, your child's task is to compare the two fractions and determine which value is larger.

Another way to play the game is to flip only two cards, creating one fraction, and ask your child to determine whether the fraction is greater than 1 or less than 1. For example, if the top card is 2 and the bottom card is 5, the resulting fraction is less than 1. If the top card is 8 and the bottom card is 3, the resulting fraction is greater than 1.

VOCAB

A *proper fraction* is one whose absolute value is less than one. For example, ½ is a proper fraction. ⅔ is also a proper fraction because its absolute value is less than one. An *improper fraction* is one whose absolute value is greater than or equal to one. The fractions ⁵⁄₂, ⁴⁄₄, and ‑⁵⁄₄ are all examples of improper fractions. Just because a fraction is improper doesn't mean it's bad or wrong—the term simply defines a concept in mathematics.

Your child can also use the fraction card game to practice simplifying fractions. For this version of the game, it's suggested that you place the card with the smaller value on top and the card with the larger value on the bottom. This approach will avoid improper and mixed fractions.

VOCAB

A *mixed fraction*, also called a *mixed number*, is the sum of a whole number and a proper fraction. For example, 3½ is a mixed fraction. If you think about it, 3½ is the same as 3 + ½. Mixed fractions, or mixed numbers, can also be negative. However, an expression like 0¼ would not really be a mixed fraction because 0 + ¼ would simply be ¼.

Once your kid has mastered the more elementary versions of the fraction card game, invite him to play the most challenging version. In this version, he'll convert the card fractions into decimals—sans calculator, of course.

Additional Card Games

These games represent only a few possible ways one can practice math with a deck of cards. Encourage your kid to brainstorm and think of other math games he can play with ordinary playing cards. If he has a younger sibling, have him think up a card math game he can use to teach his younger sibling a math concept or two. For a young child, the game can be as simple as turning over two cards and asking the young child to identify the larger value. The cards can be used to practice basic addition and subtraction, as well as other math involving fractions (e.g., the addition, subtraction, and multiplication of fractions). In a later chapter, you'll discover some ways a deck of cards can be used to introduce basic probability concepts.

Algebra Dice

Use this simple dice game to introduce your child to basic algebra. Your kid may get so caught up in the game she may not even realize she's doing algebra.

MATERIALS NEEDED:
- Pair of standard dice
- Blank sheet of paper
- Pen or marker
- Scratch paper and a pencil
- Watch or timer (optional)

ESSENTIAL

Algebra is a branch of mathematics in which symbols are used to represent numbers in equations or formulas. Typically, the symbols are letters of the alphabet, such as X or Y.

Game Setup

You'll first design a game board using the blank sheet of paper and the marker or pen. There are several variations of the game you can play. Choose whichever best suits your child's current math abilities—though don't be afraid to challenge her to think a little beyond them.

In the simplest version of the game, you'll set up the board for addition problems. Using a marker or pen, write ____ + X = ____ on the blank sheet of paper. The spaces should each be about 1½–2" in width.

Game Play

Algebra Dice is super simple to play. Have your child roll the pair of dice. Place the die with the larger value over the blank on the right side, after the equals sign. Place the other die, the one with the smaller value, over the blank on the left. Explain to your child that the X represents an unknown in the equation. Her task is to figure out what number can be put in place of X to make the equation true. Each time you roll the dice, you create a new equation with a new X to solve. The goal of the game is to solve as many Xs as possible in ten minutes. It may be easier for your child to visualize the problem if, after rolling the dice each time, she rewrites the equation on scratch paper using standard numerals in place of the dots on the dice.

A Strategy for Playing the Game

If your child hasn't yet worked with equations in math class, she can still play the game. You'll just need to provide her with a strategy for solving the unknown X.

Explain to her that the equation on the game board is like a scale—not a bathroom scale with a digital readout, but an old-time scale like the proverbial scales of justice (show her a picture from the Internet if necessary). Like those old scales, an equation has to balance out. If one side of the equation has a larger total value than the other side, the equation is out of balance.

For example, if you roll a 6 and a 2 on the dice, the equation on the game board will read $2 + X = 6$. What number could be put in place of X to make this equation balance out?

The standard way of approaching this type of problem in math is to isolate the unknown X. Since the two sides of the equation need to balance out, whatever operation is done on the left side of the equation must also be done on the right side. To isolate the X in this example, you would need to subtract 2 from the left side of the equation; then the only value remaining on the left side would be X. But when you subtract 2 from the left side, you also need to subtract 2 from the right side. 2 subtracted from 6 leaves a difference of 4. So after subtracting 2 from each side of the equation, what remains is $X = 4$. And that is the solution for the unknown X. Following this strategy, the unknown becomes known.

ESSENTIAL

Welsh scholar Robert Recorde invented the equals sign in the midsixteenth century. Prior to the equals sign, equality was written out in words. Recorde is also credited with writing the first mathematical textbooks in the English language.

Variations of the Game

One way to make Algebra Dice a bit more challenging is to allow for negative values of the unknown X. Instead of rolling the dice at the same time and placing the larger value on the right, roll each die individually and the place the first die rolled on the right and the second one rolled on the left. You will inevitably have outcomes such as $5 + X = 3$. This problem can be solved following the same strategy as outlined previously; the value of the X just turns out to be a negative number.

Another way to raise the level of challenge is to create new game boards featuring different math operations. Following are some suggested ways of setting up the game board:

$$\_\_\_\_ - X = \_\_\_\_$$
$$X - \_\_\_\_ = \_\_\_\_$$
$$\_\_\_\_ X = \_\_\_\_ \text{ or } (\_\_\_\_)(X) = \_\_\_\_$$
$$\_\_\_\_ / X = \_\_\_\_$$
$$X / \_\_\_\_ = \_\_\_\_$$
$$\_\_\_\_^2 - X = \_\_\_\_$$

Each time you introduce a new operation, you may need to walk your child through the strategy for solving for X. The same basic principle applies: The two sides of the equation should remain in balance, so whatever operation is done on the right side must be done on the left.

For example, suppose the equation that comes up in the game is $3X = 6$. The X can be isolated by dividing the left side of the equation by 3. 3X divided by 3 leaves X. The right side of the equation must also be divided by 3. 6 divided by 3 is 2, so in this case $X = 2$.

Mixing It Up

Consider playing a version of the game involving all six of the previous game boards. Label them 1 through 6. Roll a single die to determine which game board will be used that round. Then roll the dice as a pair to populate the blanks on the selected game board. As your kid progresses in her math ability, encourage her to devise new, more advanced Algebra Dice game boards.

CHAPTER 12

Geometry All Around You

Children are interested in shapes from a very young age. This chapter features activities you can use to reinforce your child's understanding of basic geometry while introducing a few new concepts. Along with your child, learn about the famous mathematicians Pythagoras, Euclid, and Descartes and their important contributions to the field of geometry. Help your kid practice identifying various geometric shapes while creating a "geometry monster." Invite your child to try the geometry scavenger hunt or one of the other activities designed to demonstrate to kids that geometry is, in fact, all around them.

Creating a Geometry Monster

One way you can introduce your child to geometric shapes is to create "geometry monsters." For this activity, you'll only need a few basic supplies and a little imagination.

MATERIALS NEEDED:
- Several sheets of construction paper
- Scissors
- Glue
- Crayons or markers
- Poster board (optional)

The point of this activity is to introduce your child to various geometric shapes in a way that's interesting and fun. Simply reading about the shapes from a textbook may work for some children, but others may benefit from a different approach, particularly those kids who favor art class over math class.

Suggest to your child that you make geometry monsters together. You and your child will be crafting "monsters" using the supplies previously listed. One suggestion is to create a monster zoo by pasting each of the monsters onto the poster board, with the goal of filling the zoo completely.

Explain to your child that there's one basic rule for building a geometry monster, and that is that each part of the monster must be an identifiable geometric shape. One way to frame the activity is to introduce a collection of shapes to your child—"monster parts"—and ask that he use each shape at least once in his design.

VOCAB

A *polygon* is a plane shape with straight sides. A *plane shape* is a two-dimensional shape.

Shapes to Use

Discuss the definition of each shape with your child as you incorporate it into a new monster design. You can stick to basic geometric shapes or introduce more advanced shapes. Here are some suggestions to get you started.

QUESTION

What's the difference between a rhombus and a square?
A *rhombus* and a *square* both have 4 equal sides, but a square—
because it's also a rectangle—has 4 right angles.

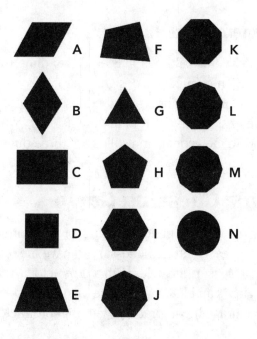

Parallelogram—a quadrilateral with 2 pairs of parallel sides (A, B, C, D)

Rhombus—a parallelogram with 4 equal sides (A, B, D)

Rectangle—a parallelogram with 4 sides and 4 right angles (C, D)

Square—a rectangle with 4 equal sides (D)

Trapezoid—a quadrilateral with 1 pair of parallel sides (E)

Trapezium—a quadrilateral with no parallel sides (F)

Triangle—a 3-sided polygon (G)
Pentagon—a 5-sided polygon (H)
Hexagon—a 6-sided polygon (I)
Heptagon—a 7-sided polygon (J)
Octagon—an 8-sided polygon (K)
Nonagon—a 9-sided polygon (L)
Decagon—a 10-sided polygon (M)
Circle—a plane shape with all of its outer points the same distance from its center (N)

A *plane* is a flat surface extending in all directions without any ends. For practical reasons, when a plane is depicted in a diagram it is shown with ends or edges.

Three-Dimensional Shapes

After your child has mastered two-dimensional shapes, consider building some new monster designs that incorporate three-dimensional shapes such as cubes, cylinders, and cones. Explain to your child that points have no dimensions, lines are one-dimensional, planes—and all plane shapes—are two-dimensional, and solids are three-dimensional.

The Angle Guessing Game

If you're going to build any kind of structure, you're going to be working with angles. Often it's necessary to have an accurate measurement of those angles. Measuring angles with a protractor is relatively easy and fun for most kids. Here's an idea you can use to make it even more fun for your child, and to encourage her to practice with that protractor.

Who invented the protractor and what was it first used for?
Thomas Blundeville, an English mathematician and writer, wrote about an instrument for measuring angles in a book published in 1589. Specifically, Blundeville used the instrument—the protractor—for making maps. Others wrote about a similar instrument around the same time, so science historians aren't sure who actually invented the protractor. But by the early seventeenth century, the protractor was in wide use among land surveyors and sea navigators.

MATERIALS NEEDED:
- Graph paper
- Pencil or pen
- Protractor
- Some kind of reward

Although the angle guessing game can be played by one player, it's definitely more fun with two players. Game play is fairly simple. The first player—Player 1—begins by drawing an angle on the graph paper. Player 2 also draws an angle on the graph paper, either the same sheet or a different sheet. (The angles can be drawn on plain paper, but graph paper will help the person drawing keep her lines straight. A number of websites offer downloadable graph paper free of charge.)

After the angles are drawn, Player 1 attempts to guess the measurement of the angle drawn by Player 2, while Player 2 attempts to guess the measurement of Player 1's angle. After both players make their guesses, the two angles are measured using a protractor. The player whose guess is closest to the actual angle measurement wins the round. Set a predetermined number of rounds of play for your game; ten is a good number. In ten rounds, you can expose your child to several different types of angles, including a right angle, a straight angle, and a few acute and obtuse angles. You might consider designating your child "the official angle measurer" and allowing her to do all the measurements in the game.

VOCAB

An *acute angle* is one with a measurement between 0 and 90 degrees. An *obtuse angle* is one with a measurement between 90 and 180 degrees. The most well-known angle is probably a *right angle*, which measures 90 degrees. A *straight angle* measures 180 degrees and looks like a straight line.

The reward is, of course, for the player who wins the most rounds. You might also consider keeping an extra prize handy, which you—as the game judge—can award to the "official angle measurer," regardless of which player wins the game.

ESSENTIAL

A standard protractor has two sets of numbers, one increasing from the left to the right, and the other increasing from the right to the left. When reading degrees on a protractor it's important to use the correct set of numbers. Ask your child to think about whether the angle being measured is acute or obtuse, for that's the determining factor in choosing which set of numbers to use.

Reflex Angles

The angle guessing game, as described so far, assumes that all the angles in the game fit on the protractor scale, meaning that they're all 180 degrees or less. A *reflex angle* is an angle that's greater than 180 degrees, but less than 360 degrees. Such an angle won't fit on the protractor scale, so measuring it requires some additional work. To find out the measurement of a reflex angle, you have to add the measurements of two angles: a 180-degree angle and a second angle. The diagram shows how to find the measurement of a reflex angle.

The measure of this angle is 180° + 85° = 265°

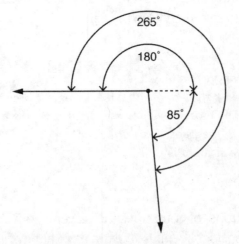

Whenever you feel your child is ready, consider adding some complexity to the game by incorporating reflex angles.

Mini Pyramids—Many Triangles

Lots of young learners are given the opportunity to build miniature pyramids as part of a social studies class project. If your child's teacher doesn't assign the Giza project, you might consider doing it at home as a family learning activity. Building pyramids is a lot of fun, and it provides you with a perfect opportunity to review triangles with your child.

MATERIALS NEEDED:
- Several sheets of card stock
- Ruler
- Scissors
- Glue
- Scotch tape
- Crayons or markers
- Sand (optional)

It's not difficult to build the pyramids. There are many approaches you and your kid can use. First, you'll have to make some basic decisions: How big do you want your pyramids to be? How many pyramids will you build? (The Giza Necropolis has three major pyramids.) How will you decorate your pyramids? Once you've made your choices, the rest is fairly straightforward. The basic purpose of this activity is to use it as an opportunity to review the geometry of triangles with your child.

Triangle Basics

The three interior angles of a triangle always add up to 180 degrees. An *equilateral triangle* has three equal sides and three equal angles (each interior angle is 60 degrees). An *isosceles triangle* has two equal sides and two equal interior angles. A *scalene triangle* has no equal sides and no equal angles.

A triangle can also be categorized based on the measurements of its interior angles. For an *acute triangle*, all of its interior angles are less than 90 degrees. A *right triangle* has one interior angle that's exactly 90 degrees. An *obtuse triangle* has an interior angle that's greater than 90 degrees.

VOCAB

A *right triangle* has one side that's longer than the other two sides. It's the side of the triangle opposite from the right angle. That side, the longest side of the right triangle, is known as the *hypotenuse*.

Back to the Build

To build a miniature pyramid, you'll need four equilateral triangles and a square base. It's best if you measure and draw the pieces on card stock before cutting them out. Help your child measure out and draw four equilateral triangles and a square base. (Note that the square base should be the same width as the bottom edge of the triangles.)

After you've drawn the pieces on card stock, cut them out and assemble them using glue. You may need to use Scotch tape on the inside of the pyramid so that the pieces hold together while the glue is drying. Also, if your child is planning to decorate the pyramid using crayons or markers, it's best that he do that before the pieces are assembled.

Another approach to decorating the pyramid is to cover the sides in glue after the pieces are assembled, and coat the pyramid with real sand. This approach can get messy, so you'll want to do it outside or over a large piece of cardboard or plastic. The sand approach, though messy, results in a more realistic-looking miniature pyramid.

QUESTION

Who was Pythagoras?
Pythagoras was a famous mathematician and philosopher who lived in Greece around 500 B.C. Sometimes referred to as the first "true" mathematician, Pythagoras believed that geometry was the highest form of mathematics, and that mathematics could help people understand the world around them. He believed that numbers have personalities. Although he and his followers contributed several important ideas to the study of mathematics, Pythagoras is most famous for the Pythagorean theorem, a formula that applies to all right triangles.

More Pyramid Activities

Ask your child if he thinks he could build a pyramid using an isosceles or scalene triangle. Encourage him to test his prediction by attempting to build a mini pyramid utilizing these other triangle shapes.

Either while building or after the initial build, you can help your child find the area of one of the triangles used in the pyramid construction. The area of a triangle is found by multiplying the base by the height and dividing the product in half. For example, if your triangle has a base of 4" and a height of 4", the triangle's area is 8 sq." ($4 \times 4 = 16$, half of which is 8).

ESSENTIAL

The *Pythagorean theorem* states that, for a right triangle, the square of the hypotenuse is equal to the sum of the squares of the other two sides. The theorem can be written in equation form as $a^2 + b^2 = c^2$, where c is the length of the hypotenuse, and a and b are the lengths of the triangle's other two sides.

In addition to being a great geometry activity, the mini pyramid project also provides you with an opportunity to discuss ancient Egyptian history with your child. He may find it interesting to know that, although experts have proposed many theories, no one has quite figured out how the ancient Egyptians constructed the actual pyramids. One thing is certain, however: Those ancient builders had a supreme understanding of geometry.

Calculating the Circumference of a Pie, Bike Wheel, Car Tire, Etc.

How many circular objects can you find around the house? Ask your child to find some circles, and then practice finding the circumference of those objects.

MATERIALS NEEDED:
- Tape measure
- Various circular objects
- Calculator

Circle Basics

Even a very young child can identify a circle, but not everyone knows what *makes* a circle a circle, technically speaking. A circle is a plane shape whose outer points are all the same distance from its center. The distance around the edge of a circle is the *circumference*. A line through the center, or midpoint, of a circle that connects two of the circle's outer points is called the *diameter*. If you cut a pie precisely in half, right down the middle, you're tracing the pie's diameter. Half of a circle's diameter is its *radius*. A radius connects a circle's center or midpoint with a point on the circle's border.

A *chord* is a straight line connecting two points on a circle's border. The diameter of a circle is a chord, but of course not all chords are the diameter. A circle's radius is not a chord, because a radius only touches one point on the circle's border.

Calculating the Circumference

The formula for calculating a circle's circumference is relatively easy to use. The circumference can be found by multiplying the circle's diameter by the numerical constant known as *pi*, denoted by the Greek symbol π. The formula is written as:

$$C = \pi \cdot d$$

C represents the circle's circumference and d represents the diameter. Because a circle's radius is half its diameter, the circumference can also be found using the formula:

$$C = 2\pi \cdot r$$

where r stands for radius.

QUESTION

What is π?
The number *pi* is represented by the sixteenth letter in the Greek alphabet, π. It is the ratio of a circle's circumference to its diameter, π = circumference/diameter. The value of π is approximately 3.1415926535, but the digits go on infinitely without repeating.

VOCAB

A *rational number* is a number that can be represented by a simple fraction. A whole number like 5 can be represented by the fraction ⁵⁄₁, so it's a rational number. All whole numbers are rational. A number like 2.5 is rational because it can be represented by the fraction ⁵⁄₂. *Irrational numbers* are numbers that can't be represented by a simple fraction. For example, the square root of 3 is approximately 1.7320508. Because the digits continue forever without repeating, the square root of 3 cannot be represented by a simple fraction and thus it's irrational. The most famous irrational number is π, a constant used in calculating a circle's circumference.

The Circle Challenge

Help your child master the circumference formula by challenging her to find several circular objects around the house and measuring the circumference of those items. If more than one child is involved, set it up as a little contest to see who can find the biggest circle, who can find the smallest circle, and who can find the most circles. If your child has trouble locating circles, you can steer her toward a few to get her started.

HERE ARE A FEW IDEAS:

- Bike tire
- Car tire
- Plate
- Ring
- Compact case
- Butter lid
- Round tabletop
- Bottom of a mug
- End of a pipe
- Circular pattern on a rug or throw
- Drumhead
- Actual pie (frozen or baked)

Encourage your child to try out both versions of the circumference formula, perhaps even on the same object. Have her choose a circle, measure its diameter, and then, using a calculator, multiply the circle's diameter by 3.14159. Or, alternatively, she can measure the radius, multiply it by 2, and multiply that product by pi. This activity will help your child learn to use a tape measure while reinforcing the basic geometry of circles.

Calculating the Area of a Circle

Consider taking the activity a step further and ask your child to calculate the area of some of the circles she found. The area of a circle is calculated using

$$A = \pi \cdot r^2$$

where A represents the circle's area and r represents the circle's radius. Note that π also shows up in the formula for the area of a circle. Not only is π a famous number, it's also very useful in geometry.

The Cartesian Treasure Map

The Cartesian Treasure Map is a fun activity you can use to reinforce your child's understanding of the coordinate system. It's essentially a board game you can make yourself.

MATERIALS NEEDED:
- Graph paper
- Felt-tip pen
- Ruler or other straight edge
- Crayons or markers

Begin with a clean sheet of graph paper (a number of websites offer downloadable graph paper free of charge). Using a straight edge and a felt-tip pen, draw two lines, dividing the page into four parts or four quadrants. If you want to be exact, you can take measurements to ensure that your lines are precisely centered. These two lines form the axes for your coordinates. Decide which axis will be your x (or horizontal) axis, and which will be your y (or vertical) axis. After you've decided, orient your page appropriately.

Number the x and y axes. The point where the two lines intersect is the *origin*, whose coordinates are 0 on the x axis and 0 and the y axis. (It's not necessary to label the origin.) From the origin, begin numbering the points to the right along the horizontal axis. As you move the pen rightward from the origin, the numbers increase (i.e., the point on the x axis one place to the right of the origin is 1, the point two places to the right of the origin is 2, and so on). As you move the pen leftward from the origin, the numbers decrease (i.e., the point on the *x* axis one place to the left of the origin is –1, the point two places to the left of the origin is –2, and so on).

As you set out to number the *y* or vertical axis, keep in mind that the numbers increase moving up the axis and decrease moving down the axis. The point on the *y* axis one place above the origin is 1, the point two places above the origin is 2, and so on. The point on the *y* axis one place below the origin is –1, the point two places below the origin is –2, and so on.

ESSENTIAL

The *Cartesian plane*, also known as the *x-y plane*, is divided into four quadrants numbered I through IV. In Quadrant I, the upper right-hand quadrant, both the *x* and *y* coordinates are positive. In Quadrant II, the upper left-hand quadrant, the *x* value is negative and the *y* value is positive. In Quadrant III, the lower left-hand quadrant, both the coordinates are negative. In Quadrant IV, the lower right-hand quadrant, the *x* value is positive and the *y* value is negative.

After you've numbered your axes, your coordinate system is ready. You could use it just like it is for a learning activity, but your child will probably have more fun if you dress it up a bit. Invite your kid to use crayons or markers to transform the page into a pirate treasure map. Keep in mind that pirate treasure maps are typically quite different from the ordinary kind of map you'd find in an automobile glove compartment. Common features on a pirate treasure map include islands, palm trees, ships, volcanoes, caves, and skulls. Make sure the number lines remain visible as your kid decorates the treasure map.

QUESTION

Who was Descartes?
René Descartes was a French philosopher and mathematician who lived in the sixteenth and seventeenth centuries. Although he made numerous contributions to science and philosophy, Descartes is best known for developing the Cartesian coordinate system (Descartes in Latin is *Cartesius*—hence the *Cartesian* coordinate system). His system provided a link between geometry and algebra by allowing the graphical depiction of algebraic equations.

Using the Map

Of course, everyone knows that an *X* on a pirate map marks the spot where treasure is buried. You could stick with one *X* per map, but there's nothing that says you can't have more than one treasure marked on your map. Mark some *X*s on the map, preferably at least one in each quadrant and one on the origin.

Create a little story for use with the activity. Have your child pretend that he's the pirate captain and he has to direct his crew to the spots on the map where the treasures are located. How will he direct them to the proper locations? Of course, he'll use Cartesian *x-y* coordinates!

The *x-y* coordinates are always given in a particular order. The *x* value is always given first, and the *y* value second. Together, a pair of *x-y* coordinates (known as an ordered pair) designates a particular point on a graph—or, in the case of this activity, a particular point on the map. The *x* value in the ordered pair gives the horizontal distance from the origin, and the *y* value gives the vertical distance from the origin.

VOCAB

The *abscissa* is another name for the *x* value in an ordered pair of coordinates. The *y* value in an ordered pair of coordinates is also called the *ordinate*.

For example, the pair of coordinates (3, 2) refers to the point that is three places to the right of the origin on the *x* axis, and two places up on the *y* axis. The pair of coordinates (–5, –10) refers to the point that's five places to the left of the origin on the *x* axis and ten places down on the *y* axis. The pair (6, –4) refers to the point that's six places to the right of the origin on the *x* axis and four places down on the *y* axis. The origin has the coordinates (0, 0).

After your child successfully "locates" all the treasures by assigning them pairs of coordinates, consider rewarding him with a real treasure. Treats work as well as gold doubloons for hungry pirate captains! You might also consider trying other activities that use the Cartesian plane. For example, work with your child to create a map of your neighborhood, and then ask him to identify coordinates for particular points in the neighborhood.

The Geometry Scavenger Hunt

Students tend to become more interested in a subject when they can see its relevance to their daily lives. The Geometry Scavenger Hunt is a simple activity you can use to help your kid learn to identify geometric shapes while gaining an appreciation for the importance of geometry in everyday life.

MATERIALS NEEDED:
- List of geometric shapes (see following)
- Pencil or pen

One person can do the geometry scavenger hunt alone, or it can be set up as a challenge involving two or more scavenger hunters. If your kid is hunting alone, challenge her to find as many shapes on the list as she can. To increase the intensity level of the hunt you can consider adding a time limit. If more than one hunter is involved, conduct the activity like a standard scavenger hunt—i.e., the hunter who finds the most shapes by the end of the game wins.

GEOMETRY SCAVENGER HUNT—LIST OF SHAPES:
1. Right angle—an angle measuring 90 degrees
2. Acute angle—an angle measuring between 0 and 90 degrees
3. Obtuse angle—an angle measuring between 90 and 180 degrees
4. Circle—a plane shape with all of its outer points the same distance from its center
5. Polygon—a plane shape with straight sides
6. Quadrilateral—a 4-sided polygon with 4 angles
7. Parallelogram—a quadrilateral with 2 pairs of parallel sides
8. Rhombus—a parallelogram with 4 equal sides
9. Rectangle—a parallelogram with 4 sides and 4 right angles
10. Square—a rectangle with 4 equal sides
11. Trapezoid—a quadrilateral with 1 pair of parallel sides
12. Trapezium—a quadrilateral with no parallel sides
13. Pentagon—a 5-sided polygon
14. Octagon—an 8-sided polygon
15. Decagon—a 10-sided polygon
16. Equilateral triangle—a triangle with three equal sides and three equal angles

17. Isosceles triangle—a triangle with two equal sides and two equal interior angles
18. Scalene triangle—a triangle with no equal sides and no equal angles
19. Acute triangle—a triangle whose interior angles are all less than 90 degrees
20. Right triangle—a triangle with one 90-degree interior angle
21. Obtuse triangle—a triangle with an interior angle that's greater than 90 degrees
22. Cube—a three-dimensional solid object with 6 identical square faces
23. Sphere—a three-dimensional (ball-shaped) object whose surface points are all equidistant from the center
24. Cylinder—a three-dimensional solid object with two parallel circular or elliptical ends and a curved outer surface
25. Cone—a three-dimensional solid object with a flat circular base that tapers to a single point

ESSENTIAL

In elementary school students primarily study what's known as *Euclidean plane geometry*, but there are other types of geometry. Plane geometry is focused on flat surfaces, or planes. In contrast, *Euclidean solid geometry* focuses on three-dimensional space. There are also several types of non-Euclidean geometry.

Encourage your kid to be creative in hunting for the shapes. The screen on a flat-screen TV is a rectangle. A drink coaster may be circular. A pattern on a rug might include many shapes in the list.

QUESTION

Who was Euclid?
Euclid was a Greek mathematician who lived around 300 B.C. and taught mathematics in Alexandria, Egypt. Often referred to as the "Father of Geometry," Euclid wrote the most important work in the field of geometry, *Elements*. One of the most studied texts in human history, Euclid's *Elements* carefully presents the axioms, theorems, constructions, and proofs that have come to be known collectively as Euclidean geometry.

The Geometry Scavenger Hunt for Younger Children

If you have younger children, try a scaled-down version of the Geometry Scavenger Hunt, using the following list.

GEOMETRY SCAVENGER HUNT—LIST OF SHAPES (SHORT VERSION):

1. Line
2. Circle
3. Square
4. Rectangle
5. Triangle
6. Star
7. Cube
8. Sphere
9. Cone
10. Pyramid

Either version of the scavenger hunt can be done at home or at any location where shapes abound. Consider trying it with your kids as a driving game the next time you set out on a family road trip.

CHAPTER 13

Statistically Speaking

It's been widely reported that the famous writer H.G. Wells once said, "Statistical thinking will one day be as necessary for efficient citizenship as the ability to read and write." The words are actually a paraphrased version of another statement Wells made regarding mathematical literacy, but the point is still valid. In today's world a great deal of information is presented in the form of statistics. Sometimes statistics are misused, or even intentionally abused, but a child who begins learning a few of the basic principles of statistics will be well on his way to becoming a better-informed citizen. The activities in this section are designed to introduce your child to a few basic, but vitally important, concepts from the world of statistics.

Mean, Median, and Mode

Statisticians are people who work with numbers every day. Statisticians don't usually work with one number at a time; ordinarily they analyze a group of numbers, which is often referred to as a *data set*, or just data. The numbers in a data set represent counts or measurements from real life. For example, if you look up the win-loss record of your favorite sports team, you're looking at data. If you count the number of students in your classroom who are wearing short sleeves versus the number who are wearing long sleeves, you're working with data.

When statisticians work with a set of data, there are certain things they typically want to know about it. For instance, they often want to know where the center of a set of data lies. There are three common methods statisticians use to find the center (i.e., point of central tendency) of a data set. Each method has a different name, and the answers they yield aren't always the same.

Mean

You've probably come across *mean* before, but it you may have heard it called a different name. Mean is the same as average. Suppose the heights of the five starting players on the Rockaway Blasters basketball team are as follows:

Joe	10 ft. (yes, that's really, really tall!)
Jenny	6 ft.
Jordan	5 ft.
Jehan	5 ft.
J.J.	4 ft.

The collection of the players' heights is a data set with 5 values. You might be able to make a guess about the central point of this data set by just eyeballing it, but there's no need to guess. The mean, or average, can easily be calculated by summing the 5 values and dividing that sum by the total number of values in the data set.

$$10 + 6 + 5 + 5 + 4 = 30$$
$$30 / 5 = 6$$

The mean height of a starting player on the Rockaway Blasters basketball team is 6 feet.

Median

After calculating the mean for the data set, you might think your work is done. But if you examine the values in the data set more closely and compare them to the mean, you may realize that 6 feet is not very representative of the typical Rockaway starting player's height. In fact, three of the players are significantly less than 6 feet tall.

You've calculated the mean correctly. The problem lies in the fact that one of the players, Joe, is a *lot* taller than all the other players. Joe's height skews the data set such that the mean is not very representative of the typical player's height. Joe is what statisticians refer to as an *outlier*, meaning that his height doesn't fit neatly with the rest of the data.

When a data set has outliers like Joe, the *median* is usually a better indicator of the data set's center. The *median* is the value that falls exactly at the halfway point in a data set. For example, in a data set composed of the values 1, 2, and 3, the point in the middle, or the median, is 2.

The easiest way to find the median is to first arrange the values in a given data set from smallest to largest. Suppose a data set contains the following values: 100, 35, 15, 20, 5.

Arranged from smallest to largest they are:

5, 15, 20, 35, 100

After the values are arranged from smallest to largest, the next step is to cross out the smallest value and the largest value in the set. Neither value is the median.

5, 15, 20, 35, ~~100~~

VOCAB

Another measure that is sometimes useful when working with data is the *range*. It's easy to calculate the range of a set of numbers. Simply subtract the smallest value in the data set from the largest value in the data set. The resulting answer is the range. For example, if the largest value is 100 and the smallest value is 5, the range is 100 − 5 = 95. The range gives you an idea of the scope of the data you're working with.

Cross out the next smallest value and the next largest value in the set. Those aren't the median, either.

5, ~~15~~, 20, ~~35~~, ~~100~~

This process of elimination is continued until there's only one remaining value—the one exactly in the middle. That value is the median. In this last example, the median is 20. But what if a data set contains an even number of values? Consider a data set made up of the following values:

60, 70, 80, 90

When the smallest and largest values are crossed out, there are two values remaining.

~~60~~, 70, 80, ~~90~~

In a situation where there are two middle values, the median is determined by finding the mean of those two middle values.

70 + 80 = 150
150 / 2 = 75

The data set 60, 70, 80, 90 has a median of 75.

Back to the Rockaway Blasters basketball team and their starting lineup. Again, the heights of the starting players are 10 feet, 6 feet, 5 feet, 5 feet, and 4 feet.

Arranged from smallest to largest, the players' heights are:

4, 5, 5, 6, 10

Following the procedure already outlined, it should be clear that the median height of the starting players is 5 feet.

4, 5, 5, 6, 10

In the case of the Rockaway Blasters starting lineup, because Joe's height is so much different from the other players, the median is a better indicator of the data set's central point than the mean.

ESSENTIAL

Measures of position are sometimes useful in analyzing a data set. Common measures of position include *quartiles* and *percentiles.* When you divide a data set into 4 equal parts, you've created quartiles. Percentiles divide a data set into 100 equal parts. The first quartile is synonymous with the 25th percentile. The second quartile is the same as the 50th percentile. Incidentally the second quartile—or the 50th percentile—is the same as the median; half the numbers in the set lie above this value and half the numbers lie below this value.

Mode

In some situations, the best representation of a typical value in a data set is given by the mode. The *mode* is simply the value in the data set that repeats most frequently. In the data set containing the heights of the Rockaway Blasters starting basketball team—4, 5, 5, 6, 10—the value 5 occurs twice (i.e., there are two players who are 5 feet tall). The mode of the data set is 5, or 5 feet.

ALERT

One shortcoming of the mode as a measure of central tendency is the fact that not every data set has mode. What if the players' heights were 4 feet, 5 feet, 6 feet, 7 feet, and 10 feet? None of the values repeat, so there's no mode. It's also the case that some data sets have more than one mode. What if the heights of the Rockaway starters were 5 feet, 5 feet, 6 feet, 6 feet, and 10 feet? The value 5 feet occurs twice in the data set and so does the value 6 feet. This data set has two modes—or, as statisticians might say, it's *bimodal*.

SOME PRACTICE WITH MEAN, MEDIAN, AND MODE:

- The next time you're at a gathering of family or friends, have your child ask everyone in attendance their age. Then the two of you can calculate the mean age of those in attendance. Also calculate the median and mode. See if you can identify any obvious outliers (i.e., friends or family members who are significantly younger or older than the others in attendance).

- Have your child ask all of her classmates how many TVs are in their home. Find the mean, median, and mode number of TVs.

- Keep track of how much money you spend each day for a month. At the end of the month, you and your child can calculate the mean amount you spent per day. Also calculate the median and mode. The results may surprise you.

Making a Pie Chart from Scratch

Organizing and presenting data is an important part of statistics. There are several ways data can be displayed visually. Data can be presented in a table, a graph, or a chart. One of the most common graphic forms for data display is the tried-and-true pie chart.

Pie Chart Basics

Everyone who has flipped through magazines or newspapers has seen pie charts. Popular periodicals like *USA Today* frequently use pie charts to present data in an easily digestible manner.

Here is an example of a pie chart that shows the causes of airline delay.

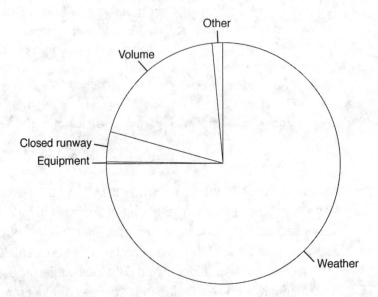

The whole circle or "pie" represents the full universe of reasons why flights might be delayed. Each section, or piece of the pie, represents a particular reason why flights may be delayed. As you might gather from examining the pie chart, the biggest reason for flight delays is weather. The least significant reason for flight delays is equipment failure. The sizes of the sections of the pie chart correspond to the data represented in the chart. Pie charts are easy to interpret when they're used properly.

Making a Pie Chart by Hand

There are a number of computer programs you can use to generate accurate pie charts. However, if your child goes through the process of creating one by hand, he'll have a better understanding of the mechanics of pie charts and of how the underlying data fits into the chart. He'll also get a little practice with some basic geometry concepts.

MATERIALS NEEDED:
- Blank paper
- Pencil
- Compass
- Protractor
- Set of colored pencils or markers

You'll want to begin by converting your "raw" data into percentages. An example will help clarify the process. Suppose you have ten people living in your household, and you have your child go around and ask each one his or her favorite flavor of ice cream. Suppose your child discovers from his survey that 5 of the people in your household like chocolate ice cream the best, 3 like vanilla the best, and 2 prefer strawberry. In percentage terms, 5/10 or 50% of the members of your household prefer chocolate, 30% prefer vanilla, and 20% like strawberry the best.

QUESTION

What is raw data?
Raw data is data that hasn't yet been processed—much like raw food is food that hasn't yet been processed. If you ask three different people their ages and write down their responses, you've gathered raw data. If you calculate the average, or mean, of those three ages, then the data has been processed; it's no longer raw data.

After your child has converted his raw data into percentages, have him pause for a moment to add up the resulting percentages. If they don't total 100%, then he needs to check over his work; the percentages should add up to 100.

The next step involves a little geometry. Keeping in mind that a whole circle is 360 degrees, he'll want to multiply each of his percentages from the first step by 360. This will give him the angles he needs to create each section of the pie chart.

50% × 360 degrees = 180 degrees
30% × 360 degrees = 108 degrees
20% × 360 degrees = 72 degrees

At this point he may want to pause and check his math again. Be sure the degrees add up to 360. If the math checks out, then he's ready to begin drawing his pie chart.

He should start by drawing a circle on a blank piece of paper using the compass. Make the circle large so that he can easily divide it into slices. There should be an indentation in the paper, in the circle's center, where the compass needle rested. From that center, he can draw a straight line to the edge of the circle. Then, using the protractor, he should measure out his first angle and draw the corresponding line on the chart. Returning to the ice cream flavor example, the first angle is 180 degrees. After measuring a 180-degree angle and drawing the line, he will have cut the pie exactly in half.

Next he'll measure out the remaining angles and draw the corresponding lines, sectioning the circle into the appropriately sized slices. In the ice cream example, there will obviously be three sections or slices.

The sections of a pie chart are typically color-coded to a key. After your child has converted the raw data into percentages and calculated and drawn the angles, he can choose a color to represent each section of the pie and shade in the sections. Lastly, he can create a color key along one side of the page explaining the meaning of each color in the pie chart.

An Additional Pie Chart Activity

After your child successfully creates the pie chart in the example, invite him to try another one from scratch. The extra step of gathering the raw data will help him see the connection between real-world information and two-dimensional charts and graphs.

The same materials are required as those listed in the previous activity. The only difference is that your child will gather his own data. Have him ask ten friends or classmates one of the following questions and carefully record the answers:

- What's your favorite sport to watch on TV?
- What's your favorite subject in school?
- What's your favorite holiday?
- What's your favorite season?

When he's gathering the data, it's important that each person surveyed give only one response. It doesn't work if someone says he likes Thanksgiving and Halloween equally, unless your child collects responses such as those into a category called "Undecided" or something similar. For the pie chart to make sense, the categories represented by the sections must be *mutually exclusive*.

Also note that if all ten respondents give a different answer, then a pie chart won't be an effective way to visually display the data.

VOCAB

When categories are *mutually exclusive* it means that items can only belong to one category at a time. For example, "dead" and "alive" are generally considered to be mutually exclusive categories. A person or an animal can't be both dead and alive at the same time. The seasons of the year are also mutually exclusive categories. You can't find a date on the calendar that falls both in the spring and the summer because the seasons have clearly defined beginnings and endings.

After your child gathers the data, guide him through the steps outlined previously. It might be interesting to try creating the pie chart using Excel or another chart generator, and then compare the computer version to the one your child created. Links to some online chart generators are listed in the Additional Resources section of this book.

Pie Chart Pitfalls

Like any graphical form of data display, the pie chart can be misused. Pie charts have been published or aired on TV in which the proportions of the pie pieces sum to a value greater than 100%. For pie charts to be accurate, the proportions of the sections must always sum to 100%.

Even if the proportions of the pie sections sum to 100%, it doesn't necessarily mean that a pie chart is the best choice for graphically displaying your data. A pie chart with too many slices is difficult to read and interpret. It's best to use a pie chart if you're only dealing with a few categories. Also, if all of the slices are roughly the same size, a pie chart doesn't provide much useful information to users.

Remember that it's best to use a pie chart when you're dealing with data that's divided into a few mutually exclusive categories, and those categories represent different-sized proportions of the whole. If your data set doesn't fit those characteristics, you'll be better off finding another way to visually display your data.

Pie Chart versus Bar Chart

The bar chart is another widely used graphical display for certain types of data. A *bar chart*—also called a *bar graph*—uses bars to represent data in various categories. The bars' heights (or lengths) are proportional to the data being presented.

ALERT

The bars on a bar chart can be vertical or horizontal. Note that in Excel a bar chart uses horizontal bars. In Excel, a chart that uses vertical bars is called a *column chart*.

Bar Chart Basics

Suppose you want to create a bar chart that shows candy bar consumption by grade for a particular elementary school for a particular month (yes, that would make it a candy bar bar chart). Suppose you gather the following data for Greenwood Elementary for the month of October:

CANDY BARS CONSUMED BY GRADE—OCTOBER

Grade	Candy Bars Consumed
Kindergarten	150
1st Grade	200
2nd Grade	250
3rd Grade	400
4th Grade	125
5th Grade	100

To create a bar chart depicting this data, you'll need paper, a pencil or pen, a ruler, and a set of fine-tip markers or colored pencils. Begin by using a straight edge to create a box that will frame your bar chart. Assuming you want to create a horizontal bar chart, write your categories along the left side of the chart, roughly equidistant apart: K, 1st, 2nd, 3rd, 4th, 5th. Be sure to give yourself enough space for the bars, and for spaces between the bars.

Using the ruler, create a scale along the bottom of your bar chart. Given the data you're graphing, you might use a scale such as 1" equals 100 candy bars." That would make the largest bar in your chart 4" tall. The kindergarten bar will be 1½", the 1st grade bar will be 2", and so on. The bars on a bar chart are often colored differently to help set them apart from one another visually. If you'd prefer a smaller bar graph, you can easily reduce the scale. Below is bar graph representing the candy bar data that uses 1" a centimeter for every 50 candy bars.

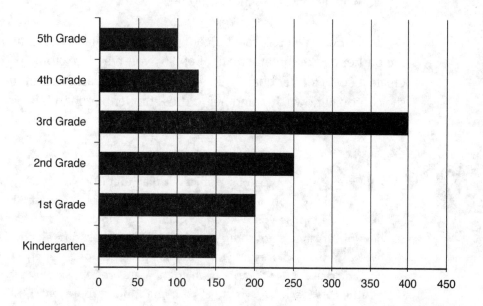

ESSENTIAL

Often people get bar charts confused with another type of graphical display called a *histogram*. A bar chart is used to present data that are grouped into discrete categories. A histogram is used to display continuous data. For instance, if you asked several of your friends to stand on a scale one at a time and you recorded their weights, you would be collecting *continuous data*. If you wrote down the hair color of each of your friends, you'd be collecting *qualitative data* and dividing the data into discrete categories. A histogram resembles a bar chart in appearance, except that in a histogram there's no gap between the bars.

Invite your child to practice creating her own bar chart. She can gather some raw data by asking four or five friends one of the following questions:

- How many states have you visited?
- How many pets have you had in your lifetime?
- How many musical instruments are in your home?
- How many cousins do you have?
- How many times have you flown in an airplane?
- How many plants are in your home?

Each friend will represent a category in your child's bar chart. Depending on her age and mathematical ability, you may have to help your child create a scale for her chart. Allow her to complete as much of the chart as she can on her own. Remind her to dress up her bar chart by coloring each of the bars a different color.

VOCAB

A *pictograph* is a type of graphical display that is very similar to a bar chart. A pictograph uses images or symbols to represent data. For example, suppose you wanted to create a graphic displaying the numbers of cars in each of three automobile categories: gas, electric, and hybrid. You could present your data using a traditional bar chart, or you could use a pictograph in which the bars are replaced by pictures of little cars (each car symbol in your chart might represent 1,000 actual cars, for instance). Like a bar chart, the symbols in a pictograph can be stacked horizontally or vertically.

Pie Chart versus Bar Chart

It probably seems like bar charts serve much the same function as pie charts. It's true that for some data you could just as easily use a pie chart as a bar chart. The consumption of candy bars by grade at Greenwood Elementary for the month of October could be presented in a pie chart instead of a bar chart, if such a presentation suits the focus or purpose of the study.

Pie charts are most effective when you want to illustrate differences in the proportions of the various categories. Bar charts are more effective when you want to show differences in the actual numbers contained in the various categories. Suppose, for example, the underlying goal of the Greenwood Elementary study is to reduce candy bar consumption among all grades. In that case, the overall numbers of candy bars consumed by each grade would be more useful than the proportion consumed by grade level. If you really are interested in the proportion of candy bars consumed by each grade level, then a pie chart will serve your purposes well.

Learning Probability with Playing Cards

People frequently tend to miscalculate the likelihood, or probability, of various events occurring. Some of the rules of probability are complex and best suited for a college-level course or an advanced-level high school course. But some of the basics of probability can be understood by a student in elementary school. The following activities will introduce your child to some basic aspects of probability theory.

MATERIALS NEEDED:
- Standard deck of playing cards
- Blank sheet of paper
- Pen or pencil

First remove the jokers from the deck so that you have fifty-two total cards. If your child isn't familiar with cards, show her four suits and the various card denominations. Two of the suits are black (clubs and spades) and the other two are red (hearts and diamonds). There are thirteen cards in each suit: the numbers 2 through 10, the three face cards, and one ace. To learn about probability using the card deck, it's best to arrange the cards face up on the table in their respective suits. Explain to your kid that you're going to leave the cards face up, but she should imagine that the cards have all been turned face down.

Classical probability is one of the more common approaches to calculating probability. The approach applies to situations in which all the outcomes are equally likely. Based on classical probability, the likelihood of a particular event occurring is equal to the number of favorable outcomes divided by the number of total possible outcomes. For instance, if you're rolling a single die the number of possible outcomes is 6. If you're interested in the probability of rolling an even number on the die, there would be 3 favorable outcomes. Thus, using the classical approach, the probability of rolling an even number is $\frac{3}{6}$, or 0.5.

Now ask your kid the following questions:

IF SOMEONE WERE DRAWING A CARD AT RANDOM (UNSEEN), WHAT IS THE LIKELIHOOD THAT PERSON WOULD CHOOSE:

1. A heart
2. A red card
3. A king
4. The king of hearts
5. A king or a heart

Some Probability Basics

Probability can be expressed as a fraction, in decimal form, or as a percentage. For example, you might hear the weatherman say there's a 40% chance of rain later in the week. The weatherman is making a statement about probability.

The probability of anything occurring is always somewhere between 0 and 1 (0% and 100%), inclusive. An event can never have a 110% probability of occurring. Probability also can't be negative. There could never a –15% chance of rain later in the week, for instance.

It's probably fairly easy to see that the probability of drawing a heart is $^{13}/_{52}$, since there are 13 hearts and 52 total cards. That, of course, simplifies to ¼ or 0.25.

The Special Rule of Addition

The probability of drawing a red card will be greater than ¼ since there are more red cards in the deck than hearts. One of the basic rules of probability is the *special rule of addition*, which says that the probability of A or B occurring is the same as the probability of A occurring plus the probability of B occurring, as long as A and B are mutually exclusive. In this case, A and B are mutually exclusive because a card can't be both a heart and a diamond—a single card can only belong to one suit. Therefore the probability of drawing a red card is the probability of drawing a heart plus the probability of drawing a diamond, or ¼ + ¼ = ½.

ESSENTIAL

The *complement rule* is another useful probability rule. Complementary events are events whose probabilities sum to 1. In a standard deck of cards (sans jokers), drawing a red card and drawing a black card are complementary events. Since you know that the probability of drawing a red card is ½, you instantly know that the probability of drawing a black card is ½, because the two events are complementary.

The General Rule of Addition

There are 4 kings in the deck, so the probability of drawing a king is $^{4}/_{52}$, which simplifies to $^{1}/_{13}$ or 0.077. Likewise, you can see that the probability of drawing the king of hearts is $^{1}/_{52}$, or 0.01923, since there's only 1 such card in the deck.

The special rule of addition doesn't work for calculating the likelihood of drawing a king or a heart. If you've followed along with the entire activity so far, you've already seen that the probability of drawing a heart is $^{13}/_{52}$. Following the special rule of addition, the probability of drawing a king plus the probability of drawing a heart would be $^{4}/_{52}$ + $^{13}/_{52}$ = $^{17}/_{52}$. But that answer is not quite correct. With the cards spread out in front of you face up, you can see that there are 13 hearts and 3 kings that aren't hearts. So the likelihood of drawing a king or a heart is actually $16/52$.

The reason the special rule of addition doesn't work in this case is because the category "king" and the category "heart" are not mutually exclusive. There is overlap between the two categories because the king of hearts belongs to both categories. When A and B aren't mutually exclusive, you have to rely on another probability rule, the *general rule of addition*.

The general rule of addition says that the probability of A or B occurring is the probability of A occurring plus the probability of B occurring, minus the probability of A and B both occurring. Thus the probability of drawing the king of hearts is equal to the probability of drawing a king plus the probability of drawing a heart, less the probability of drawing the king of hearts, or:

$$4/52 + 13/52 - 1/52 = 16/52$$

Extending the Activity

There are several ways you can extend the probability playing card activity. Ask your child to calculate the probability for each of the following scenarios.

IF SOMEONE WERE DRAWING A CARD AT RANDOM (UNSEEN), WHAT IS THE LIKELIHOOD THAT PERSON WOULD CHOOSE:
1. A club or spade
2. A face card
3. An ace
4. The ace of spades
5. An ace or a spade

Encourage your child to try using the special rule of addition to solve #1 and the general rule of addition to solve #5.

Another way to extend the activity is to choose one of the probabilities related to the card deck and test it out. For example, the probability of drawing a red card is $1/2$. Invite your kid to turn the cards face down, shuffle them, draw a card at random, and record whether it's a red or black card. Repeat the shuffle and draw twenty times or so, making sure to replace the card after each draw. Consult the record and see if a red card was drawn approximately half the time. Repeat the experiment for another of the card probabilities.

Learning Probability with Dice

Games of chance are all about probability. In fact, the first rules of probability were devised because a French nobleman wanted to gain a better understanding of a particular casino game. His appeal to mathematician Blaise Pascal, and Pascal's subsequent correspondence with mathematician Pierre de Fermat, led to the birth of probability theory.

Earlier in this chapter, two basic rules of probability—the special rule of addition and the general rule of addition—were introduced using a card activity. Here, another important probability rule is introduced using a simple dice activity.

MATERIALS NEEDED:
- Pair of dice
- Blank paper
- Pen or pencil

Probability for a Single Throw

Start with a single die. Ask your child what her favorite number is between 1 and 6. Then ask if she can figure out the likelihood of rolling her favorite number on a die. It should be fairly easy for her to see that the probability of rolling any number between 1 and 6 is ⅙. This is a simple calculation based on the notion of classical probability.

ESSENTIAL

Classical probability is only one approach that is used to calculate the likelihood of various events occurring. *Empirical probability* relies on using information from the past to determine probabilities for future events. For example, suppose that you have a mouse that, over the course of a month, appears in your house 3 mornings out of 4. The probability of the mouse appearing on any particular future morning would be ¾, or 0.75, based on the notion of empirical probability.

Probability for Multiple Throws

It's easy to calculate the likelihood of rolling any particular number on one throw of a die. But what about multiple throws? Suppose your child said her favorite number on a die was 5. The probability of rolling a 5 on a single throw of the die is $\frac{1}{6}$. What's the probability of throwing two 5s in a row?

Neither the special rule nor the general rule of addition will help answer that question. Both of those additive rules apply to situations in which you want to find the probability of A *or* B occurring. Calculating the probability of throwing two 5s on a die is about finding the probability of A *and* B occurring. Specifically, you want to know the probability of throwing a 5 and then another 5 on a die. For a problem like this, you'll want to use a basic probability rule known as the *special rule of multiplication*. The special rule of multiplication is used when you want to find the likelihood of A *and* B occurring. It's important to note that the special rule of multiplication only works in cases where A and B are independent events.

VOCAB

Two events are considered *independent events* if the occurrence of one has no effect on the probability of the other occurring. For instance, the probability of drawing a black card from a standard 52-card deck is $\frac{1}{2}$. If you draw a black card and subsequently put it back in the deck, the probability of drawing a black card a second time remains $\frac{1}{2}$. The first draw and the second draw would be independent events. However, if you draw a black card and keep it out of the deck, the probability of drawing a second black card is no longer $\frac{1}{2}$. In this case, the first draw and the second draw are not independent because the first draw impacts the probability of the second draw.

The special rule of multiplication is easy to use. It states that if A and B are independent events, the probability of A and B both occurring is equal to the probability of A occurring times the probability of B occurring.

The probability of rolling a 5 on the first roll of a die is $\frac{1}{6}$. Think of that as event A. The probability of rolling a 5 on the second roll of a die—event B—is also $\frac{1}{6}$. So the probability of rolling two 5s in a row is $(\frac{1}{6}) \times (\frac{1}{6}) = \frac{1}{36}$.

With paper, a pen, and a little time, you can prove to yourself that the special rule of multiplication works. Invite your child to write out on a sheet of paper all the possible arrangements of two throws of a die. She can actually draw pictures of dice with dots, if it helps her visualize the problem.

One possible arrangement is a 1 on the first throw of the die, and a 1 on the second throw. Another possible arrangement is a 1 on the first throw and a 2 on the second throw, and so on. When your child finishes drawing out the possibilities, there should be 36 different arrangements depicted on the page. How many of those arrangements include a 5 on the first roll and a 5 on the second roll? Only 1 of them does: 1 out of 36 possible arrangements. But this is a somewhat time-consuming way to solve the problem. The special rule of multiplication yields the answer much more quickly.

Note that when the events are not independent, the calculation of probability becomes more involved. A discussion of probability in those situations is better suited for an advanced-level class in high school or college.

VOCAB

Aside from classical probability and empirical probability, there's another approach to estimating the probability of an event (or events) happening. *Subjective probability* is an approach that's used when the other approaches can't be employed. Subjective probability estimates are based on the best information available. Sometimes such an estimate is referred to as "expert opinion." In truth, a subjective probability estimate is essentially a special type of educated guess.

Extending the Activity

Ask your child to calculate the probability of each of the following events. Remind her to use the special rule of multiplication where it's appropriate.

FIND THE PROBABILITY OF EACH OF THE FOLLOWING EVENTS:
1. Rolling an even number on a single die
2. Rolling two 5s in a row on a die
3. Rolling three 5s in a row on a die

4. Flipping a coin and having it turn up heads
5. Flipping two heads in a row on a coin
6. Flipping ten heads in a row on a coin

The special rule of multiplication works for any number of independent events. The probability of A and B and C occurring can be found using the special rule of multiplication as long as the three events are independent. So the probability of rolling three 5s in a row on a die is ($\frac{1}{6}$) × ($\frac{1}{6}$) × ($\frac{1}{6}$), which equals $\frac{1}{216}$, or 0.00463.

CHAPTER 14

Money Math

Some kids seem to pick up mathematical concepts more easily when dollar signs are attached to the numbers. If that's true for your child, it may be that your kid is destined to become a Wall Street wizard one day. Or it may just be that the dollar signs help your child see the relevance of the math. This chapter's activities will introduce your child to mathematical concepts that are often used in the fields of economics and finance. Hopefully, your kid will also pick up a few tips about sound money management while learning some math.

How Many Zeros Are in a Quadrillion?

The zero is undoubtedly one of the greatest inventions in the history of mankind. If you doubt that statement, just take a moment to think about what our number system would be like without it. Instead of having ten digits—0, 1, 2, 3, 4, 5, 6, 7, 8, and 9—we would need a unique digit for every number used. If you counted 100 of something, you couldn't write it as a 1 followed by two zeros. You would have to write it using unique symbols. Perhaps it would be written as 1ğž or 1¢φ. Can you image how complicated our number system would be without the zero? When most people think of a number with a whole bunch of zeros, they immediately think of money. The information in this section pertains to zeros whether they're part of a monetary figure or not.

QUESTION

Who invented the zero?
The ancient Babylonians used a mark to indicate that a number was absent from a column, but it wasn't exactly the same concept as the zero used today. The first mathematical operations involving zero were formalized in India around A.D. 650. But it was Middle Eastern mathematicians who gave the zero its mathematical properties and introduced the zero symbol.

The Importance of Place Value

The number system most commonly used today is known as the decimal or base 10 system. The value of a particular digit depends on its *place value*, or where it lies in the number. The place to the immediate left of the decimal is the ones place. Immediately left of that is the tens place. Left of that is the hundreds place, then the thousands place, then the ten thousands place, and so on.

To the immediate right of the decimal is the tenths place. To the right of that is the hundredths place. Right of that is the thousandths place, then the ten thousandths place, and so on. Of course, when it comes to dollar amounts, the number is usually rounded to the hundredths decimal place.

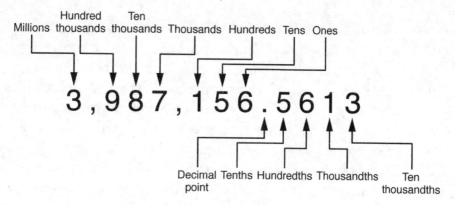

Decimal Place Value Chart

The zero serves as a placeholder. For example, if you write the number one hundred and one in digits you'll write 101. The 1 in the hundreds place indicates 1 hundred, the 0 in the tens place indicates 0 tens, and the 1 in the ones place indicates 1. Without the zero you would have to write 11, but that wouldn't carry the same value as 101. With the zero as a placeholder in the tens place, you know that you're dealing with a number whose value is at least one hundred.

VOCAB

Infinity is an abstract concept in mathematics that refers to a number too big to be counted or expressed. It also refers to a line or a space that is never-ending. Infinity is often represented by the symbol ∞.

The Place Value Game

Try this simple game that will help reinforce your child's understanding of place value in the decimal or base 10 number system.

MATERIALS NEEDED:

- Blank paper
- Black marker or felt-tip pen
- Pencil and eraser
- Pair of dice
- Watch or timer

Using the black marker, create spaces on the paper for the millions place through the ten thousandths place. Be sure to include the decimal, which will serve as a reference point. When you're finished, you should have seven spaces to the left of the decimal point and four spaces to the right of the decimal. You can use the place value chart provided as a guide.

After you've created your game board, randomly choose digits to populate the spaces. You can roll a single die repeatedly and use the resulting numbers to populate the spaces, or you can use an online random number generator, or you can simply pick numbers from thin air. When you're finished, you should have all eleven spaces filled with a number. You might consider using a pencil to populate the spaces so you can erase the numbers and reuse the game board.

To begin the game, have your child roll a single die and note the resulting number. He should look for that on the game board. Be sure to set the timer—he has ten seconds from the time he rolls the die to identify the place value of the number on the die. For example, suppose he rolls a 2 on the die. He should look for a 2 on the game board. Suppose there is a 2 in the thousands place. He has until the timer runs out to say "thousands place." If he does so within the time limit, he wins the round. If the number on the die appears in more than one place on the game board, he may choose one place value to identify.

If your kid rolls a 2 and there are no 2s on the game board, then have him roll again. He should alternate between rolling a single die and the pair so that values over 6 will be included in the game. When he rolls the pair of dice he should promptly add the dots on the dice and look for that number on the game board. If the numbers on the dice sum to 10, 11, or 12, then he may disregard the dice and just identify the place value of any number on the board he wishes. Play until your child has successfully identified the place value of each digit on the game board, then erase the numbers and try again with new numbers. You can also consider trying an extension of the game where you add a dollar sign on the left side and only carry the decimals to the hundredths place. You might find that your child has an easier time identifying place values when the numbers are dollar amounts.

ESSENTIAL

One famous large number is the *googol*, which is 10 raised to the hundredth power, or 10^{100}. Written out, a googol would be 1 followed by 100 zeros. The googol doesn't have any special significance in mathematics, but it did inspire the name of an extremely well-known search engine.

Really Big Numbers

What's the biggest possible number in the universe? The truth is there's no limit on how large (or how small) a number can get. Most people know that a million comes after a thousand, and that a billion comes after a million. Lots of people also know that a trillion comes after a billion. But what comes after a trillion? Take a look at the list below to find out.

REALLY BIG NUMBERS:

- A million has 6 zeros: 1,000,000
- A billion has 9 zeros: 1,000,000,000
- A trillion has 12 zeros: 1,000,000,000,000
- A quadrillion has 15 zeros: 1,000,000,000,000,000
- A quintillion has 18 zeros: 1,000,000,000,000,000,000
- A sextillion has 21 zeros: 1,000,000,000,000,000,000,000

And the numbers get bigger (and the names stranger) than a sextillion. To cite a few examples, an undecillion has 36 zeros, a quattuordecillion has 45 zeros, and a novemdecillion has 60 zeros!

QUESTION

Do we ever really need to count to a trillion?
You'll need to count to well over a trillion if you're going to count the United States' national debt. At the beginning of 2015, the U.S. national debt stood at over $18 trillion, which is a whole lot of money! Fortunately, the United States is a big country with lots of assets and resources at its disposal. Still, many Americans are concerned about the country having a debt with so many zeros.

Decimals and Money

For a long time, money transactions have been used as a way to teach young people about mathematical operations. A large part of understanding money math involves knowing how to work with decimals. The following activities are designed to help introduce your child to the basic decimal math she needs to comprehend various monetary transactions.

MATERIALS NEEDED:
- Paper currency in denominations of 1 up to 20
- Reasonably large pile of coins of varying denominations
- Blank paper
- Pen or pencil

QUESTION

Where did the terms *dollar* and *cent* come from?
The word *cent* comes from the Latin *centum,* which means hundred. At one time cent meant one hundred, but its meaning later shifted to mean "hundredth part." The word *dollar* comes from the Flemish word *daler* (or *thaler* in German), which was a name for a coin from a specific region. The term dollar was first used for currency in the United States in the late eighteenth century.

Adding and Subtracting Money

When adding or subtracting decimals, you just need to line up the decimal points and then the problem is essentially like any other addition or subtraction problem. A great way to encourage your child to practice is to lay out different arrangements of currency and coins and ask her to add or subtract the amounts, using scratch paper if necessary.

VOCAB

Profit and *loss* are familiar terms to a lot of people. Both of them involve decimal addition and subtraction. To calculate a company's profit, you first have to add up all the company's revenues over a given period. *Revenues* are the monetary amounts the company receives from selling its goods or services. The company's costs also have to be added up for the same period. These include dollar amounts the company pays for rent, advertising, wages, etc. Profit is calculated by subtracting the company's total costs from its total revenues. If the resulting amount is positive, then the company earned a profit. If the resulting amount is a negative value, then the company incurred a loss over the period.

Money Multiplication

There are numerous contexts in which multiplication is used with monetary units. One example is gross pay—the amount a worker receives for working X number of hours at X dollars per hour. Another example is sales tax. Discounts and sales prices also involve money multiplication.

The easiest way to multiply decimals by hand is to leave out the decimals while completing the multiplication, and then add in the decimals last. For example, suppose you're purchasing an item at a store—say a new softball bat—and the price is $40. Suppose also that the sales tax where you live is 8%. You need to know how much you'll have to pay in total for the bat so you know whether you brought along enough money or not.

Sales tax rates are typically stated in percentage terms, but they can easily be converted into decimals. Simply remove the "%" symbol and divide by 100. Thus, 8% in decimal form is 0.08. The price of the bat, $40, multiplied by 0.08— ignoring the decimal—is 40 × 8 = 320. That's not the final answer, of course. Because there are two decimal places in 0.08, you must move the decimal over two places in your answer as well, making it 3.20. The tax on the softball bat is $3.20, so the total amount you'll have to pay at the register is $43.20.

ESSENTIAL

A shortcut for calculating the total price of item including the sales tax is to multiply the price by 1 + the sales tax rate in decimal terms. In the example here, $40 × 1.08 = $43.20.

Money Division

There are plenty of situations in which you might be called upon to use division with monetary units. Suppose you have $10 and you'd like to know how many 80¢ packs of gum you can buy. An amount denominated in cents can easily be converted to decimals. Simply drop the "¢" symbol and divide by 100. The price of a pack of gum in this example can be written as $0.80 instead of 80¢.

To divide $10 by $0.80 it would be helpful to first include decimal, or cent, places in the dividend. Dropping the dollar signs would give you 10.00/0.80.

If you then drop the decimals, you have an ordinary long division problem: 1,000/80.

The quotient of 1,000/80 is 12.5. There's no need to do anything more; division is all about ratios, and the ratio 1,000 to 80 is the same as the ratio 10.00 to 0.80. If you have $10 in your pocket you can buy 12.5 packs of gum that cost 80¢ each, as long as you live in a state and town with no sales tax.

Practicing with Real Money

One of the best ways to help kids learn about money is set up ways for them to practice with real money. It's also a great way to help them practice decimal math. A great activity to start with is a money journal—a written record of all the money your child spends and receives over a given period. Help your kid set up columns in her journal for money receipts and outflows. Encourage her to keep a running balance, which should offer her ample opportunity to practice adding and subtracting decimals. It will also help prepare her to manage a checking or debit card account one day. She can also practice decimal multiplication by calculating any sales taxes paid on items she purchases.

After your child keeps a money journal for a month, she's ready to sit down and prepare an actual budget. A budget is similar to a money journal except instead of focusing on expenditures and receipts as they occur, a budget projects future spending and income. A budget is a way to establish goals for your money. Even for a kid whose income and expenditures are relatively small, a budget can be an invaluable learning tool.

Calculating Percentage Change

Lots of numerical measures change over time, and oftentimes people are interested in tracking those changes. For example, temperatures, prices, incomes, and home values all change over time. One common method of evaluating the change in numerical values over time is to calculate the percentage change in those values. There are many potential applications for percentage change, but it's probably most commonly used in the fields of business, economics, and finance.

Absolute Change

Suppose you've been working for $100,000 per year and then you receive a raise. Your new salary is $110,000. Clearly you are earning $10,000 more per year after the raise. That $10,000 increase is the *absolute change* in your income.

Absolute change is just basic subtraction, and it can be calculated for any two values with common units (or units that can be converted to common units). For instance, you can easily calculate the absolute change in temperature if the temperature rises from 80°F to 90°F over the course of a given week. You can also calculate the absolute change if one of your temperature values is given to you in Celsius, since temperatures in Celsius can be converted to Fahrenheit and vice versa. But what if one value is in terms of inches and another value is in terms of dollars? In such a case, calculating the change between the two values would have no meaning (unless you're dealing with a product that is sold by the inch).

Percentage Increase

While knowing the absolute change between two values can be useful, people are often interested in knowing the percentage change. Returning to the example involving the raise, $10,000 was the absolute change in income. The percentage change in income is 10%. How is that calculated?

The basic formula for calculating the percentage change is:

Percentage Change from Old Value to New Value =
(New Value–Old Value) / |Old Value|

After finding your answer you'll want to multiply by 100 and add the "%" symbol to make the number a percentage. So using the numbers from the change in income example, you would write:

Percentage Change from Old Income to New Income =
($110,000 – $100,000) / $100,000

The resulting answer is 0.10, or 10% when converted to percentage terms. In other words, if your income rises from $100,000 per year to $110,000 per year, then you received a 10% raise.

VOCAB

Absolute value refers to the value of a real number without reference to its sign. Absolute value is denoted by "| |" with the number between the two symbols. With absolute value, you're interested in the magnitude of a number, or how far it lies from 0 on the number line. A positive number would therefore remain positive and a negative number would also be positive. For example, |5| is 5 and |–2| is 2.

Percentage Decrease

What if your income decreased instead of increased? Would you use the same formula to find the percentage decrease in your income? The answer is yes—the formula works for calculating both increases and decreases.

Suppose that instead of receiving a raise, your salary is reduced from $100,000 to $90,000. You would enter the numbers into the formula as follows:

Percentage Change from Old Income to New Income = ($90,000 – $100,000) / $100,000

The resulting answer, in percentage terms, is –10%. In other words, if your income falls from $100,000 per year to $90,000 per year, then you're receiving 10% less per year after the salary cut.

Interesting Percentage Change Activities

Encourage your child to track some numerical measures and calculate the percentage change in those values over some time period. A few ideas are listed here:

FIND THE PERCENTAGE CHANGE IN:
- Price of gasoline over a week
- Temperature over a week or month
- His own height over a year (if he recorded his height around this time a year ago)
- Price of (some favorite toy) over a month
- Number of games won by (favorite pro or college sports team) over a year

Note for the last one on the list, your child will have to track down the win record of his favorite team on the same date the previous year (which shouldn't be difficult to do online). The percentage change would indicate the degree to which the team is doing better or worse than the previous year.

Another Way to Calculate Percentage Change

It's always good to know more than one way of doing something. Percentage change can be calculated using the formula that's already been presented. But there is another method that also works every time. The alternative formula is:

Percentage Change from Old Value to New Value =
[(New Value / Old Value) − 1] × 100

Using the first example presented in this section, the numbers would be entered into the formula as follows:

Percentage Change from Old Income to New Income =
[($110,000 / $100,000) − 1] × 100

The resulting answer is 10, or 10% after the percent symbol is added. If there's a reduction from the old value to the new value, then the resulting answer will be negative.

Money's Value over Time

One of the best-kept secrets about money is how its value changes over time. Actually it's not really a secret, but many people seem to ignore or overlook the concept of the time value of money. The younger you are when you learn about the time value of money, the greater your opportunity to take advantage of it.

Simple Interest

When you keep your money in the bank—in a savings account or certain other types of accounts—the bank pays you for keeping it there. The money the bank pays you is known as *interest*. Interest is expressed in percentage terms. Just to make the math straightforward, suppose the bank is paying interest of 5% annually to hold your money. Note that the bank doesn't just park your money; the bank actually uses your money to make loans to borrowers who are looking to buy houses, cars, businesses, and other big-ticket items.

Suppose you put $100 in your account at the beginning of the year. How much would you have in your account at the end of the year, assuming you didn't make any other deposits or any withdrawals during the year? Your end-of-year balance would be equal to your beginning balance plus the interest you earned over the year. If the bank pays 5% interest on a yearly basis, the amount of interest earned over the year would be $100 × 5%, or $5. (Note that 5% in decimal form is 0.05, so 100 × 0.05 = 5.) Your balance at the end of the year would therefore be $100 + $5 = $105.

ESSENTIAL

There's a shortcut you can use to calculate the ending year balance, given an interest rate. It's similar to the shortcut for calculating the total price of item including the appropriate sales tax. Simply multiply the beginning balance by 1 + the annual interest rate in decimal terms to arrive at the ending account balance. Using the example given, $100 × 1.05 = $105.

Compound Interest

The beautiful thing about interest paid on bank deposits is that it keeps on accumulating as long as there's money in the account. Not only does the bank pay interest on the initial amount you deposited, but the bank also pays interest on the interest your account previously earned. This is known as *compound interest*, and it makes saving money a lot of fun.

For example, at the end of year two, you would have $110.25 in your account, assuming you didn't make any additional deposits in the second year. That amount is found by multiplying $105 by 5% (or 0.05) and adding that value—which is the interest earned in the second year—to your account balance at the end of the first year.

$105 \times 5\% = \$5.25$. And $\$105 + \$5.25 = \$110.25$

Take a few moments and help your child calculate what the balance will be at the end year three, again assuming that no additional deposits and no withdrawals are made during the third year. If she understands decimal math, she should be able to figure out that the account balance at the end of year three will be approximately $115.76 (calculated by $110.25 × 1.05).

A Formula for Calculating Compound Interest

Suppose you left the $100 in the bank for ten years, and the bank paid 5% interest per year. You could calculate the ending balance by hand using the method already outlined. There is a faster way to arrive at the answer, but it requires a bit more math ability. The formula for calculating compound interest for interest compounded annually is:

$$PV \times (1 + r)^n = FV$$

where PV is the present value or starting account balance, r is the yearly interest rate (in decimal form), n is the number of periods, and FV is the future value, or the ending balance of the account. At the end of ten years, your account that started with $100 will have a balance of:

$$\$100 \times (1.05)^{10} = \$162.89$$

It's interesting to note that after fourteen years, the account will have a balance of approximately $198. Within fourteen years, your money will have nearly doubled, thanks to the magic of compound interest. Note that the formula becomes slightly more complex if the interest is compounded semiannually, quarterly, monthly, or daily.

A Savings Plan

Perhaps after explaining compound interest to your child, you can help her create a savings plan. There's a formula that determines how much money you would have in an account if you were to save a set amount on a regular basis. Suppose your child managed to save $1,200 per year, depositing that amount at the end of each year, for forty years. At a 5% annual interest rate, after forty years, she would have about $144,960 in her account. Without interest payments she would only have $1,200 × 40 = $48,000. See the difference compound interest makes over time? People who begin saving while they're young and save consistently over a number of years can accumulate a large amount of money.

> An *annuity* is a steam of equal payments made at regular intervals. The future value of an annuity can be found using the formula FV = P × [((1 + r)^n − 1) / r], where P is the periodic payment, r is the annual interest rate, and n is the number of years. A person who saves $1,200 per year at 5% interest will have $1,200 × [((1.05)^{40} − 1) / 0.05] = $144,960 at the end of forty years. Note that the formula is slightly different if the period payments are made at the beginning of the month instead of at the end of the month.

Compound interest problems can get complicated, depending on the particulars of the problem. There are financial calculators, software programs, and online calculators to help solve more advanced problems. The main purpose of this section is to highlight the concept of the time value of money and to introduce some of the basic math involved in these important financial calculations.

Extra Practice

To be sure your child understands basic time value of money calculations, invite her to try the following problems.

CALCULATE THE FUTURE VALUE, OR ENDING ACCOUNT BALANCE, IN EACH OF THE FOLLOWING SCENARIOS:
1. The beginning balance is $1,000, the yearly interest rate is 4%, the number of years is 4.
2. The beginning balance is $1,000, the yearly interest rate is 1%, the number of years is 4.
3. The beginning balance is $1,000, the yearly interest rate is 4%, the number of years is 12.

4. The beginning balance is $1,000, the yearly interest rate is 8%, the number of years is 4.

5. The beginning balance is $2,000, the yearly interest rate is 4%, the number of years is 4.

The previous scenarios allow your child to analyze the impact of changing various numbers in the formula.

ANSWERS:
1. $1,000 \times (1.04)^4 = $1,169.86$
2. $1,000 \times (1.01)^4 = $1,040.60$
3. $1,000 \times (1.04)^{12} = $1,601.03$
4. $1,000 \times (1.08)^4 = $1,360.49$
5. $2,000 \times (1.04)^4 = $2,339.72$

The Rule of 72

The "rule of 72" is one of those great math shortcuts every kid should learn in elementary school, but not all are presented the opportunity. It works in any context which involves a growth rate. People often use it to examine population growth, for instance. However, the rule is used most frequently in financial applications.

Applying the Rule of 72

The rule of 72 gives an estimate of the number of years it takes some amount to double at a given rate of growth. It could be used to estimate how long it'll take a particular nation's population to double, given a particular population growth rate. It's frequently utilized to estimate the length of time it will take a monetary investment to double at a particular interest rate.

Suppose you put money into an account that pays 10% annual interest. To use the rule of 72, you simply divide 72 by the interest rate (as a whole number rather than a decimal). The resulting number is the estimate in years of how long it will take the money in your account to double. In this case it would take about 72 / 10 = 7.2 years for your money to double.

ESSENTIAL

The rule of 72 is often used to estimate future inflation, another important concept from the world of finance and economics. *Inflation* is a general rise in the overall level of prices, and it's usually expressed on an annualized basis. If the rate of yearly inflation were 4%, for example, overall prices would double in about 18 years (calculated by 72 / 4 = 18).

Alternate Uses of the Rule of 72

Instead of using the rule of 72 to estimate the number of years it would take your investment to double, you could use it to calculate the interest rate you would need to receive in order for your money to double. Suppose you need your nest egg to double in 15 years so that you can retire comfortably. According to the rule, 72 / X = 15, where X is the rate of interest that doubles your money. Rearranging this equation gives you 72 / 15 = X, and solving for X yields 4.8. So, based on the rule of 72, you would need to find an investment that pays an annual return of approximately 4.8% if you want your money to double in 15 years.

Practicing with the Rule of 72

Invite your child to try a little practice with the rule of 72. Give her a pencil and some scratch paper and have her go through each of the scenarios below.

USE THE RULE OF 72 TO SOLVE EACH OF THE FOLLOWING SCENARIOS:
1. If the population of Country Y is growing at an annual rate of 3%, how long will it take the population of Country Y to double?
2. If inflation is rising at 6% per year, how long will it take overall prices to double?
3. If your savings account pays interest of 1% per year, how long will it take your savings to double?
4. If you need your money to double in 10 years, what yearly interest rate do you need to receive on your investment?
5. If Country Z's Gross Domestic Product (GDP) is growing at 2.5% per year, how long will it take the country's GDP to double?

ANSWERS:

1. 72 / 3 = 24 years
2. 72 / 6 = 12 years
3. 72 / 1 = 72 years
4. 72 / x = 10, so x = 7.2%
5. 72 / 2.5 = 28.8 years

ESSENTIAL

Sometimes people use the rule of 69 or the rule of 70 instead of the rule of 72. Essentially when the growth process involves continuous compounding, or when the rate is small (0.5% or less), the rule of 69 provides a better estimate of the doubling time. If the rate of growth is between 0.5% and about 5%, the rule of 70 provides a better estimate. The rule of 72 becomes less accurate if the growth rate is very high.

The Limits of the Rule of 72

The rule of 72 is a shortcut that provides an estimate, and estimates are rarely completely accurate. The rule provides more accurate estimates when the rate of growth falls within certain parameters. Also, the rule assumes that no other factors change that would affect the rate of growth over time. For example, if you use the rule of 72 to estimate the length of time it would take the population to double, you're assuming that no factors change that would impact the population growth rate. What if an improvement in healthcare technology increases life expectancy, thus increasing the overall level of population? Or what if the fertility rate decreases over time?

In addition to these shortcomings, the rule of 72 doesn't acknowledge that some growth processes have natural limits. If you're a family that records your child's height over time, try having her calculate the growth rate in her height from last year to this year (you can use the percentage change formula presented earlier in this chapter). Then ask her to use the rule of 72 to determine how long it would take her to double in height. Ask her to discuss whether she believes she really could grow twice as tall as she is now. Hopefully she'll be able to see that the rule of 72 is a useful mathematical shortcut, but, like all shortcuts, it has limitations and thus can't be applied in all situations.

CHAPTER 15

STEM Kits, Games, Apps, and Magazines

In addition to all the hands-on STEM activities listed in this book that involve household items, a number of options exist for readymade learning activities and materials. This chapter lists dozens of such options, ranging from science kits to card games to learning apps to STEM-related magazines. There's surely some resource among those listed that will appeal to your child's specific interests and grade level.

STEM-Related Kits

There's nothing in the world that fires a kid's imagination like a well-designed science kit. There are kits on the market relating to nearly every STEM subject, designed for children of varying grade levels. The companies listed here are the largest and most well-known manufacturers of STEM-related learning kits. If you're looking for a good science kit for your child, you'll want to start by browsing the websites of these companies.

Thames & Kosmos—*www.thamesandkosmos.com*

Thames & Kosmos produces a wide array of science kits covering nearly every area of science, for ages five and up. For ages eight to nine, Thames & Kosmos offers kits exploring electronics, rocket science, solar mechanics, optical science, motors and generators, space exploration, solar cooking science, and dinosaur fossils, among others. For ages ten and up, Thames & Kosmos offers kits such as Smart Car Robotics, Candy Chemistry, Genetics & DNA, Volcanoes & Earthquakes, Perfume Science, and Crystal Growing. The company also has a number of kits available that focus on the environment and alternative energy. Representative kits include: Climate and Weather, Global Water Quality, Recycled Paper Press, Physics Solar Workshop, Solar Car, Solar Boat, Fuel Cell X7, Hydropower, Wind Power, and Sustainable Earth Lab.

4M Industrial Development Limited—*www.4m-ind.com*

4M is a Hong Kong–based maker of educational toys, many of them STEM related. 4M offers a number of moderately priced STEM toys and kits for various age levels. Some of the kits include the Tin Can Robot, the Mousetrap Racer, the Doodling Robot, the Bottle Catamaran, the Robot Duck, the Electric Plane Launcher, the Enviro Battery, the Windmill Generator, the Micro Rocket, the Pocket Volcano, the Dynamo Circuit Board, the Glow Dinosaur Skull, and Glow Mini Stars.

ScienceWiz—*www.sciencewiz.com*

ScienceWiz offers an array of kits designed to teach kids of various ages fundamental scientific concepts through hands-on play. ScienceWiz kits cover topics such as physics, chemistry, energy, electricity, light, magnetism, inventions, and rocks. ScienceWiz also offers thinking games such as Cool Circuits, and activity kits such as Super Crystals and Stinky Rocks.

SmartLab Toys—www.smartlabtoys.com

SmartLab Toys creates educational toys for young people ages three to twelve that include a book component. SmartLab offers a number of exciting STEM-related toys with names such as Demolition Lab, Solar System Adventure, Design-A-Saurs, It's Alive! Slime Lab, Star Dome Planetarium, Weird & Wacky Contraption Lab, That's Gross Science Lab, Inhuman Squishy Zombie, Squishy Human Body, Amazing Squishy Brain, Amazing Squishy T. Rex, Smartphone Science, Glow-in-the-Dark Lab, All-Natural Spa Day, You-Build-It Headphones, Bug Playground, Blast-Off Rocker Racer, and You-Track-It Weather Lab.

POOF—http://poof-slinky.com/product-category/scientific-explorer

POOF is a well-established toy company with a portfolio of products that include numerous STEM-related kits. Representative kits include Ice Cream Science Kit, Sci-Fi Slime Kit, Amusement Park Science Kit, Electrified Energy Lab, Wacky Weird Weather Kit, Lava-Blasting Volcano Kit, Tasty Science Kit, Sports Science Kit, All About Volcanoes Kit, Solar Energy Mini Lab, Crystal Radio Mini Lab, Kitchen Chemistry Mini Lab, Tornado Maker Kit, Our Amazing Mummies Kit, Fingerprint Science Mini Lab, and Young Architect Kit.

OWI Incorporated—www.owirobot.com

OWI offers a series of technology kits available in five different difficulty levels. The levels range from beginner to advanced, with some kits more geared toward grade school kids and others better suited for adults. OWI offers solar kits, salt water fuel cell kits, robotics kits, and aluminum bug and dino kits.

Smithsonian—www.SmithsonianStore.com

A line of science kits carrying the Smithsonian name is available for sale at numerous retail outlets, including online outlets. Hand Crank Radio, Astro Lab Planetarium, Rock & Gem Dig, Prehistoric Sea Monsters, Crystal

Growing, Frog Lab, Weather Center, Gummy Bug Lab, and Cool Circuits Electronics Lab are some of the kits available under the Smithsonian brand.

Be Amazing! Toys—*www.beamazingtoys.com*

Be Amazing! Toys bills itself as a maker of "educational, creative, and fun science kits and toys that teach real science in a way that makes kids say 'Wow! How does that work?'" Representative kits include Big Bag of Science, Brain Tickling Science, Epic Bubbles, Slime Factory, Wired Science, and This Is Rocket Science.

The Young Scientists Club—*www.theyoungscientistsclub.com*

The Young Scientist Club offers several series of STEM-related kits, including the Young Scientist series, the Magic School Bus series, the Adventure Science series, and the Nature series. Some of the kits are aimed kids ages five to eight, and others are geared toward young people ages nine to twelve. Representative kits include Magnets, Recycling, Minerals, Crystals, Bacteria and Fungi, Heart and Lungs, Digestive System, Bones and Muscles, Circuits and Electromagnets, Stars, Planets, Forces, Volcano Madness, Famous Scientists and Their Experiments, Math Explosion, Awesome Bubbles, and Science on a Fossil Dig. Representative kits in the Magic School Bus series include Growing Crazy Crystals, Engineering Lab, Weather Lab, Slime and Polymer Lab, Chemistry Lab, and Microscope Lab.

Elenco—*www.elenco.com*

Elenco, a company founded by engineers, produces a line of educational science toys and kits including robotics kits, electronic project labs, Engino Construction kits, Tree of Knowledge kits, and the award-winning Snap Circuits kits. The Snap Circuits kit teaches kids the basics of electricity by allowing them to build working circuit boards. The standard kit, designed for ages eight to fifteen, includes over sixty pieces that can be used to create more than 300 electronics projects. Elenco also offers Snap Circuits Lights, the Alternative Green Energy Kit, and Snap Circuits Jr. for younger children.

Discover with Dr. Cool—*www.discoverwithdrcool.com*

Discover with Dr. Cool produces a selection of kits focusing on various facets of earth science, including geology, insects and bugs, paleontology and dinosaurs, and break-open geodes. The company offers several discounted bundles for the homeschool market.

Ravensburger—*www.ravensburger.com*

Ravensburger, best known for its puzzles and games, produces a line of science kits under its Science X brand. Ravensburger's Science X kits include Electronics and Circuitry, Secret Codes, Crystals & Gemstones, Fueling Future Cars, Dinosaurs, Magnetic Magic, 3D Optics, Nature's Energy, Crystal Magic, and CSI Crime Scene Investigation. Ravensburger's science kits are designed either for ages eight and up, or ages ten and up.

LEGO Education—*http://education.lego.com*

LEGO is, of course, one of the best-known toy companies in the world. But not everyone is aware of the high-tech educational kits offered by LEGO Education. LEGO Education offers kits that teach robotics, engineering, and programming. Many of the kits include programmable moving parts. LEGO Education has kits appropriate for elementary-aged kids through the high school level. The LEGO Mindstorms robotics sets are among the most advanced science kits on the market, featuring designs that can be programmed to operate via smartphone.

STEM Board Games and Card Games

In addition to many excellent online STEM games and apps, a number of companies offer "low-tech" games designed to teach STEM basics. Several popular STEM-related board games and card games are listed here.

Robot Turtles—*www.robotturtles.com*

Robot Turtles is a low-tech learning game that teaches some high-tech skills. The board game, for two to five players, "sneakily teaches" the basics of programming. Designed for kids ages four and up, Robot Turtles was launched on Kickstarter, where it became the most-backed board game in the crowdfunding site's history.

Totally Gross—The Game of Science— *www.university-games.co.uk*

A popular board game from University Games, Totally Gross—The Game of Science features "queasy questions" and gross-out challenges. Combining elements of chemistry, biology, and other science disciplines, Totally Gross—The Game of Science requires a player to complete a lab experiment in order to win the game. Designed for two to four players, the game is best suited for ages eight to fourteen.

Think Big Science Life Science Game— *www.learningresources.com*

Think Big Science Life Science Game comes complete with a unique three-dimensional game board and game cards featuring graphs, charts, diagrams, and pictures. Players climb the tower as they answer color-coded, standards-based questions about the human body, animals, plants, food chains, and more. Manufactured by Learning Resources, the game is geared toward kids ages eight to ten.

SomeBody—*www.talicor.com*

A combination puzzle and trivia game, players of SomeBody place body parts on the body boards, learning vocabulary and body functions as they compete to win. Suited for ages six to ten, SomeBody can be played by two to four players at a time.

Antimatter Matters: A Quantum Physics Board Game— *www.elbowfish.myshopify.com*

In the board game Antimatter Matters, players assume the role of scientists on an orbiting space lab. Players try to be the first to build an atom from individually captured elementary particles. Designed for two to six players, Antimatter Matters can be played in multiple modes so that players of differing ages and skill levels may participate in the same game. Produced by independent game studio Elbowfish, the game is recommended for ages eleven and up.

STRAIN: The Bioengineering Game—
www.copernicustoys.com

In STRAIN: The Bioengineering Game, players try to outsmart each other to build the mightiest organisms while avoiding getting infected. Strain: The Bioengineering Game is a card game for players ages ten and up.

Laser Maze Beam-Bending Logic Game—
www.thinkfun.com/lasermaze

ThinkFun's Laser Maze Beam-Bending Logic Game requires players to direct a real laser beam through a series of mind-challenging mazes. The game, suited for ages eight to fifteen, helps players build sequential reasoning and planning skills.

Math Explosion and Science Explosion—
www.theyoungscientistsclub.com

Produced by The Young Scientists Club under the Magic School Bus brand, Math Explosion and Science Explosion are two games designed to teach kids ages five and above key STEM concepts in a fun and exciting way. The player who gets his or her math or science facts correct first gets to explode the volcano. Both games are designed for two to four players.

NewPath Learning Curriculum Mastery Games—
www.newpathlearning.com

NewPath Learning produces digital learning resources, but the company also offers research-based board games in a series called the Curriculum Mastery Games. The games, developed by teachers and tested in classrooms, meet current national and state standards. Different games in the series target different subject areas and grade levels.

Professor Noggin's Card Games—
www.professornoggin.com/index.shtml

Professor Noggin produces a series of award-winning educational card games, with several STEM themes available, including the Human Body, Earth Science, Dinosaurs, Outer Space, Famous Inventions, and more. For players ages seven and up, the Professor Noggin games offer two levels of difficulty so that younger children can play alongside older siblings or adults.

Science Bingo et al.—*www.lucybingogames.com*

Lucy Hammett Games, which bills itself as an old-fashioned toy company, produces educational picture bingo games. A number of the company's bingo games are STEM related. Representative titles include Science Bingo, Space Bingo, Ocean Bingo, Wildlife Bingo, Nature Bingo, Weather Bingo, and Bug Bingo.

STEM Apps

With handheld computer devices more popular than ever, apps have become an excellent avenue for fun, interactive learning. There are loads of learning apps available online; a few popular ones are listed below. Many of the apps listed here focus on teaching kids basic programming skills using interactive games.

Hopscotch—*www.gethopscotch.com*

Hopscotch is a free app for the iPhone and iPad that teaches kids core programming concepts, such as sequencing, abstraction, values, and conditionals. Hopscotch allows kids to design their own games, animations, digital art, and more. The app is designed for ages nine to eleven.

Move the Turtle—*www.movetheturtle.com*

Move the Turtle is an app designed to teach basic programming to kids ages five and up. The app's learning process has been "gamified," with advancing levels. Move the Turtle is available, for a fee, for the iPhone and the iPad.

Lightbot—*www.lightbot.com/hocflash.html*

Lightbot is a puzzle game that allows kids to move a robot using visual programs. The game teaches programming concepts such as loops, procedures, and conditionals. The app, which is available for a fee, comes in two versions: one designed for ages six to eight, and the other for ages nine to eleven.

Daisy the Dinosaur—*www.mindleaptech.com/apps/daisy-the-dinosaur/*

Daisy the Dinosaur offers a simple drag-and-drop introduction to basic programing. The iPad app is available free of charge.

Cargo-Bot—*www.twolivesleft.com/CargoBot*

Cargo-Bot is a puzzle game in which the player programs a robotic arm to move crates. The game teaches basic coding skills in a multilevel fashion. Cargo-Bot touts itself as being the first game programmed entirely on an iPad using Codea. Cargo-Bot is an iPad app available free of charge.

Cato's Hike—*http://hwahba.com/catoshike/*

Cato's Hike: A Programming and Logic Odyssey is a story-based game that takes players through various mazes, requiring them to use the logic of computer programming to guide their character. Players can work with beginning-level commands or advanced commands such as branches, loops, goto commands, and if/then commands. Cato's Hike is available, for a fee, for the iPhone, iPad, and iPod Touch.

Monster Physics—*https://itunes.apple.com/us/app/monster-physics/id505046678*

Monster Physics is an app for ages eight and up that teaches players some of the basic laws of physics by challenging them to solve problems or build contraptions. Monster Physics is available, for a fee, for the iPhone and iPad.

Robot School—*www.robotschoolapp.com*

Robot School: Learn to Code is a programming game for ages seven and up featuring a robot, R-obbie, who crashed his spaceship in a distant galaxy and needs help getting back home. Robot School: Learn to Code is available, for a fee, for the iPhone and iPad.

Hackety Hack—*www.hackety.com*

Hackety Hack teaches the basics of the Ruby programming language, which is used for many web and desktop applications. Hackety Hack is an open-source app that runs on Mac, Windows, and Linux operating systems.

Coins Genius—*https://itunes.apple.com/us/app/ coins-genius-crazy-coin-counting/id362006211*

Coins Genius bills itself as a "crazy coin counting flash cards game for kids." The app, which challenges kids to add coin values quickly, is available for a fee for the iPhone, iPad, and iPod Touch.

Other Online Learning Resources

Apps aren't the only online resources available for learning about STEM subjects. Other web-based tools exist that offer kids the opportunity to learn coding, build websites, create animations, and other intriguing applications. Several exceptional educational sites are listed here.

Scratch—*www.scratch.mit.edu*

Scratch is a site developed and maintained at MIT for the purpose of teaching basic programming concepts to young people ages eight to sixteen. A visual programming language, Scratch allows user to build games, animations, interactive stories, and art. Scratch runs on Windows, Mac, and Linux, and is free to download.

Code.org—*www.code.org*

Code.org is a nonprofit dedicated to expanding participation in computer science by making it available in more schools. Code.org also aims to increase participation in computer sciences by women and underrepresented students of color. Code.org has some heavy-hitting corporate partners, such as Amazon, Facebook, Microsoft, and Google. Its online platform, Code Studio (*studio.code.org*), offers several free tutorials and courses that teach computer science fundamentals and programming.

Stencyl—*www.stencyl.com*

Stencyl is an online game-creation software that allows users to design games and publish them to iOS, Android, Flash, Windows, Mac, and Linux. Stencyl utilizes freemium-style pricing, with a free starter version available, as well as paid plans that offer more functionality.

Alice—*www.alice.org*

Alice is a 3D programming environment that allows users to create animations for videos or interactive games. Designed to be a student's first exposure to object-oriented programming, Alice is free to download and use.

Code Monster—*www.crunchzilla.com/code-monster*

Code Monster, produced by Crunchzilla, is a free online tutorial designed to teach programming basics to kids. Code Monster offers a simple introduction to elementary programming concepts such as variables, functions, loops, and conditionals. A highly interactive learning tool, Code Monster displays the code on one side of the screen and the results of the code on the other side of the screen.

Codecademy—*www.codecademy.com*

Codecademy offers a fun, social introduction to programming for higher-level students. Codecademy students learn programming skills and Javascript in an interactive manner, receiving feedback as they code. As students reach certain milestones, they earn badges and are invited to share their progress with friends.

CoderDojo—*www.coderdojo.com*

CoderDojo is a worldwide network of independent community-based youth programming clubs. CoderDojo club members learn to code and to develop programs, games, apps, and websites in a fun, social environment. Geared for young people ages seven to seventeen, CoderDojo clubs are led by volunteers and are free of charge to participants.

Made with Code—*www.madewithcode.com*

Made with Code is one of Google's initiatives to inspire girls to get involved in coding. Made with Code's website features introductory coding projects designed for girls who've never tried coding, as well as a resources page for girls who are ready to take their skills to the next level. Some of Made with Code's introductory projects include Music Mixer, Accessorizer, Kaleidoscope, and GIF. The site also features an online community designed to connect girl coders around the world.

Teaching Kids Programming— *http://teachingkidsprogramming.com*

Teaching Kids Programming (TKP) offers free, open-source Java course-ware designed to teach programming concepts to young people. Utilizing the Socratic method to keep kids engaged, TKP classes cover concepts such as loops, variables, conditionals, recursion, and concatenation.

Shodor—*www.shodor.org*

Shodor is a vast open resource for computational science education. Shodor's mission is "to improve math and science education through the effective use of modeling and simulation technologies—'computational science.'" Shodor develops interactive models, simulations, and other educational tools, and makes them available online by subject and by education level. Shodor's free resources include learning activities for students and lesson plans for teachers.

STEM-Related Magazines

One way to encourage your kid to embrace STEM learning is to get her a subscription to a quality science-based magazine. Magazines are a great way to keep your young learner up-to-date on the latest in science news. You can be sure the information in a reputable science magazine has been curated by an expert, which isn't necessarily the case for a number of web articles. A few excellent options are listed here.

Odyssey—www.odysseymagazine.com

Odyssey is a well-known science magazine for young people covering a wide array of scientific fields, including biology, physics, and environmental science. The magazine frequently highlights careers in science, and offers readers opportunities to enter science, math, and writing contests. *Odyssey* is aimed at young people ages nine to fourteen.

National Geographic Kids— http://kids.nationalgeographic.com

National Geographic Kids is a well-established magazine published by the National Geographic Society. *National Geographic Kids*, similar in scope to the adult version of the magazine, features articles on topics such as wildlife, technology, archeology, and geography. The magazine is geared toward young people ages six to fourteen. The National Geographic Society also publishes a related magazine for younger children—*National Geographic Little Kids*.

Ranger Rick—www.nwf.org/Kids/Ranger-Rick.aspx

Ranger Rick is a longtime favorite of children interested in nature and wildlife. Filled with activities aimed at promoting nature and outdoor activities, *Ranger Rick* is suited for kids ages seven and up (*Ranger Rick Jr.* is the version for kids ages four to seven). *Ranger Rick*, which is published by the National Wildlife Federation, also promotes responsible environmental stewardship. Additionally, *Ranger Rick*'s website offers games, apps, and other learning activities for kids and families.

OWL—www.owlkids.com/magazines/owl

OWL magazine, geared toward kids ages nine to thirteen, features articles and activities related to science, technology, engineering, math, and art. A typical issue of *OWL* includes quizzes, comics, hands-on activities, tech news, innovations, and interviews with experts.

Zoobooks—www.zoobooks.com

Zoobooks, published by Wildlife Education Ltd., is perfect for the budding zoologist, or any kid interested in animals. Aimed at kids ages six to twelve, *Zoobooks* features great animal photographs and informative articles. *Zoobooks* began as a publication available for purchase at zoo kiosks. Due to popular demand, the magazines have been made available on a subscription basis. Each issue is themed around an animal or animal group, and articles provide in-depth information about animal habits and habitats.

Muse—www.musemagkids.com

Muse is a popular kids' magazine that bills itself as "the magazine of life, the universe, and pie throwing." Suited for young people ages nine to fourteen, *Muse* features articles relating to the earth sciences, physics, math, and more.

Ask—www.askmagkids.com

Ask is an arts and sciences magazine for kids ages seven to ten. *Ask* includes articles on a wide array of interesting topics, many of them STEM related. The magazine also features games, puzzles, cartoons, and other fun activities. *Ask*'s interactive website offers free games, crafts, recipes, and more.

SuperScience, Science World, and Science Spin—http://classroommagazines.scholastic.com/

Scholastic offers a host of STEM-related magazines for kids covering various age ranges. *SuperScience* is aimed at students in third to sixth grades. *Science World* is for students in sixth to tenth grades. *Science Spin* has three versions spanning readers from kindergarten to sixth grades. The focus of all of Scholastic's science periodicals is the same: to provide science information that's "too new for textbooks." *Science World* is available for general purchase on Amazon (subscription or individual issues); *SuperScience* and *Science Spin* are available for purchase by schools.

CHAPTER 16

STEM Summer Camps, Enrichment Classes, Online Classes, and Job Shadowing

Summer camps aren't what they used to be. These days, numerous opportunities exist for kids to learn important STEM skills, such as computer programming and robotics, during the summer. Likewise, many options exist for extracurricular STEM learning in the form of afterschool and online enrichment classes. Many of these enrichment classes are designed to be fun and experiential, like the STEM summer camps. This chapter lists dozens of extracurricular STEM-based learning opportunities for kids, including summer camps, afterschool classes, and online classes. In addition, the chapter offers some guidelines and suggestions you might consider if you wish to involve your child in a STEM-related job-shadowing experience.

STEM Summer Camps and Enrichment Classes

In every major city, as well as in many smaller communities, opportunities abound for kids to engage STEM subjects outside the classroom. These enrichment opportunities take the form of afterschool classes, summer camps, winter break camps, spring break camps, in-school field trips, and birthday party programs. The following providers of STEM-related youth enrichment programs share some similarities, but each approaches its mission from a slightly different angle. Compare the options available in your area and choose the one that best suits your child's interests and aptitude.

Mad Science Group—*www.madscience.org*

Mad Science is a Canadian-based franchise company that offers science-based summer camps, afterschool enrichment classes, in-school field trips, and birthday programs for kids from preschool through middle school. Mad Science is a well-established company, operating in hundreds of locations throughout North America and around the world. Mad Science offers programs relating to nearly every area of science. The company's programs include titles such as Science of Magic, Red Hot Robots, Fun Physics, Slime Time, Crazy Chemworks, Techno Safari, Secret Agent Lab, Jet Cadets, and Planet Rock!

Bricks 4 Kidz—*www.bricks4kidz.com*

Bricks 4 Kidz is one of the many companies offering enrichment classes and summer camps for kids focusing on engineering, architecture, and robotics. Bricks 4 Kidz has franchises across North America and in numerous countries overseas. Bricks 4 Kidz utilizes kits from LEGO Education along with proprietary builds and other materials for its classes.

Engineering for Kids—*www.engineeringforkids.com*

Engineering for Kids is another company that offers a suite of programs designed to introduce kids up to age fourteen to STEM-related subjects in over 100 locations in the United States and several locations overseas. Engineering for Kids offers camps, afterschool classes, weekend programs, and birthday parties. Engineering for Kids' afterschool and evening classes are focused on a specific discipline of engineering such as civil, electrical, or aerospace engineering. The company's camps are thematic, focusing on a variety of engineering fields within a given theme. Engineering for Kids offers nearly 300 individual lessons, covering a very wide variety of engineering disciplines, requiring students to use math and physics concepts to solve engineering challenges. Each Engineering for Kids lesson is aligned to five different sets of state and national educational standards.

All About Learning—*www.allaboutlearning.co/default.php*

All About Learning provides STEM-related enrichment classes and summer camps for kids from kindergarten through eighth grade utilizing LEGO Education kits and LEGO elements. Representative programs include Gears and Gadgets, FUN-gineering, Collision Cars, Vehicle Brick Building, Video Game Making, and Journey Into Space.

IMACS—*www.imacs.org*

For students in grades one to twelve, IMACS (the Institute for Mathematics and Computer Science) offers afterschool, weekend, and homeschool classes as well as a summer camp. Working solo and in teams, IMACS students learn how to think logically and creatively while having fun with games, puzzles, stories, and other engaging activities. The IMACS Hi-Tech Summer Camp program engages students with logic puzzles, computer programming, virtual robotics, and electronics. Advanced students entering grades nine to twelve may also enroll in IMACS's university-level programs in mathematical logic and computer science. Afterschool, weekend, and homeschool classes include Mathematics Enrichment, Computer Enrichment, University-Level Logic for Mathematics, and University-Level Computer Science. IMACS and its affiliates operate teaching centers in several states. IMACS also offers select components of their curriculum online.

Play Well TEKnologies—*www.play-well.org*

Play Well TEKnologies offers LEGO-inspired engineering classes, summer camps, and birthday party programs for kids from kindergarten through eighth grade. Play Well TEKnologies's classes and camps are available in over 2,000 locations nationwide.

iD Tech—*www.idtech.com*

iD Tech is a provider of tech-based summer day camps and overnight camps for students ages six to seventeen. iD Tech's camps are offered at some of the most prestigious college campuses in the country. The company's camps cover topics such as programming, video game design, 3D modeling, robotics, and digital arts. iD Tech has a unique all-girls' program in place for girls ages ten to fifteen called Alexa Café.

Digital Media Academy—*www.digitalmediaacademy.org*

In addition to offering continuing studies classes for adults, Digital Media Academy (DMA) provides tech-based summer camps for young people ages six to eighteen. Based in several university campuses around the country, DMA's youth camps cover such topics as programming and app development, robotics and engineering, 3D modeling and animation, filmmaking and visual effects, game design and development, and sports and technology.

Additional STEM Enrichment Class and Camp Providers

In addition to the organizations listed so far, a number of companies offer STEM-related camps and/or enrichment classes on a regional basis. Emagination, Snapology, i2 Camp, Sarah's Science, High Touch High Tech, and Ideaventions are just a few. Also, many community colleges offer STEM-related summer camps, winter break camps, and spring break camps for elementary and high school students.

When choosing an enrichment class for your child, keep in mind that STEM subjects are challenging by their very nature. In the words of IMACS president Terry Kaufman, "Students who want to pursue university degrees and a career in STEM should develop the skills needed to persevere through difficult coursework *before* entering college. Facing real intellectual challenge for the first time at college when the consequences are more serious is a circumstance you should help your child avoid. When comparing STEM-related programs, choose one that will challenge your child within a supportive environment while still being enjoyable. Non-rigorous programs might be fun now, but they won't benefit your child as much in the long run."

Online STEM Classes

A number of companies and organizations offer online STEM classes for kids. Some of the classes are targeted at homeschoolers and offer a complete science curriculum. Others are supplemental in nature. Online classes are especially good for kids interested in learning coding, as coding isn't taught in every school. Some of the options for online STEM classes are listed here.

Supercharged Science—*www.superchargedscience.com*

Created by a former NASA scientist and college instructor, Supercharged Science offers a complete online science program for homeschoolers. The program teaches science using a combination of videos, live teleclasses, reading, and exercises. It's designed so that parents don't have to know science themselves in order for their kids to participate. Supercharged Science offers curricula for grades one through twelve. Its services are available on a monthly subscription basis.

Time4Learning—*www.time4learning.com*

Time4Learning's curriculum covers kindergarten to twelfth grade and is appropriate for homeschool, afterschool, and summer skill building. The sixth grade through twelfth grade curricula are correlated to state standards. The kindergarten to fifth grade materials don't necessarily correlate to state standards, and so they're included as a free bonus. Time4Learning's lessons are delivered using a combination of multimedia lessons, videos, printable worksheets, assessments, and online and offline projects.

Real Science 4 Kids—*www.gravitaspublications.com/online-classes*

Real Science 4 Kids is a publication-based science program with some online classes available in the core subjects. Unlike most online science programs for kids, each of Real Science 4 Kids' online classes has an actual teacher's name listed as the course instructor. The courses are offered for a flat fee per course.

Youth Digital—*www.youthdigital.com*

Youth Digital offers technology courses for kids ages eight to fourteen through a highly interactive learning platform. Youth Digital offers courses in Java coding, computer programming, digital illustration, 3D animation, game design, and app design. Youth Digital's online classes are offered for a flat fee per course. The fee gains a student access to the course and materials for a full year.

Tynker—*www.tynker.com*

Tynker offers programming education through interactive self-paced courses and game-based activities. In additional to grade-based curricula for schools, Tynker offers classes for individual students as well as instructor-led summer camps and afterschool clubs. Classes for individual students are provided for a flat fee per course.

Homeschool Programming, Inc.— *www.homeschoolprogramming.com*

Homeschool Programming, Inc., founded by homeschooling parents, offers online programming courses for kids in fourth grade and up. Its kids track includes classes in beginning and advanced web design, as well as Windows programming and game programing. The company's teen track features classes in Windows programming, game programming, and Java and Android programming. The courses are offered for a flat fee per course, and several packages are available.

Gamestar Mechanic—*www.gamestarmechanic.com*

Gamestar Mechanic offers game-based classes and quests that teach users how to create their own video games. The site also allows users to publish their games and join an online community of game designers.

Pluralsight—*www.pluralsight.com/kids*

Pluralsight's main bread and butter consists of online training courses for professional developers and IT administrators, but it offers a few free online courses for kids. The kids' courses cover basic programming, app building, and basic HTML.

Kodable—*www.kodable.com*

Kodable's online program is designed for classroom use. Its services are available for purchase on a classroom by classroom basis, or on a school-wide basis. Kodable offers a free basic service that can be sampled by one classroom.

Quick Study Labs—*www.quickstudylabs.com*

Quick Study Labs offers electronics classes for kids ages eight and up. In addition to electronics, Quick Study Labs offers online courses in robotics and green technology. The classes are offered for a flat fee per course.

Khan Academy—*www.khanacademy.org*

Khan Academy is a well-known nonprofit organization that provides free educational resources covering a vast array of fields. Khan Academy's offerings consist primarily of online video tutorials.

Job Shadowing

Job shadowing isn't a new idea. "Take Our Daughters and Sons to Work Day" (*www.daughtersandsonstowork.org*) is a familiar concept to most people. In fact, as part of a national campaign, Groundhog Day has been renamed "National Groundhog Job Shadow Day."

Job shadowing expands the concept of "Take Our Daughters and Sons to Work Day" beyond the workplaces of a child's own parents. It creates possibilities for a child to visit any workplace and learn about any career in which she has an interest. Job shadowing is a useful way to expose a young person to any career field, but it's particularly useful in motivating kids to pursue STEM careers.

Job Shadowing in the STEM Fields

A job-shadowing experience isn't the same as an internship, nor is it a fieldtrip. Typically it involves an individual student following, or *shadowing*, a professional through his regular workday or workweek. The point is for the student to get a good idea of the daily activities a particular job entails. Most job-shadowing experiences will also include some time for the student to ask questions.

Job shadowing is a good idea for any career field, but it's an especially good way to expose young people to various careers in the STEM fields. Most would agree that STEM fields are underrepresented on TV and in movies. Unless a child's parents or other family members are directly employed in STEM fields, the child will likely have little knowledge of careers in those fields.

A study published in the *Journal of Applied Communication Research* found that high school students tend to become more motivated to enter STEM careers after they've had an opportunity to visit workplaces where such jobs take place. Job shadowing is often done for students at the college and high school levels, but younger students can also benefit from job-shadowing experiences. In fact, some employers believe that middle school is the best time to the plant the seed in a young person's mind with respect to STEM careers. Following are some suggestions for finding job-shadowing opportunities in the STEM fields.

Finding Job-Shadowing Opportunities

Although many people are beginning to recognize the value of job shadowing in promoting the STEM fields, there aren't yet any broad-based nationwide programs set up to connect interested students with job-shadowing opportunities. Most existing job-shadowing programs are local or regional in scope. Companies that heavily rely on STEM skills, such as Boeing, Procter & Gamble, and Lockheed Martin have in the past offered job-shadowing opportunities in some of the cities where their facilities are located. NASA has also offered some job-shadowing opportunities in the past; however, the agency's educational programming will always be subject to budgetary considerations.

The best way to begin seeking out a STEM job-shadowing arrangement for your child is to first consult your school's guidance counselor. You might be pleasantly surprised and discover that your child's school already has a program in place, or at least an available list of job-shadowing resources. If the school guidance counselor has no resources to offer, take your search to the Internet. Start with companies and other organizations in your area that are known to employ STEM workers. Likely candidates include technology firms, research facilities, manufacturing companies, and hospitals. Contact the HR departments at those companies and ask about the possibility of setting up a job shadow for your child. If you have a community college in your area, you can contact individual department chairs in the STEM fields and ask for ideas. Most community colleges have strong ties to STEM employers in their service areas. If you know an individual employee, even only casually, consider approaching that person directly. A sample letter (or e-mail) proposing a job shadow is included at the end of this section.

Virtual Job Shadowing

In an ideal world, your child's school would have a rich job-shadowing program in place for its students. If your kid's school hasn't established a job-shadowing program, there may be practical reasons why it hasn't happened. First, if you live in a rural area, there may be limited opportunities for such arrangements. Also, safety concerns may prevent some companies from offering job-shadowing arrangements, particularly to younger children. As an alternative to on-the-ground shadowing, you could consider setting up a virtual job shadow for your child.

A number of websites provide virtual job-shadowing experiences for students. VirtualJobShadow.com offers its services to institutional users, such as schools, and also to individuals. In addition to its virtual job-shadowing service, the site offers resources to help with college searches, as well as internship and job searches. The site's resources are appropriate for students from middle school through college. JobShadow.com offers interviews with individuals in many different career fields, including a number of STEM fields. Although the site doesn't offer true job shadowing—the interviews are written, with no accompanying video—JobShadow.com's resources are available free of charge. Other sites featuring career videos include America's Career InfoNet (*www.acinet.org*), MyPlan.com, and JobsTVnews.com.

Getting the Most Out of a Job-Shadowing Experience

Before the job shadow visit, check ahead (or have your child check ahead) to find out what clothing is appropriate for the visit. It's also a good idea to find out ahead of time whether it's acceptable for your child to ask questions during the visit, or whether questions should be saved for a separate interview. Encourage your child to take notes during the visit, but not to let notetaking distract her from fully absorbing the experience. Reflecting on the job-shadow experience following the visit, either in writing or using an audio recorder, is something else your child may wish to consider. Also, don't forget to encourage your child to write a thank-you note to the individual, or individuals, who hosted the job shadow.

Sample Job-Shadowing Letter of Request

Dear (*Job-Shadowing Prospect's Name*):

I am writing to you about a potential job-shadowing arrangement. Currently I'm a student at (*Name of School*), and I'm very much interested in exploring (*Name of Career Field*) as a possible career path. After studying all the material I can find online and in the library related to (*Name of Career Field*), I'm eager to learn more. Your name was given to me by (*Name of School Counselor or Source of Prospect's Name*) as a person who would likely have some valuable insights to share.

If you're able to work it into your busy schedule, I would greatly appreciate the opportunity to shadow you for part of a day as you perform your usual work duties. I would remain quiet while I observe you working, unless you invite me to ask questions during the job shadowing.

Additionally, I would like to ask if I may interview you at the end of my visit, so that I may ask any questions that occur to me during the shadowing. I promise to keep the interview as brief as possible.

I understand that this is a big request, but I would be forever grateful for the opportunity to learn about (*Name of Career Field*) firsthand from a professional such as you. I am willing to do the visit at whatever time best suits your schedule.

You can reach me in the afternoons and early evenings at (*Your Phone Number*) or anytime by e-mail at (*Your E-mail Address or Parent's E-mail*

Address). I look forward to your response, and I very much look forward to the possibility of visiting with you in the near future.

Thank you for your time and consideration.

Sincerely,
(*Your Name*)

P.S. If you're not able to accommodate my visit, but you know of another professional in the area who possibly can, I would greatly appreciate a referral to that person.

CHAPTER 17

STEM Activities for the Car

Many of the activities in this book require various household materials to execute. This chapter features activities you can do with your child while traveling in the car. The activities are educational and they can be done at no cost. Try using these activities to make the time fly by on your next family road trip.

Math Rock, Paper, Scissors

The standard Rock, Paper, Scissors game has probably been a favorite travel game for as long as automobiles have been around. The standard Rock, Paper, Scissors game sometimes involves a punishment—a hard wrist slap—delivered to the round's loser by the winner. Whether you play with the wrist slap or not, you can make Rock, Paper, Scissors an educational math game by incorporating one simple modification. After playing a round, the loser gets a chance to redeem himself by answering a math question posed by a neutral party (i.e., a parent in the front seat). The questions may be drawn from any area of math the players have studied in school. There are several available questions in the "Making Math Matter" chapter in this book (Chapter 11).

You can also try another variation of the game: Science Rock, Paper Scissors. In this variation, the loser of a round gets a chance to redeem herself by answering a science question, based on whatever topics she is currently studying in science class.

Science Connections

Science Connections, a variation of a popular travel game, is simple to play. Decide who in the car is going first and settle on the order of play. The first player begins the game by naming a science term. The second player must state another term that is related to the first term. For example, suppose the first player says, "physics." The second player could say something like "Einstein" or "theory of relativity." The third player states a term related to the second term, and so on. When a player is unable to think of a related term within a given amount of time (say, ten seconds), she is eliminated. Play continues until there's only one player remaining. If there's disagreement about whether or not a term is related to a previously stated term, the issue can be settled by majority vote. Remember, though, that it's just a game, and the more lighthearted you keep it, the more fun it will be.

Science Categories

Science Categories is very similar to Science Connections with one basic difference. The first player names a science category rather than a term. Each subsequent player then names something that falls within that category. For instance, the first player might say "planets" as a category. The other players would then take turns naming planets, with game play mirroring the Science Connections game. Some ideas for possible categories are listed here. The categories range from fairly basic to more advanced.

CATEGORIES FOR THE SCIENCE CATEGORIES GAME:

- Planets
- Elements from the periodic table
- Famous scientists
- Famous inventors
- Reptiles
- Amphibians
- Mammals
- Dinosaurs
- Plants
- Insects
- Minerals
- Star constellations
- Types of scientist

Geometry Scavenger Hunt—Travel Version

The Geometry Scavenger Hunt is described in Chapter 12. This activity can easily be done in the car on a family trip, even without pencil and paper. For the travel version, players take turns naming shapes. As soon as a player names a shape, everyone in the car involved in the game begins searching for that shape somewhere in the vicinity. The first player to spot the shape wins the round. For safety purposes, it might be best if the driver stays out of the game. Alternatively, the driver can be appointed the official shape namer for all the game's rounds. Play the game for ten rounds. The winner who wins the most out of ten rounds is the ultimate winner of the game. See the Geometry Scavenger Hunt activity in Chapter 12 for shape ideas.

License Plate Game—Math Version

Many people have played the standard version of the license plate game, which involves players attempting to spot plates from as many of the fifty states as possible. The math version of the game adds an educational component.

In the math version of the license plate game, players in the car search for particular types of numbers on license plates. The game is a great way to introduce or reinforce some basic math definitions. Following is a list of number types, accompanied by their definitions.

BE THE FIRST TO FIND EACH OF THE FOLLOWING ON A LICENSE PLATE:

- **A whole number**—a non-negative number that's not a fraction or decimal. Whole numbers are the counting numbers, starting with 0. Finding a whole number on a license plate should be as easy as spotting the broad side of a barn.
- **An integer**—like whole numbers, but also including negative numbers. 0 is an integer. So are –1, –2, –3, and so on. Fractions and decimal numbers are not integers. Since license plates don't include negative numbers, spotting an integer will be the same as spotting a whole number in the game (however, including integers in the game will allow you an opportunity to review the term with your child).
- **An even number**—an integer that can be divided exactly by 2, without leaving a remainder. 0 is an even number, as are –2 and –4.
- **An odd number**—an integer that is not a multiple of 2.
- **A prime number**—a whole number greater than 1 that can only be divided evenly by 1 and itself. 3 is a prime number because it can only be divided evenly by 3 or by 1. 2 is also a prime number. Other examples of prime numbers include 5, 7, 11, 13, 17, 19, and 23.
- **A composite number**—a whole number greater than 1 that's not a prime number. In other words, a composite number is a positive integer greater than 1 that has another divisor besides 1 and itself. 4 is a composite number because it has 2 as a divisor, in addition to 1 and 4. Other examples of composite numbers include 6, 8, 9, and 10.
- **A rational number**—a number that can be represented by a simple fraction. A whole number like 4 can be represented by the fraction $\frac{4}{1}$, so it's a rational number. All whole numbers are rational. A number like 3.5 is rational because it can be represented by the fraction $\frac{7}{2}$. For the purposes of the license plate game, spotting a rational number will be the same as spotting a whole number.
- **An irrational number**—a number that can't be represented by a simple fraction. The square root of 3 is approximately 1.7320508. Because

the digits continue forever without repeating, the square root of 3 cannot be represented by a simple fraction, and thus it's irrational. The most famous irrational number is π, whose digits also continue without repeating. This would be a trick question in the game, since license plates don't generally include irrational numbers.

- **A factor of 12**—a number that divides into 12 without leaving a remainder (i.e., 1, 2, 3, 4, 6, and 12).
- **A factor of 21**—these include 1, 3, 7, and 21.
- **A factor of 25**—these include 1, 5, and 25.
- **A factor of 36**—these include 1, 2, 3, 4, 6, 9, 12, 18, and 36.
- **A factor of 45**—these include 1, 3, 5, 9, 15, and 45.
- **A factor of 100**—these include 1, 2, 4, 5, 10, 20, 25, 50, and 100.
- **A factor of** ____ (fill in the blank).

First to Reach 100

First to Reach 100 is a math game well-suited for road trips. When the game begins, each player starts searching for numbers in the vicinity. Likely places to look include license plates, billboards, address markers, and street signs. When a player spots a number, she calls it out. Once a number has been called out, no other player can use that same source. For example, suppose a player spots the number 8 on a billboard. Once the player calls out that 8, no other player can use that billboard as a source. The player then looks for another number to add to 8, multiply by 8, subtract from 8, or divide by 8 to move closer to 100. Suppose after spotting the 8, the player spies a 9 on a license plate. The player would say, "times 9 equals 72." Now the player seeks another number she can add to 72, multiply by 72, subtract from 72, or divide by 72 to move closer to 100.

The ultimate goal of the game is to be the first player to reach 100 *exactly*. If a player reaches 101, she must find a 1 to subtract from 101 in order to win the game. It helps if a neutral party (i.e., a parent in the front seat) monitors all the mathematical operations to ensure they're carried out correctly. The game can also be played by one child, with the goal being to reach 100 before the end of the trip, or within a predetermined amount of time.

Finish the Sequence

Finish the Sequence may not be the game for everyone—it's certainly not Tic-Tac-Toe. But if your kid is the rare kind who lives and breathes math, or the type who enjoys puzzles and mind-benders, give the game a try on your next trip. It may help to have a notepad and pen handy for the game.

For each of the following sequences, state the next number in the sequence. Answers and explanations are in parentheses.

2, 4, 6, 8, __ (**10** . . . increasing multiples of 2)

2, 4, 8, 16, __ (**32** . . . each number doubles the previous number)

4, 9, 16, 25 __ (**36** . . . 2 squared, 3 squared, 4 squared, 5 squared, and 6 squared)

2, 4, 16, 256, __ (**65,536** . . . each number, starting with 4, is the product of the previous number twice, so $256 \times 256 = 65,536$)

10, 19, 27, 34, __ (**40** . . . $10 + 9 = 19$, $19 + 8 = 27$, $27 + 7 = 34$, $34 + 6 = 40$)

100, 93, 86, 79, __ (**72** . . . $100 - 7 = 93$, $93 - 7 = 86$, $86 - 7 = 79$, $79 - 7 = 72$)

1, 1, 2, 3, 5, 8, __ (**13** . . . this is the beginning of the famous Fibonacci sequence, which starts with two 1s and then successively adds the two previous terms: $1 + 1 = 2$, $1 + 2 = 3$, $2 + 3 = 5$, $3 + 5 = 8$, $5 + 8 = 13$)

ESSENTIAL

Fibonacci, an Italian mathematician who lived in the thirteenth century, derived his famous sequence by examining the pattern via which rabbits multiply. Amazingly, the Fibonacci numbers show up many places in nature, a fact that has intrigued scientists for centuries. Fibonacci numbers can be found in the array of seeds in a sunflower, the spiral pattern in pinecones, the branching pattern in some flowers and trees, and in the family structure of honeybees.

If your child enjoys Finish the Sequence, continue playing with sequences you invent yourself. Also consider inviting your child to create some series that you complete. Inventing numerical sequences and completing them are both great critical-thinking activities.

The Birthday Problem

The Birthday Problem is a well-known scenario in statistics that is fun to test out in real life. The problem begins with a simple question: If you have 23 people in a room, what's the likelihood that 2 of them share the same birth date? When considering the question, ignore February 29, which of course doesn't come around every year. Also, only consider the date of birth, not the year.

You might assume it would be very unlikely for 2 or more individuals in a group of 23 to share the same birth date, but actually the probability is higher than most people would expect. The probability is greater than 50 percent that 2 or more people in a group of 23 will share a birth date. The statistical explanation, which is somewhat advanced, is presented here:

Using the special multiplication rule (presented in Chapter 13), you can calculate the probability that 2 people in a group of 23 do *not* share a birthday as follows:

$$\frac{365}{365} \times \frac{364}{365} \times \frac{363}{365} \times \ldots \times \frac{343}{365} = 0.4927$$

This expression states that the probability of the 2nd person not sharing a birthday with the 1st person is $\frac{364}{365}$, the likelihood of the 3rd person not sharing a birthday with the 1st or 2nd person is $\frac{363}{365}$, and so on.

If the probability of 2 people in 23 not sharing a birthday is 0.4927, then the probability of 2 of them sharing a birthday can be calculated as follows:

$1 - 0.4927 = 0.5073$ or 50.7 percent

The Birthday Problem is a great activity to try out at a gathering of 23 or more people. But it can also be done as a travel game, even if you're not traveling with 22 other passengers. There are a couple ways you can approach the Birthday Problem as a travel game. If you have, say, 4 people in the car, you can begin with the birth dates of those 4 individuals. Then if each of the 5 can think of 4 other birth dates of people he or she knows, you'll have a sample of at least 24 birth dates. Another way you can approach the problem as a travel game is to have someone (*not* the driver) text people and ask their birth dates. If you repeat this activity several times, asking different subjects for their birth dates, you should have a birthday match on roughly every other trial. Incidentally, if you ask 57 different people their birth dates, there's a 99 percent likelihood that 2 of the 57 will share a birthday. The Birthday Problem may seem like a paradox, but it has a solid statistical explanation.

Science Fiction or Science Fact?

Science Fiction or Science Fact is a game you can play anywhere, and it's a game that is constantly changing. The basic premise of the game isn't complicated. One person makes a statement relating to some scientific development, and then another person determines whether that statement is science fact or science fiction. The game is constantly changing because, of course, the frontiers of science are always advancing.

Some ideas are listed here which you can use for the game. You can also find ideas by reading magazines such as *Scientific American*, *Popular Science*, or *iD* (*Ideas and Discoveries*). These following statements represent science facts that probably sound like science fiction to most people.

SCIENCE FACTS THAT SOUND LIKE SCIENCE FICTION:
- Robots have been developed that climb walls like insects
- Medical researchers have succeeded in creating artificial blood
- Organisms exist that can survive in scalding water
- An invisibility device has been developed which uses lenses to cloak a small object
- Scientists have modified silkworms to create silk that's stronger than steel
- Some Earth organisms have survived in space without a space suit or other protection
- Astronomers have discovered that planets can exist in systems with multiple suns
- The FDA has approved a bionic eye that enables blind people to see
- Scientists have teleported individual atoms from one location to another
- Cyborgs—human beings who have robot parts implanted or permanently attached—really exist

For statements of pure science fiction, you can be as creative as you want. Just to get your juices flowing, a few statements of pure science fiction are listed here.

STATEMENTS OF PURE SCIENCE FICTION (FOR THE TIME BEING):

- Scientists have cloned dinosaurs from fossils
- Astronomers have spotted alien life forms on Europa, one of Jupiter's moons
- A mineral was discovered that, when digested, can completely stop the aging process
- Military researchers have invented a suit that enables soldiers to hover in the air
- A helicopter was invented that can fly underwater
- Japan's space agency has developed an escalator that carries humans to space
- Bioengineers dug up a corpse and brought it back to life using nanotechnology
- A monkey was genetically modified to give birth to a human baby
- Archaeologists have discovered evidence that the Greek god Zeus once really existed
- Technology exists that can send astronauts to neighboring star systems
- Dog breeders have bred a special new breed of dog that doesn't eat or go to the bathroom

In some cases, there have been hoaxes in which science fiction has been portrayed as science fact. For example, a statement about British scientists cloning dinosaurs from fossils was released some time ago, but it was proved to be a prank. As you search for additional material for the Science Fiction or Science Fact game, be sure to choose your sources carefully.

Appendix A: Additional Resources

Science Museums by State

Alabama
U.S. Space and Rocket Center—Huntsville
www.rocketcenter.com

McWane Science Center—Birmingham
www.mcwane.org

Sci-Quest Hands-on Science Center—Huntsville
www.sci-quest.org

Southern Museum of Flight—Birmingham
www.southernmuseumofflight.org

Alaska
Alaska Museum of Science & Nature—Anchorage
www.alaskamuseum.org

Alaska Aviation Museum—Anchorage
www.alaskaairmuseum.org

Arizona
Arizona Science Center—Phoenix
www.azscience.org

Earth Science Museum—Phoenix
www.earthsciencemuseum.org

Center for Meteorite Studies—Tempe
http://meteorites.asu.edu

Arizona Museum of Natural History—Mesa
www.azmnh.org

The University of Arizona Mineral Museum—Tucson
www.uamineralmuseum.org

Arizona-Sonora Desert Museum—Tucson
www.desertmuseum.org

Discovery Park Campus—Safford
www.eac.edu/discoverypark

National Solar Observatory: Kitt Peak—Tucson
http://nsokp.nso.edu

Southwest Museum of Engineering, Communications and Computation—Glendale
www.smecc.org

Arkansas
Museum of Discovery—Little Rock
www.museumofdiscovery.org

Mid-America Science Museum—Piney
www.midamericamuseum.org

The Arts & Science Center for Southeast Arkansas—Pine Bluff
www.asc701.org

California

California Science Center—Los Angeles
www.californiasciencecenter.org

California Academy of Sciences—San Francisco
www.calacademy.org

World of Wonders Science Museum—Lodi
www.wowsciencemuseum.org

Discovery Cube—Los Angeles
www.discoverycube.org/la

Discovery Cube—Orange County
www.discoverycube.org/oc

Exploratorium—San Francisco
www.exploratorium.edu

Gateway Science Museum—Chico
www.csuchico.edu/gateway

The Discovery Museum Science & Space
Center—Sacramento
www.thediscovery.org

Reuben H. Fleet Science Center—San Diego
www.rhfleet.org

The Lawrence Hall of Science—Berkeley
www.lawrencehallofscience.org

Western Science Center—Hemet
www.westerncentermuseum.org

Explorit Science Center—Davis
www.explorit.org

Chabot Space & Science Center—Oakland
www.chabotspace.org

Columbia Memorial Space Center—Downey
http://columbiaspacescience.org

CuriOdyssey—San Mateo
www.curiodyssey.org

San Diego Air & Space Museum—San Diego
www.sandiegoairandspace.org

KidZone Museum—Truckee
www.kidzonemuseum.org

The Tech Museum of Innovation—San Jose,
Saratoga, Los Gatos
www.thetech.org

Youth Science Institute—San Jose
www.ysi-ca.org

Griffith Observatory—Los Angeles
www.griffithobservatory.org

Museum of Paleontology—Berkley
www.ucmp.berkeley.edu

Fossil Discovery Center of Madera
County—Chowchilla
www.maderamammoths.org

Children's Natural History Museum—Fremont
http://cnhm.msnucleus.org

Birch Aquarium at Scripps Institution of
Oceanography—La Jolla
www.aquarium.ucsd.edu

Great Valley Museum—Modesto
www.mjc.edu/instruction/sme/gvm

STAR Eco Station—Culver City
www.ecostation.org

Natural History Museum of Los Angeles
County—Los Angeles
www.nhm.org/site

Aerospace Museum of California—McClellan
www.aerospaceca.org

Kidspace Children's Museum—Pasadena
www.kidspacemuseum.org

Riverside Metropolitan Museum—Riverside
www.riversideca.gov/museum

Colorado
Denver Museum of Nature & Science—Denver
www.dmns.org

Fort Collins Museum of Discovery—Fort Collins
www.fcmod.org

Morrison Natural History Museum—Morrison
www.mnhm.org/246/
Morrison-Natural-History-Museum

Wings Over the Rockies Air & Space
Museum—Denver
www.wingsmuseum.org

The Children's Museum of Denver—Denver
www.mychildsmuseum.org

Colorado School of Mines Geology
Museum—Golden
www.mines.edu/Geology_Museum

Peterson Air & Space Museum—Colorado
Springs
www.petemuseum.org

World of Wonder Children's Museum—Lafayette
www.wowchildrensmuseum.org

Museum of Western Colorado—Grand Junction
www.museumofwesternco.com

Dinosaur Ridge—Morrison
www.dinoridge.org

Florissant Fossil Beds National
Monument—Divide
www.nps.gov/flfo/index.htm

Rocky Mountain Dinosaur Research Center—
Woodland Park
www.rmdrc.com

Georgetown Energy Museum—Georgetown
www.georgetownenergymuseum.org

Mountain Top Children's Museum—Breckenridge
www.mtntopmuseum.org

Ryan Geology Museum—Alamosa
www.adams.edu/academics/earthscience/
ryan-geology-museum.php

Connecticut

Connecticut Science Center—Hartford
www.ctsciencecenter.org

Discovery Museum and Planetarium—Bridgeport
www.discoverymuseum.org

Connecticut State Museum of Natural
History—Storrs
www.cac.uconn.edu/mnhhome.html

New England Air Museum—Windsor Locks
www.neam.org

Dinosaur State Park—Rocky Hill
www.dinosaurstatepark.org

Connecticut Air & Space Center—Stratford
http://cascstratford.wordpress.com

Delaware

Delaware Museum of Natural
History—Wilmington
www.delmnh.org

Delaware Mineralogical Society—Wilmington
www.delminsociety.net

Iron Hill Museum—Newark
www.ironhill-museum.org

Delaware Children's Museum—Wilmington
www.delawarechildrensmuseum.org

Florida

Kennedy Space Center—Titusville
www.kennedyspacecenter.com

Museum of Discovery and Science—Fort
Lauderdale
www.mods.org/home.html

Museum of Science & Industry—Tampa
www.mosi.org

Orlando Science Center—Orlando
www.osc.org

South Florida Science Center and Aquarium—
West Palm Beach
www.sfsciencecenter.org

Patricia and Phillip Frost Museum of
Science—Miami
www.miamisci.org

Museum of Arts & Sciences—Daytona Beach
www.moas.org/main.cfm

Florida Museum of Natural History—Gainesville
www.flmnh.ufl.edu

Air Force Space & Missile Museum—Cape
Canaveral
www.afspacemuseum.org

Eastern Florida State College Planetarium &
Observatory—Cocoa
*www.easternflorida.edu/community-resources/
planetarium*

Calusa Nature Center & Planetarium—Fort Myers
www.calusanature.org

Children's Science Explorium—Boca Raton
www.scienceexplorium.org

Emerald Coast Science Center—Fort Walton
Beach
www.ecscience.org

Explorations V Children's Museum—Lakeland
www.explorationsv.com

FPL Energy Encounter—Jensen Beach
www.fpl.com/community/energy-encounter.html

Jacksonville University Life Sciences
Museum—Jacksonville
*www.ju.edu/biology/Pages/Life-Sciences-
Museum.aspx*

Science and Technology Education Innovation
Center—St. Petersburg
www.sciencecenterofpinellas.org/eic

Science & Discovery Center of Northwest
Florida—Panama City
www.scienceanddiscoverycenter.org

Georgia
Tellus Science Museum—Cartersville
www.tellusmuseum.org

Fernbank Science Center—Atlanta
www.fernbank.edu

Fernbank Museum of National History—Atlanta
www.fernbankmuseum.org

Museum of Arts and Sciences—Macon
www.masmacon.com

Coca-Cola Space Science Center—Columbus
www.ccssc.org

David J. Sencer CDC Museum—Atlanta
www.cdc.gov/museum

Elachee Nature Science Center—Gainesville
www.elachee.org

Georgia Museum of Natural History—Athens
http://naturalhistory.uga.edu

Interactive Neighborhood for Kids—Gainesville
www.inkfun.org

Museum of Aviation—Robins AFB, Warner
Robins
www.museumofaviation.org

Hawaii
Bernice Pauahi Bishop Museum—Honolulu
www.bishopmuseum.org

Hawaii Children's Discovery Center—Honolulu
www.discoverycenterhawaii.org

Astronaut Ellison S. Onizuka Space
Center—Kailua-Kona
www.aloha.net/~tashima

'Imiloa Astronomy Center of Hawaii—Hilo
www.imiloahawaii.org

Idaho

Discovery Center of Idaho—Boise
www.dcidaho.org

Idaho Museum of Natural History—Pocatello
www.imnh.isu.edu/home

Herrett Center for Arts and Science—Twin Falls
herrett.csi.edu

Idaho Museum of Mining & Geology—Boise
www.idahomuseum.org

Illinois

Museum of Science and Industry—Chicago
www.msichicago.org

SciTech Hands On Museum—Aurora
www.scitechmuseum.org

Discovery Center Museum—Rockford
www.discoverycentermuseum.org

Adler Planetarium—Chicago
www.adlerplanetarium.org

Cernan Earth and Space Center—River Grove
www.triton.edu/cernan

Children's Discovery Museum—Normal
www.childrensdiscoverymuseum.net

The Field Museum—Chicago
www.fieldmuseum.org

Illinois State Museum—Springfield
www.museum.state.il.us

International Museum of Surgical Science—Chicago
www.imss.org

Kidzeum of Health and Science—Springfield
www.kidzeum.org

Leon M. Lederman Science Education Center—Batavia
http://ed.fnal.gov/lsc/index.shtml

Midwest Museum of Natural History—Sycamore
www.mmnh.org

Orpheum Children's Science Museum—Champaign
www.orpheumkids.net

Indiana

Indiana State Museum—Indianapolis
www.indianamuseum.org

WonderLab Museum of Science, Health and Technology—Bloomington
www.wonderlab.org

Science Central—Fort Wayne
www.sciencecentral.org

Terre Haute Children's Museum—Terre Haute
www.terrehautechildrensmuseum.com

HealthWorks! Kids' Museum—South Bend
www.healthworkskids.org

Hoosier Air Museum—Auburn
www.hoosierairmuseum.org

Muncie Children's Museum—Muncie
www.munciemuseum.com

Iowa
Science Center of Iowa—Des Moines
www.sciowa.org

The Putnam Museum & Space
Center—Davenport
www.putnam.org

Bluedorn Science Imaginarium—Waterloo
www.bluedornscienceimaginarium.org

Grout Museum of History & Science—Waterloo
www.groutmuseumdistrict.org

Kansas
Kansas Cosmosphere and Space
Center—Hutchinson
www.cosmo.org

Banner Creek Science Center &
Observatory—Holton
www.bcscience.myevent.com

The Kansas Children's Discovery Center—Topeka
www.kansasdiscovery.org

Exploration Place—Wichita
www.exploration.org

Flint Hills Discovery Center—Manhattan
www.flinthillsdiscovery.org

Kansas Meteorite Museum and Nature
Center—Haviland
www.kansasmeteorite.com

St. John Science Museum—St. John
www.stjohnsciencemuseum.org

Sternberg Museum of Natural History—Hays
http://sternberg.fhsu.edu

Lake Afton Public Observatory—Wichita
www.webs.wichita.edu/lapo

Johnston Geology Museum—Emporia
www.emporia.edu/~es/museum/

Kentucky
Kentucky Science Center—Louisville
http://ksciencecenter.org

Owensboro Museum of Science &
History—Owensboro
www.owensboromuseum.org

The Aviation Museum of Kentucky—Lexington
www.aviationky.org

East Kentucky Science Center—Prestonsburg
www.bigsandy.kctcs.edu/eksc

Explorium of Lexington—Lexington
www.explorium.com

Louisiana

Louisiana Art & Science Museum—Baton Rouge
www.lasm.org

Lafayette Science Museum—Lafayette
www.lafayettesciencemuseum.org

Sci-Port: Louisiana's Science Center—Shreveport
www.sciport.org

Louisiana Children's Museum—New Orleans
www.lcm.org

Northeast Louisiana Children's
Museum—Monroe
www.nelcm.org

Chennault Aviation & Military Museum—Monroe
www.chennaultmuseum.org

The Children's Museum—Lake Charles
www.swlakids.org

Maine

Children's Discovery Museum—Augusta
www.childrensdiscoverymuseum.org

Children's Museum & Theatre of
Maine—Portland
www.kitetails.org

George B. Dorr Museum of Natural History—Bar
Harbor
www.coa.edu/dorr-museum-microsite.htm

The Maine Air Museum—Bangor
www.maineairmuseum.com/page/942/home

Maine State Aquarium—West Boothbay Harbor
www.maine.gov/dmr/rm/aquarium/index.html

Northern Main Museum of Science—Presque Isle
http://pages.umpi.edu/~nmms/

The Peary-MacMillan Arctic Museum—Brunswick
www.bowdoin.edu/arctic-museum

The Maine Discovery Museum—Bangor
www.mainediscoverymuseum.org

Maryland

Maryland Science Center—Baltimore
www.mdsci.org

Discovery Station at Hagerstown—Hagerstown
www.discoverystation.org

Goddard Space Flight Center—Greenbelt
www.nasa.gov/centers/goddard/home

National Electronics Museum—Linthicum
www.nationalelectronicsmuseum.org

National Museum of Health and Medicine—
Silver Spring
www.medicalmuseum.mil

National Children's Museum—National Harbor
www.ccm.org

Hagerstown Aviation Museum—Hagerstown
www.hagerstownaviationmuseum.org

Chesapeake Children's Museum—Annapolis
www.theccm.org

The Glen L. Martin Maryland Aviation Museum—Middle River
www.mdairmuseum.org

Massachusetts
Museum of Science—Boston
www.mos.org

EcoTarium—Worcester
www.ecotarium.org

Springfield Science Museum—Springfield
www.springfieldmuseums.org/the_museums/science/

Blue Hill Observatory & Science Center—Milton
www.bluehill.org

Boston Children's Museum—Boston
www.bostonchildrensmuseum.org

Cape Cod Children's Museum—Mashpee
http://capecodchildrensmuseum.org

The Cape Cod Museum of Natural History—Brewster
www.ccmnh.org

The Discovery Museums—Acton
www.discoverymuseums.org

Waterworks Museum—Boston
www.waterworksmuseum.org

MIT Museum—Cambridge
http://web.mit.edu/museum/

Nash Dinosaur Track Site and Rock Shop—South Hadley
www.nashdinosaurtracks.com

Michigan
Cranbrook Institute of Science—Bloomfield Hills
http://science.cranbrook.edu/

Michigan Science Center—Detroit
www.mi-sci.org

Ann Arbor Hands-On Museum—Ann Arbor
www.aahom.org

Sloan Museum—Flint
www.sloanlongway.org/Sloan-Museum

Air Zoo—Portage
www.airzoo.org

A.E. Seaman Mineral Museum—Houghton
www.museum.mtu.edu

Impression-5 Science Center—Lansing
www.impression5.org

Abrams Planetarium—East Lansing
www.pa.msu.edu/abrams

Alden B. Dow Museum of Science & Art—Midland
www.mcfta.org/museums/alden-b-dow-museum-of-science-and-art

Carr-Fles Planetarium—Muskegon
www.muskegoncc.edu/astronomy/carr-fles-planetarium

Minnesota

Science Museum of Minnesota—Saint Paul
www.smm.org

Minnesota Children's Museum—Saint Paul
www.mcm.org

The Bell Museum of Natural
History—Minneapolis
www.bellmuseum.umn.edu

Duluth Children's Museum—Duluth
www.duluthchildrensmuseum.org

The Works Museum—Bloomington
www.theworks.org

Headwaters Science Center—Bemidji
www.hscbemidji.org

Mississippi

Mississippi Museum of Natural Science—Jackson
www.mdwfp.com/museum.aspx

INFINITY Science Center—Stennis Space Center
www.visitinfinity.com

Dunn-Seiler Geology Museum—Starkville
http://geosciences.msstate.edu/museum.htm

Missouri

Saint Louis Science Center—St. Louis
www.slsc.org

Science City at Union Station—Kansas City
www.unionstation.org/sciencecity

Discovery Center of Springfield—Springfield
http://www.discoverycenter.org/

Missouri Plant Science Center—Mexico
www.mopsc.org

The Space Center—Bonne Terre
www.space-mo.org

The Magic House, St. Louis Children's Museum—St. Louis
www.magichouse.org

Montana

ExplorationWorks!—Helena
www.explorationworks.org

American Computer & Robotics
Museum—Bozeman
www.compustory.com

spectrUM Discovery Area—Missoula
http://spectrum.umt.edu/

Montana Natural History Center—Missoula
www.montananaturalist.org

Children's Museum of Bozeman—Bozeman
www.cmbozeman.org

Great Plains Dinosaur Museum & Field
Station—Malta
www.greatplainsdinosaurs.org

Two Medicine Dinosaur Center—Bynum
www.tmdinosaur.org

Nebraska

Strategic Air & Space Museum—Ashland
http://sasmuseum.com

Alia Arram Children's Museum—Kearney
www.kearneychildrensmuseum.org

The Edgerton Explorit Center—Aurora
www.edgerton.org

Omaha Children's Museum—Omaha
www.ocm.org

Trailside Museum of Natural History at Fort
Robinson State Park—Crawford
www.trailside.unl.edu

Lincoln Children's Museum—Lincoln
www.lincolnchildrensmuseum.org

Nevada

The Terry Lee Wells Nevada Discovery
Museum—Reno
www.nvdm.org

The National Atomic Testing Museum—Las
Vegas
www.nationalatomictestingmuseum.org

The Children's Museum of Northern Nevada—
Carson City
www.cmnn.org

Fleischmann Planetarium & Science
Center—Reno
http://planetarium.unr.nevada.edu/

Las Vegas Natural History Museum—Las Vegas
www.lvnhm.org

DISCOVERY Children's Museum—Las Vegas
www.discoverykidslv.org

New Hampshire

SEE Science Center—Manchester
www.see-sciencecenter.org

The Seacoast Science Center—Rye
www.seacoastsciencecenter.org

McAuliffe-Shepard Discovery Center—Concord
www.starhop.com

Mount Washington Observatory—North Conway
www.mountwashington.org

The Aviation Museum of New
Hampshire—Londonderry
www.nhahs.org

Children's Museum of New Hampshire—Dover
www.childrens-museum.org

New Jersey

Liberty Science Center—Jersey City
www.lsc.org

Garden State Discovery Museum—Cherry Hill
www.discoverymuseum.com

Aviation Hall of Fame of New Jersey—Teterboro
www.njahof.org

Monmouth Museum—Lincroft
www.monmouthmuseum.org

InfoAge Science History Museum—Wall
www.infoage.org

The Franklin Mineral Museum and Nature
Center—Franklin
www.franklinmineralmuseum.com

New Mexico

New Mexico Museum of Natural History and
Science—Albuquerque
www.nmnaturalhistory.org

The National Museum of Nuclear Science &
History—Albuquerque
www.nuclearmuseum.org

Bradbury Science Museum—Los Alamos
http://lanl.gov/museum/

Explora—Albuquerque
www.explora.us/en

E3 Children's Museum & Science
Center—Farmington
www.fmtn.org/e3

The New Mexico Museum of Space
History—Alamogordo
www.nmspacemuseum.org

Museum of Southwestern Biology—Albuquerque
www.msb.unm.edu

New York

New York Hall of Science—Corona
www.nysci.org

American Museum of Natural History—New
York
www.amnh.org

Science Museum of Long Island—Plandome
www.smli.org

Long Island Science Center—Riverhead
www.lisciencecenter.org

Goudreau Museum of Mathematics in Art and
Science—New Hyde Park
www.mathmuseum.org

Sony Wonder Technology Lab—New York
www.sonywondertechlab.com

Lucile M. Wright Air Museum—Jamestown
http://wrightairmuseum.com

Staten Island Museum—Staten Island
www.statenislandmuseum.org

Roberson Museum and Science
Center—Binghamton
www.roberson.org

Rochester Museum & Science Center—Rochester
www.rmsc.org

The CNSE Children's Museum of Science and
Technology—Troy
www.cmost.org

Museum of Innovation and
Science—Schenectady
www.schenectadymuseum.org

Buffalo Museum of Science—Buffalo
www.sciencebuff.org/site/

Milton J. Rubenstein Museum of Science &
Technology—Syracuse
www.most.org

National Museum of Mathematics—New York
www.momath.org

New York State Museum—Albany
www.nysm.nysed.gov

Paleontological Research Institution and Its
Museum of the Earth—Ithaca
www.priweb.org

Sciencenter—Ithaca
www.sciencenter.org

Empire State Aerosciences Museum—Glenville
www.esam.org

The Frank S. McCullough, Jr. Hawkins Point
Visitors Center and Boat Launch—Massena
www.nypa.gov/vc/stlaw.htm

Niagara Aerospace Museum—Niagara Falls
http://wnyaerospace.org

Intrepid Sea, Air & Space Museum—New York
www.intrepidmuseum.org

Children's Museum of Manhattan—New York
www.cmom.org

Brookhaven National Laboratory—Upton
www.bnl.gov/education/static/slc

Children's Museum of History, Science &
Technology—Utica
www.museum4kids.net

DNA Learning Center—Cold Spring Harbor
www.dnalc.org

Science Discovery Center—Oneonta
www.oneonta.edu/sdc

North Carolina

Museum of Life and Science—Durham
www.lifeandscience.org

North Carolina Museum of Natural
Sciences—Raleigh
www.naturalsciences.org

SciWorks—Winston-Salem
www.sciworks.org

Discovery Place—Charlotte
www.discoveryplace.org

Colburn Earth Science Museum—Asheville
www.colburnmuseum.org

Imagination Station Science & History
Museum—Wilson
http://scienceandhistory.org

Greensboro Science Center—Greensboro
www.greensboroscience.org

Cape Fear Museum—Wilmington
www.capefearmuseum.com

Morehead Planetarium & Science Center—
Chapel Hill
http://moreheadplanetarium.org

Pack Place Education, Arts & Science
Center—Asheville
www.packplace.org

The Imperial Centre for the Arts & Sciences—
Rocky Mount
www.imperialcentre.org

North Dakota
Gateway to Science—Bismarck
www.gatewaytoscience.org

Dakota Dinosaur Museum—Dickinson
www.dakotadino.com

Dakota Territory Air Museum—Minot
www.dakotaterritoryairmuseum.com

Fargo Air Museum—Fargo
http://fargoairmuseum.org

Ohio
Center of Science and Industry—Columbus
www.cosi.org

Museum of Natural History &
Science—Cincinnati
www.cincymuseum.org/sciencemuseum

International Women's Air & Space
Museum—Cleveland
www.iwasm.org

Great Lakes Science Center—Cleveland
www.greatscience.com

Drake Planetarium & Science Center—Cincinnati
www.drakeplanetarium.org

Armstrong Air & Space Museum—Wapakoneta
www.armstrongmuseum.org

Lake Erie Nature & Science Center—Bay Village
www.lensc.org

Boonshoft Museum of Discovery—Dayton
www.boonshoftmuseum.org

Duke Energy Children's Museum—Cincinnati
www.cincymuseum.org/childrensmuseum

Imagination Station—Toledo
http://imaginationstationtoledo.org

Orton Geological Museum - Columbus
http://ortongeologicalmuseum.osu.edu

Oklahoma
Science Museum Oklahoma—Oklahoma City
www.sciencemuseumoklahoma.com

Tulsa Air and Space Museum & Planetarium—Tulsa
www.tulsaairandspacemuseum.org

Stafford Air & Space Museum—Weatherford
www.staffordmuseum.com

Museum of Natural History—Alva
www.nwosu.edu/museum

Museum of Osteology—Oklahoma City
www.museumofosteology.org

Shattuck Windmill Museum—Shattuck
www.shattuckwindmillmuseum.org

Oregon
Oregon Museum of Science and Industry—Portland
www.omsi.edu

Science Factory Children's Museum & Exploration Dome—Eugene
www.sciencefactory.org

Evergreen Aviation & Space Museum—McMinnville
http://evergreenmuseum.org

Columbia George Discovery Center & Museum—The Dalles
www.gorgediscovery.org

Crater Rock Museum—Central Point
www.craterrock.com

ScienceWorks Hands-On Museum—Ashland
www.scienceworksmuseum.org

Oregon Air & Space Museum—Eugene
www.oasm.info

Oregon Paleo Lands Institute—Fossil
www.oregonpaleolandscenter.com

Pennsylvania
Da Vinci Science Center—Allentown
www.davincisciencecenter.org

Lancaster Science Factory—Lancaster
www.lancastersciencefactory.org

The Franklin Institute—Philadelphia
www.fi.edu

The Academy of Natural Sciences of Drexel University—Philadelphia
www.ansp.org

Carnegie Museum of Natural History—Pittsburgh
www.carnegiemnh.org

Carnegie Science Center—Pittsburgh
www.carnegiesciencecenter.org

Coolspring Power Museum—Coolspring
www.coolspringpowermuseum.org

Delaware County Institute of Science—Media
www.delcoscience.org

Wagner Free Institute of Science—Philadelphia
www.wagnerfreeinstitute.org

Rhode Island

Museum of Natural History and
Planetarium—Providence
www.providenceri.com/museum

Rhode Island Computer Museum—North
Kingstown
www.ricomputermuseum.org

Providence Children's Museum—Providence
www.childrenmuseum.org

The Quonset Air Museum—North Kingstown
www.quonsetairmuseum.com

South Carolina

South Carolina State Museum—Columbia
http://scmuseum.org

The Children's Museum of South Carolina—
Myrtle Beach
http://cmsckids.org

World of Energy—Seneca
www.duke-energy.com/visitor-centers/world-of-energy.asp

South Dakota

South Dakota Discovery Center—Pierre
www.sd-discovery.org

The Museum of Wildlife, Science &
Industry—Webster
www.sdmuseum.org

Children's Museum of South Dakota—Brookings
www.prairieplay.org

Museum of Geology—Rapid City
www.sdsmt.edu/Academics/Museum-of-Geology/Home

South Dakota Air and Space Museum—Ellsworth
AFB
www.sdairandspacemuseum.com

Tennessee

American Museum of Science & Energy—Oak
Ridge
www.amse.org

Adventure Science Center—Nashville
www.adventuresci.org

The Hands On Science Center—Tullahoma
www.hosc.org

The Children's Museum of Memphis—Memphis
www.cmom.com

Creative Discovery Museum—Chattanooga
www.cdmfun.org

The Muse Knoxville—Knoxville
www.themuseknoxville.com

Hands On! Regional Museum—Johnson City
www.handsonmuseum.org

Tennessee Museum of Aviation—Sevierville
www.tnairmuseum.com

Texas

Forth Worth Museum of Science and History—Forth Worth
www.fwmuseum.org

Perot Museum of Nature and Science—Dallas
www.perotmuseum.org

The Houston Museum of Natural Science—Houston
www.hmns.org

Texas Memorial Museum—Austin
www.utexas.edu/tmm

Heard Natural Science Museum & Wildlife Sanctuary—McKinney
www.heardmuseum.org

Corpus Christi Museum of Science and History—Corpus Christi
www.ccmuseum.com

Austin Nature & Science Center—Austin
www.austintexas.gov/department/austin-nature-and-science-center

The Heath Museum—Houston
www.thehealthmuseum.org

Discovery Science Place—Tyler
www.discoveryscienceplace.org

The Center for the Arts & Sciences—Clute
www.bcfas.org

International Museum of Art & Science—McAllen
www.imasonline.org/dev

River Legacy Living Science Center—Arlington
www.riverlegacy.org

Science Spectrum and Omni Theatre—Lubbock
www.sciencespectrum.org

Don Harrington Discovery Center—Amarillo
www.discoverycenteramarillo.org

Hill Country Science Mill—Johnson City
www.sciencemill.org

El Paso Exploreum—El Paso
www.elpasoexploreum.org

Insights El Paso Science Center—El Paso
www.insightselpaso.org

Children's Museum of Houston—Houston
www.cmhouston.org

Frontiers of Flight Museum—Dallas
www.flightmuseum.com/

Lone Star Flight Museum—Galveston
www.lsfm.org

Utah

The Leonardo—Salt Lake City
www.theleonardo.org

Natural History Museum of Utah—Salt Lake City
www.nhmu.utah.edu

Discovery Gateway—Salt Lake City
www.discoverygateway.org

The Loveland Living Planet Aquarium—Draper
www.thelivingplanet.com/index.php

TheMonte L. Bean Life Science Museum—Provo
http://mlbean.byu.edu

The BYU Museum of Paleontology—Provo
www.geology.byu.edu/museum

The Dinosaur Museum—Blanding
http://dinosaur-museum.org

Ogden Eccles Dinosaur Park—Ogden
http://dinosaurpark.org

Cleveland-Lloyd Dinosaur Quarry—Elmo
www.blm.gov/ut/st/en/fo/price/recreation/quarry.html

Vermont

Montshire Museum of Science—Norwich
www.montshire.org

Fairbanks Museum & Planetarium—St. Johnsbury
www.fairbanksmuseum.org

The Hartness-Porter Museum of Amateur Telescope Making—Springfield
www.stellafane.org/history/early/museum-home.html

American Precision Museum—Windsor
www.americanprecision.org

Virginia

Science Museum of Virginia—Richmond
www.smv.org

Virginia Aquarium & Marine Science Center—Virginia Beach
www.virginiaaquarium.com

Science Museum of Western Virginia—Roanoke
www.smwv.org

Danville Science Center—Danville
www.dsc.smv.org

Children's Museum of Richmond—Richmond
www.c-mor.org

Museum of Geosciences—Blacksburg
www.outreach.geos.vt.edu/museum

Virginia Museum of Natural History—Martinsville
www.vmnh.net

Virginia Discovery Museum—Charlottesville
www.vadm.org

Children's Museum of Virginia—Portsmouth
www.childrensmuseumva.com

Virginia Aviation Museum—Richmond
www.vam.smv.org

Virginia Air & Space Center—Hampton
www.vasc.org

Washington

Pacific Science Center—Seattle
www.pacificsciencecenter.org

SPARK Museum of Electrical
Invention—Bellingham
www.sparkmuseum.org

Living Computer Museum—Seattle
www.livingcomputermuseum.org

The Museum of Flight—Seattle
www.museumofflight.org

Palouse Discovery Science Center—Pullman
www.palousescience.net

Mobius Science Center—Spokane
http://mobiusspokane.org/mobius-science-center

Future of Flight Aviation Center & Boeing
Tour—Mukilteo
www.futureofflight.org

Imagine Children's Museum—Everett
www.imaginecm.org

Port Townsend Marine Science Center—Port
Townsend
www.ptmsc.org

McAllister Museum of Aviation—Yakima
www.mcallistermuseum.org

West Virginia

Children's Discovery Museum of West
Virginia—Morgantown
www.cdmwv.org

The Clay Center's Avampato Discovery
Museum—Charleston
www.theclaycenter.org/science/science-sciencegalleries.aspx

Lost World Caverns—Lewisburg
www.lostworldcaverns.com

Wisconsin

Weis Earth Science Museum—Menasha
www.uwfox.uwc.edu/wesm

Discovery World—Milwaukee
www.discoveryworld.org

Dinosaur Discovery Museum—Kenosha
www.kenosha.org/wp-dinosaur/

UW-Madison Geology Museum—Madison
www.geologymuseum.org

EAA AirVenture Museum—Oshkosh
www.eaa.org/en/eaa-museum

Above & Beyond Children's
Museum—Sheboygan
http://abkids.org

Cable Natural History Museum—Cable
http://cablemuseum.org

Chippewa Falls Museum of Industry & Technology—Chippewa Falls
www.cfmit.org

Tommy Bartlett Exploratory—Wisconsin Dells
www.tommybartlett.com/exploratory/

Madison Children's Museum—Madison
http://madisonchildrensmuseum.org

Wyoming
The Wyoming Dinosaur Center—Thermopolis
www.wyodino.org

Tate Geological Museum—Casper
www.caspercollege.edu/tate

The Glenrock Paleontological Museum—Glenrock
http://paleon.org

Fossil Butte National Monument—Kemmerer
http://nps.gov/fobu/index.htm

District of Columbia
Smithsonian National Air and Space Museum—Washington, D.C.
www.airandspace.si.edu

Smithsonian National Museum of Natural History—Washington, D.C.
www.mnh.si.edu

Koshland Science Museum of the National Academy of Sciences—Washington, D.C.
www.koshland-science-museum.org

STEM Career Websites for Kids

AIBS
www.aibs.org/careers/
A site chock-full of information for students interested in careers in biology, from the American Institute of Biological Sciences.

Be an Engineer
www.beanengineer.com/
Sponsored by ExxonMobil, this site offers stories from and about real engineers in addition to information about various engineering fields.

Biotech Careers
www.biotech-careers.org
A site from Bio-Link providing information for students interested in biotech careers, including videos, on-the-job photos, articles, and internship resources.

Careers in Chemistry
www.acs.org/content/acs/en/careers.html
Sponsored by the American Chemical Society, this site features descriptions of a variety of different careers in chemistry, along with numerous professional resources.

Computing Careers
http://computingcareers.acm.org
A site from the Association for Computing Machinery offering information on computing degrees and careers, along with cool computing news.

Cool Science Careers

www.coolsciencecareers.rice.edu

An interesting interactive site from the Center for Technology in Teaching and Learning from Rice University, offering the Profession Pathfinder game, which matches users with science careers based on interests.

Discover Engineering

www.discovere.org

A community focused on encouraging students to pursue engineering careers; includes an engineering career outlook and information on various engineering fields.

Dream It Do It

www.themanufacturinginstitute.org/Image/ Dream-It-Do-It/Dream-It-Do-It.aspx

A site from the Manufacturing Institute aimed at educating people about careers in high-tech manufacturing.

Engineering, Go for It!

www.egfi-k12.org

Associated with the American Society for Engineering Education (ASEE), Engineering, Go for It! offers lots of advice and interesting information related to careers in engineering.

Engineer Girl

www.engineergirl.org

A site sponsored by Lockheed Martin offering resources to encourage girls to pursue engineering careers.

Gotta Have IT

www.ncwit.org/resources/gotta-have-it

A site of the National Center for Women & Information Technology associated with an educational kit for a K-to-12 audience. The kit, which promotes IT careers, is for all students, but is especially aimed at young girls.

IEEE Spark

spark.ieee.org

An online publication aimed at students ages 14 to 18, IEEE Spark offers career profiles, college prep tips, learning activities, news articles, comics, and more. Published by the Institute of Electrical and Electronics Engineers, the site's goal is to inspire young people to pursue careers relating to technology and engineering.

LifeWorks

www.nihlifeworks.org/feature/index.htm

An interactive career exploration site aimed at middle and high school students, with parents and teachers offering detailed information on more than 100 careers in the medical field.

Social Science Careers

www.socialsciencecareers.org

An online guide to careers in the social sciences, including articles and information on relevant degree programs.

STEMCareer

http://stemcareer.com/students

A site with tons of resources related to STEM careers, colleges, internships, and self-learning websites.

STEM-Works

www.stem-works.com

STEM-Works offers a plethora of resources for parents, teachers, and STEM professionals. The site also offers activities and information on STEM jobs.

Southwest Fisheries Science Center

http://swfsc.noaa.gov/textblock.aspx?id=54

A site for anyone interested in marine biology as a career, offering information on degree programs and career outlooks from the National Oceanic and Atmospheric Administration.

Choosing a STEM Career

www.pbslearningmedia.org/resource/ wpsu09-stemcareers.text.lpchoosingSTEMcareer/ choosing-a-stem-career/

A multimedia collection of resources from PBS Learning Media, including videos, articles, and worksheets. The site's resources are aimed at students in grades six to twelve.

Other Useful STEM Websites

24/7 Science

www.lawrencehallofscience.org/kidsite

Sponsored by the Lawrence Hall of Science, the site offers a collection of fun, interactive learning activities and games, all STEM related.

Anatomy Arcade

www.anatomyarcade.com

Anatomy Arcade makes studying human anatomy fun and thrilling through interactive flash games and other activities.

Arrick Robotics

www.arrickrobotics.com/robots.html

A site chock-full of resources about various types of robots, including instructions on how to build your own robot.

Bill Nye Science Guy

www.billnye.com

Videos, home demos, and other STEM-related resources from one of the most famous science teachers on television.

Brainrush

www.brainrush.com

A site featuring adaptive learning games that anyone can play and share.

Bugscope

http://bugscope.beckman.uiuc.edu

Bugscope offers users the opportunity to interactively control an $800,000 scanning electron microscope, and to send questions to scientists via an interactive chat tool.

Catch the Science Bug

www.sciencebug.org

A TV show and traveling educational program, Catch the Science Bug offers a site with free puzzles and other learning activities.

ChemiCroc

www.chemicroc.com

ChemiCroc, sponsored by the Chemical Business Association of the UK, offers interactive help for kids learning chemistry basics.

Computer Science Education Week

http://csedweek.org/learn

Designed to promote Computer Science Education Week, the site offers tutorials for beginning coders as well as unplugged learning activities.

Dot Diva

www.dotdiva.org

Dot Diva is an online community for young women interested in computing.

Edheads

www.edheads.org

Edheads provides free math and science games and activities—keyed to state and national standards—aimed at bolstering kids' creative thinking skills.

E is for EXPLORE!

www.eisforexplore.blogspot.com

E is for EXPLORE! is a collection of resources for parents and teachers interested in helping young people learn about STEM subjects.

Energy Kids

www.energy.gov/science-innovation/science-education

From the U.S. Department of Energy, a site offering resources to teach kids all about energy.

enggHeads e-Circuit Box

www.enggheads.com/e-circuitbox/circuit.html

enggHeads e-Circuit Box is an interactive online tool that allows users to learn about electronics by drawing electrical circuits using symbols.

Happy Earth Day Coloring and Activities Book

www.epa.gov/region5/earthday/happy/happy.pdf

A downloadable PDF coloring and activities book from the EPA that highlights Earth Day.

EPA Students

www2.epa.gov/students

An educational website from the Environmental Protection Agency.

Explorations Through Time

www.ucmp.berkeley.edu/education/explotime.html

Explorations Through Time, a project of the University of California Museum of Paleontology, offers a series of interactive modules focusing on Earth's paleontological history.

Extreme Science

www.extremescience.com

A website that covers the extremes of science, including science-related world records and miscellaneous facts.

Funology

www.funology.com

A site offering STEM-related games, experiments, recipes, magic tricks, and more.

Healthline's Human Body Maps

www.healthline.com/human-body-maps

Healthine's Human Body Maps is an interactive tool that allows users to search the various layers of the human anatomy in 3D.

Junior FIRST LEGO League

www.usfirst.org/roboticsprograms/jr.fll
A site chock-full of information relating to the Junior First Lego League competitions.

Kids Ahead

www.kidsahead.com
Articles, activities, and video games relating to space, animals, robotics, and many other STEM subjects.

Kinetic City

http://kineticcity.com
A site offering games, challenges, experiments, and other activities from the American Association for the Advancement of Science.

Maker Faire

www.makerfaire.com
Sponsored by Intel, this site promotes the Maker Faire movement for tech enthusiasts of all ages.

MathMovesU

www.mathmovesu.com
Games and other resources designed to get kids excited about learning math.

My Doctor Games

www.mydoctorgames.com/cat/biology-games
My Doctor Games features fun and funny games that help kids and adults understand genetics, cycles, and biological systems.

NASA Education for Students

www.nasa.gov/audience/forstudents/index.html
A website with the latest news about the space agency's activities and opportunities for students.

National Geographic Kids

http://kids.nationalgeographic.com
Tons of intriguing learning resources from the National Geographic Society.

Nova

www.pbs.org/wgbh/nova
The popular PBS show's website features videos and articles on all manner of STEM subjects.

Online Chart Tool

www.onlinecharttool.com
Online Chart Tool is a site that allows users to design and share various types of charts and graphs, all for free.

Science Bob

http://sciencebob.com
Another prominent science teacher offers science fair ideas, experiments, games, and other STEM activities.

Science Buddies

www.sciencebuddies.org
A great source for science project ideas, along with information on science careers and resources for teachers.

Science Kids

www.sciencekids.co.nz/gamesactivities.html
A site absolutely loaded with games, experiments, quizzes, and other activities designed to promote STEM learning among children.

SciJinks

http://scijinks.jpl.nasa.gov
A website that's all about the weather from the National Oceanic and Atmospheric Administration.

Squishy Circuits

http://courseweb.stthomas.edu/apthomas/ SquishyCircuits/index.htm
Squishy Circuits from the Playful Learning Lab at the University of St. Thomas is a project that allows students to create circuits and learn about electronics using play dough.

STEMconnector

www.stemconnector.org
A site that bills itself as the one-stop shop for STEM information. It includes resources and events organized by state, as well as a daily newsletter.

STEM Fuse

http://stemfuse.com
A website offering STEM-based curricula for teachers, designed by teachers.

Study Jams!

http://studyjams.scholastic.com/studyjams/
Study Jams from Scholastic is a collection of STEM-related songs designed to help kids remember key information.

Tech with Tia

www.techwithtia.com
A site providing resources to help teachers incorporate technology in their pedagogy.

Time for Kids Environment

www.timeforkids.com/minisite/environment
This site from *Time* magazine offers tons of articles relating to environmental issues.

Untamed Science

www.untamedscience.com
Untamed Science offers fun, engaging science videos covering biology, biodiversity, and science filmmaking.

Weather Wiz Kids

www.weatherwizkids.com
Designed by a real live meteorologist, this website offers resources to teach kids all about the weather.

We Choose the Moon

www.wechoosethemoon.org
A site featuring an interactive re-creation of NASA's first mission to the moon, sponsored by the Kennedy Library and Museum.

Women in STEM

www.whitehouse.gov/administration/eop/ostp/ women
Articles, videos, and other resources from the Office of Science and Technology Policy relating to women in STEM.

Wonderville

www.wonderville.ca/browse/fun_science
Wonderville's purpose is to get kids excited about science via online games and activities.

Appendix B: Bibliography

Aczel, Amir D. *Chance: A Guide To Gambling, Love, The Stock Market, & Just About Everything Else.* (New York: Thunder's Mouth Press, 2004).

Adkins, Rodney C. "America Desperately Needs More STEM Students. Here's How To Get Them." Forbes Leadership Forum. Forbes, July 2012. Accessed 11 February 2015. *www.forbes.com/ sites/forbesleadershipforum/2012/07/09/america- desperately-needs-more-stem-students-heres-how-to- get-them/*

Al-Khalili, Jim. *The House of Wisdom: How Arabic Science Saved Ancient Knowledge and Gave Us the Renaissance.* (New York: The Penguin Press, 2011).

"America's Pressing Challenge—Building a Stronger Foundation." *A Companion to Science and Engineering Indicators 2006.* National Science Board, February 2006. Accessed 27 January 2015. *www.nsf.gov/statistics/nsb0602/*

Bellis, Mary. "The History of Bingo." *About.com Inventors*, no date. Accessed 16 January 2015. *www.inventors.about.com/library/inventors/ blbingo.htm*

Birch, Hayley, Mun Keat Looi, and Colin Stuart. *The Big Questions in Science.* (London: André Deutsch, 2013).

Bordenstein, Seth. "The History of Science: When Was The Word 'Scientist' First Used?" *Symbionticism*, 29 April 2013. Accessed 17 January 2015. *www.symbionticism.blogspot.com/2013/04/ the-history-of-science-when-was-word.html*

Borzo, Gene. "Scholars and Scientists Explore Factors Underlying Serendipitous Discoveries." UChicago News. The University of Chicago, 19 June 2014. Accessed 16 January 2015. *http://news. uchicago.edu/article/2014/06/19/scholars-and- scientists-explore-factors-underlying-serendipitous- discoveries*

Boudreaux, Kevin A. "Periodic Trends— Electronegativity." Department of Chemistry. Anglo State University, no date. Accessed 15 January 2015. *www.angelo.edu/faculty/kboudrea/periodic/ trends_electronegativity.htm*

Bourne, Murray. "al-Khwarizmi, the Father of Algebra." *Interactive Mathematics*, December 2014. Accessed 19 January 2015. *www.intmath.com/ basic-algebra/al-khwarizmi-father-algebra.php*

Cardona, Maria. "Why the National STEM Education Fund Is So Important." *Huff Post Tech*, updated 28 July 2013. Accessed 11 February 2015. *www.huffingtonpost.com/maria-cardona/ why-national-stem-education-fund-is-so- important_b_3314124.html*

Carradice, Phil. "Robert Recorde, The Man Who Invented the Equals Sign." BBC Wales, 3 June 2010. Accessed 18 January 2015. *www.bbc.co.uk/blogs/wales/posts/robert_recorde*

Carroll, Bradley W. "Eureka! The Achievements of Archimedes." Department of Physics. Webster State University, no date. Accessed 7 January 2015. *http://physics.weber.edu/carroll/Archimedes/default.htm*

Carter, J. Stein. "Photosynthesis." University of Cincinnati, Clermont College, 13 January 2014. Accessed 1 February 2015. *http://biology.clc.uc.edu/courses/bio104/photosyn.htm*

Chang, Raymond. *Chemistry.* (New York: McGraw Hill, 2007).

Cherry, Kendra. "Introduction to Research Methods: Theory and Hypothesis." *About Education*, no date. Accessed 23 January 2015. *www.psychology.about.com/od/researchmethods/ss/expdesintro_2.htm*

Coolmath. Coolmath.com LLC, no date. Accessed 8 January 2015. *www.coolmath.com*

"Dandi: Salt March." UCLA College, no date. Accessed 20 January 2015. *www.sscnet.ucla.edu/southasia/History/Gandhi/Dandi.html*

"Data Services." Astronomical Applications Department. U.S. Naval Observatory, no date. Accessed 7 January 2015. *http://aa.usno.navy.mil/data/index.php*

DeAngelis, Stephen F. "STEM Education: Why It's Important." *Enterra Solutions*, 14 March 2014. Accessed 12 February 2015. *www.enterrasolutions.com/2014/03/stem-education-important.html*

"Deciduous." Minnesota Department of Natural Resources, no date. Accessed 1 February 2015. *www.dnr.state.mn.us/trees_shrubs/deciduous/index.html*

Dickens, Donna. "27 Science Fictions That Became Science Facts In 2012." BuzzFeed News, 19 December 2012. Accessed 22 January 2015. *www.buzzfeed.com/donnad/27-science-fictions-that-became-science-facts-in-2 - .vbMGGllJKn*

"Dmitri Mendeleev." *The Development of the Periodic Table*. Royal Society of Chemistry, no date. Accessed 15 January 2015. *www.rsc.org/education/teachers/resources/periodictable/pre16/develop/mendeleev.htm*

Douglass, Charlene. "Euclid." *Math Open Reference*, 2007. Accessed 12 January 2015. *www.mathopenref.com/euclid.html*

Douglass, Charlene. "Pythagoras." *Math Open Reference*, 2005. Accessed 14 January 2015. *www.mathopenref.com/pythagoras.html*

"Drops on a Penny." *Science World Resources*. Science World at Telus World of Science, no date. Accessed 23 January 2015. *www.scienceworld.ca/resources/activities/drops-penny*

Dunn, Katie. "Why Is STEM Important in K–12 Education?" Daily Genius, no date. Accessed 12 January 2015. *www.dailygenius.com/ stem-important-k-12-education*

"DuPont Neoprene Polychloroprene." DuPont, no date. Accessed 4 January 2015. *www.dupont.com/ products-and-services/plastics-polymers-resins/ elastomers/brands/neoprene-polychloroprene.html*

Eberle, Francis. "Why STEM Education Is Important." *InTech Magazine*, ISA Publications, September 2010. Accessed 27 January 2015. *www.isa.org/standards-and-publications/isa-publications/intech-magazine/2010/september/ why-stem-education-is-important/*

"Elementary Science Experiments, Penny Drops." *Kids-Fun-Science*. Ring of Fire Science Company, no date. Accessed 24 January 2015. *www.kids-fun-science.com/elementary-science-experiments.html*

"The Rebirth of Rails, episode 4: Energy & Dynamic Breaking." *The GE Show*, no date. Accessed 2 January 2015. *www.ge.com/thegeshow/rails/*

"Etymology of the Term Dollar." *The Titi Tudorancea Bulletin*, 12 June 2008. Accessed 24 January 2015. *www.tititudorancea.com/z/etymology_of_the_ term_dollar.htm*

"Euclid." *Famous Scientists*, no date. Accessed 12 January 2015. *www.famousscientists.org/euclid/*

Evans, Barry. "Serendipity in Science." *The North Coast Journal*, August 2010. Accessed 16 January 2015. *www.northcoastjournal.com/humboldt/ serendipity-in-science/Content?oid=2131243*

"Eye Color." *Stanford at The Tech: Understanding Genetics*, no date. Accessed 10 February 2015. *http://genetics.thetech.org/genetic-categories/ eye-color*

"Fibonacci Number." *MathWorld*. Wolfram, no date. Accessed 20 February 2015. *www.mathworld .wolfram.com/FibonacciNumber.html*

"Forget Algebra—Is Statistics Necessary?" *Statistics Learning Centre*, 6 August 2012. Accessed 16 January 2015. *www.learnandteachstatistics. wordpress.com/2012/08/06/stats-not-algebra/*

"Fuel Cell Vehicles." U.S. Department of Energy, no date. Accessed 12 January 2015. *www.fueleconomy .gov/feg/fuelcell.shtml*

Gardner, Jerry D., Arthur A. Ciociola, and Malcolm Robinson. "Measurement of meal-stimulated gastric acid secretion by in vivo gastric autotitration." *Journal of Applied Physiology*, vol 92, (2002): 427–434.

Gilbert, Gay. "Arizona's State Trees Foothill Palo Verde and Blue Palo Verde." *The Arizona Native Plant Society*, no date. Accessed 1 February 2015. *www.aznps.com/statetree.php*

Giovinazzo, Paul. "The Fatal Current." New Jersey State Council of Electrical Contractors Associations Bulletin, vol. 2, no. 13 (February 1987). Accessed 8 January 2015. *www.physics.ohio-state.edu/~p616/safety/fatal_current.html*

Glessner, Josh. "Seeking Information for Listing in STEM Book." *Engineering for Kids*, 12 February 2015. E-mail survey.

Gottlieb, Anthony. "The Limits of Science." *Intelligent Life—The Economist*, 2010. Accessed 23 January 2015. *www.moreintelligentlife.com/content/ideas/anthony-gottlieb/limits-science*

Grossman, John P., and Glenn R. Bell. "Spaceship Earth: Epcot Canter's Gateway to Tomorrow." Tampa Steel Erecting Co. *Modern Steel Construction*, 4th Quarter (1982). Accessed 12 January 2015. *tampasteelerecting.com/images/epcot.pdf*

Hale, Jamie. "Understanding Research Methodology 5: Applied and Basic Research." Psych Central: World of Psychology, no date. Accessed 23 January 2015. *www.psychcentral.com/blog/archives/2011/05/12/understanding-research-methodology-5-applied-and-basic-research/*

Hare, Jonathan. "Newton's Experiments—air pressure and bell jar." *The Creative Science Centre*. The University of Sussex, no date. Accessed 5 January 2015. *www.creative-science.org.uk/bell_jar.html*

Hatfield, Gary. "René Descartes." *The Stanford Encyclopedia of Philosophy* (Spring 2015 Edition). Edward N. Zalta (ed.), The Metaphysics Research Lab, Center for the Study of Language and Information, no date. Accessed 20 January 2015. *http://plato.stanford.edu/entries/descartes/*

Helmenstine, Anne Marie. "Scientific Method Steps." *About Education*, no date. Accessed 16 January 2015. *www.chemistry.about.com/od/lecturenotesl3/a/sciencemethod.htm*

"Hexadecimal Numbering System." *Electronics Tutorials*. Basic Electronics Tutorials by Wayne Storr, no date. Accessed 29 January 2015. *www.electronics-tutorials.ws/binary/bin_3.html*

"History of Bingo." *Winning with Numbers*, no date. Accessed 16 January 2015. *www.winningwithnumbers.com/bingo/history/*

Holm, Paige. "Water and Hydration." The University of Arizona, no date. Accessed 5 February 2015. *www.health.arizona.edu/health_topics/nutrition/general/waterhydration.htm*

Hom, Elaine J. "What Is STEM Education?" *LiveScience*, February 2014. Accessed 27 January 2015. *www.livescience.com/43296-what-is-stem-education.html*

Hom, Elaine J. "What Is The Fibonacci Sequence?" *LiveScience*, June 2013. Accessed 14 February 2015. *www.livescience.com/37470-fibonacci-sequence.html*

"How Do Batteries Work?" Northwestern University, Qualitative Reasoning Group, no date. Accessed 17 January 2015. *www.qrg.northwestern.edu/projects/vss/docs/power/2-how-do-batteries-work.html*

"How Many Drops?" *TeachEngineering*, no date. Accessed 23 January 2015. *www.teachengineering.org/view_lesson.php?url=collection/duk_/lessons/duk_drops_mary_less/duk_drops_mary_less.xml*

Huffman, Carl. "Pythagoras." *The Stanford Encyclopedia of Philosophy* (Summer 2014 edition). Edward N. Zalta (ed.), The Metaphysics Research Lab, Center for the Study of Language and Information, no date. Accessed 14 January 2015. *http://plato.stanford.edu/archives/sum2014/entries/pythagoras*

"Hun Dread No Longer." *Membean*, no date. Accessed 1 February 2015. *www.membean.com/wrotds/cent-hundred*

Inglis-Arkell, Esther. "10 Pseudo-Science Theories We'd Like to See Retired Forever." Io9, June 2014. Accessed 24 January 2015. *www.io9.com/10-pseudo-science-theories-wed-like-to-see-retired-fore-1592128908*

Jahn, Jody L.S., and Karen K. Myers. "Vocational Anticipatory Socialization of Adolescents: Messages, Sources, and Frameworks That Influence Interest in STEM Careers." *Journal of Applied Communication Research*, vol 42 (2014): 85–106.

Kauffman, George B., Stewart W. Mason, and Raymond B. Seymour. "Happy and Unhappy Balls: Neoprene and Polynorbornene." *Journal of Chemical Education*, vol 67, (March 1990): 198–199.

Kaufman, Terry, IMACS. "Seeking Information for Listing in STEM Book," 3 February 2015. E-mail Survey.

Kelly, Brian. "The State of STEM and Jobs." *U.S. News & World Report*, Sept. 2012. Accessed 28 January 2015. *www.usnews.com/news/articles/2012/09/21/the-state-of-stem-and-jobs*

Kuntzleman, Tom. "Soap Boat 2.0." *Chemical Education Xchange*, Oct. 2013. Accessed 13 January 2015. *www.jce.divched.org/blog/soap-boat-20*

Lamb, Robert. "How Are Fibonacci Numbers Expressed In Nature?" *HowStuffWorks*, no date. Accessed 22 February 2015. *http://science.howstuffworks.com/math-concepts/fibonacci-nature.htm*

"Large Number." *MathWorld*. Wolfram, no date. Accessed 28 January 2015. *www.mathworld.wolfram.com/LargeNumber.html*

Levitt, Steven D., and Stephen J. Dubner. *Freakonomics: A Rogue Economist Explores the Hidden Side of Everything.* (New York: William Morrow, 2005).

Lev-Ram, Michael. "The Business Case for STEM Education." *Fortune*, January 2015. Accessed 10 February 2015. *www.fortune.com/2015/01/22/the-business-case-for-stem-education/*

Lind, Douglas A., William G. Marchal, and Samuel A. Wathen. *Statistical Techniques in Business & Economics*, 15th Edition. (New York: McGraw-Hill, 2012).

"Magnetic Pole Reversal Happens All The (Geologic) Time." The Earth's Magnetic Field. NASA, 2012. Accessed 10 January 2015. *www.nasa.gov/topics/earth/features/2012-poleReversal.html*

"Marie and Pierre Curie." *Famous Physicists and Astronomers*. University of Zagreb in Croatia, March 1996. Accessed 9 January 2015. *www.phy.pmf.unizg.hr/~dpaar/fizicari/xcurie.html*

Maston, John. "The Origin of Zero." *Scientific American*, August 2001. Accessed 22 January 2015. *www.scientificamerican.com/article/history-of-zero/*

Math is Fun, no date. Accessed 10 January 2015. *www.mathsisfun.com*

McCormack. "Propulsion Systems" from "Space Handbook: Astronautics and Its Applications." H. Res. 496 (85th Cong.) NASA History Program Office, no date. Accessed 15 January 2015. *http://history.nasa.gov/conghand/propulsn.htm*

McCoy, Kristin. "Mousetrap Cars." MESA. University of California-Irvine, July 2010. Accessed 14 January 2015. *http://mesa.eng.uci.edu/Resources/Students/Mousetrap_Car_General.pdf*

"Measurement of pH." Georgia State University, no date. Accessed 15 January 2015. *http://hyperphysics.phy-astr.gsu.edu/hbase/chemical/ph.html*

Morales, Tatiana. "More Fires Sparked at Gas Pump." CBS News, August 2004. Accessed 8 January 2015. *www.cbsnews.com/news/more-fires-sparked-at-gas-pump/*

"More Than a Million." *FactMonster*. Family Education Network, Pearson Education, no date. Accessed 28 January 2015. *www.factmonster.com/ipka/A0769538.html*

Morella, Michael. "Many High Schoolers Giving Up on STEM." *U.S. News & World Report*, January 2013. Accessed 29 January 2015. *www.usnews.com/news/blogs/stem-education/2013/01/31/report-many-high-schoolers-giving-up-on-stem*

Morgan, Tracy. "The Importance of Extracurricular STEM Education." *TeenLife Blog*, January 2015. Accessed 29 January 2015. *www.teenlife.com/blogs/articles/the-importance-of-extra-curricular-stem-learning*

"Mousetrap Vehicle Out and Back." Electrical Engineering. New Mexico Tech, no date. Accessed 14 January 2015. *www.ee.nmt.edu/~tubesing/so/SO_Rules_C_div_High_Sch/MousetrapVehicle11C.pdf*

"Muslim Journeys, Item #173: The Impact of Alhazen's Optics on How We See the World." *Bridging Cultures Bookshelf*, no date. Accessed 21 January 2015. *http://bridgingcultures.neh.gov/muslimjourneys/items/show/173*

Nagel, David. "Job Shadowing Can Get More Students Interested in STEM Careers." *The Journal*, February 2014. Accessed 27 January 2015. *http://thejournal.com/articles/2014/02/13/job-shadowing-can-get-students-more-interested-in-stem-careers.aspx*

Newitz, Annalee. "One of the World's First Statements About the Scientific Method." *Io9*, April 2014. Accessed 22 January 2015. *www.io9.com/one-of-the-worlds-first-statements-about-the-scientific-1564545837*

"Neodymium Magnets." CMS Magnetics, no date. Accessed 9 January 2015. *www.magnet4sale.com/neodymium-ndfeb-rare-earth-magnets/*

"Norsorex." Startech Advanced Materials GmbH, no date. Accessed 3 January 2015. *www.astrotech.at/index.php/norsorex.html*

"Observable Human Characteristics." Genetic Science Learning Center. University of Utah, no date. Accessed 10 February 2015. *http://learn.genetics.utah.edu/content/inheritance/observable/*

Oladipo, Jennifer. "Students Branch Out with STEM Job Shadowing." *Upstate Business Journal*, August 2013. Accessed 27 January 2015. *www.upstatebusinessjournal.com/news/students-branch-out-with-stem-job-shadowing/*

"On-Time Arrival Performance National (December 2014)." *Airline On-Time Statistics and Delay Causes*. Bureau of Transportation Studies, no date. Accessed 17 January 2015. *www.transtats.bts.gov/OT_Delay/OT_DelayCause1.asp*

Peavler, Rosemary. "How Do You Calculate the Present Value of an Annuity Due?" About Money, no date. Accessed 30 January 2015. *http://bizfinance.about.com/od/interestrates/f/calculate-the-present-value-annuity-due.htm*

"Periodic Table." Los Alamos National Laboratory, no date. Accessed 15 January 2015. *http://periodic.lanl.gov/index.shtml*

"Periodic Table." Royal Society of Chemistry, no date. Accessed 15 January 2015. *www.rsc.org/periodic-table*

"Permanent Magnet: Excerpts from Henry's Student's Notebook." Joseph Henry Project. Princeton University, August 2012. Accessed 9 January 2015. *www.princeton.edu/ssp/joseph-henry-project/permanent-magnet/*

"Pets by the Numbers: Pet ownership survey data and the HSUS's estimates on pets adopted from or euthanized in U.S. shelters in 2012 and 2013." The Humane Society, January 2014. Accessed 12 January 2015. *www.humanesociety.org/issues/pet_overpopulation/facts/pet_ownership_statistics.html*

"Plant Nutrients." North Carolina Department of Agriculture & Consumer Services, no date. Accessed 1 February 2015. *www.ncagr.gov/cyber/kidswrld/plant/nutrient.htm*

"Protractor." National Museum of American History. Smithsonian, no date. Accessed 17 January 2015. *www.americanhistory.si.edu/collections/object-groups/protractors*

"Q & A: The Human Body's Resistance." Department of Physics. University of Illinois at Urbana-Champaign, no date. Accessed 8 January 2015. *https://van.physics.illinois.edu/qa/listing.php?id=6793h*

"Real-Time Insight Into the Market for Entry-Level STEM Jobs." *Burning Glass Careers in Focus.* Burning Glass Technologies, February 2014. Accessed 27 January 2015. *www.burning-glass.com/media/3326/Real-Time Insight Into The Market For Entry-Level STEM Jobs.pdf*

Renney, Charles, Ashley Brewer, and Tiddo Jonathan Mooibroek. "Easy Demonstration of the Marangoni Effect by Prolonged and Directional Motion: "Soap Boat 2.0"." *Journal of Chemical Education*, 90 (10), (2013): 1353–1357.

Science Buddies Staff. "Measuring Surface Tension of Water with a Penny." *Science Buddies*, Oct. 2014. Accessed 23 January 2015. *www.sciencebuddies.org/science-fair-projects/project_ideas/Chem_p021.shtml*

"Science At Multiple Levels." *Understanding Science.* University of California Museum of Paleontology, no date. Accessed 24 January 2015. *http://undsci.berkeley.edu/article/0_0_0/howscienceworks_19*

"Science Fiction or Science Fact?" NASA, no date. Accessed 22 January 2015. *http://www.nasa.gov/multimedia/mmgallery/fact_fiction_nonflash_prt.htm*

"Science Has Limits: A Few Things That Science Does Not Do." *Understanding Science.* University of California Museum of Paleontology, no date. Accessed 22 January 2015. *http://undsci.berkeley.edu/article/0_0_0/whatisscience_12*

"Static Electricity in Petroleum Stations." SESA–ESSA prevention service. South African Flameproof Association, no date. Accessed 8 January 2015. *www.flp.co.za/Portals/23/Documents/General/SHELL-Safetyandpetrol.pdf*

Stauffer, Cindy. "Gas pump death a warning." Lancaster Online, March 2010. Accessed 8 January 2015. *http://lancasteronline.com/news/gas-pump-death-a-warning/article_044caba2-83ce-590f-b1f5-12e964e3d8b1.html*

"Steps of the Scientific Method." *Science Buddies*, no date. Accessed 14 January 2015. *www.sciencebuddies.org/science-fair-projects/project_scientific_method.shtml*

Strieby, Sandra. "Comparing Conifers and Deciduous Trees." *Botanical Rambles*, Washington Native Plant Society, July 2013. Accessed 1 February 2015. *www.wnps.org/blog/conifers-deciduous-trees/*

"Surface Tension." Georgia State University, no date. Accessed 13 January 2015. *http://hyperphysics.phy-astr.gsu.edu/hbase/surten.html*

Syed, Ibrahim B. "Al-Khwarizmi: The Father of Algebra." *Pioneers of Islamic History.* Onislam, Oct. 2011. Accessed 19 January 2015. *www.onislam. net/english/reading-islam/research-studies/islamic-history/454243-al-khwarizmi-the-father-of-algebra .html*

"Taxonomy of Fields and Their Subfields." *National Academy of Sciences*, July 2006. Accessed 15 January 2015. *http://sites.nationalacademies.org/ PGA/Resdoc/PGA_044522*

"The Best New Railway Station Design." *Design Curial*, October 2013. Accessed 11 January 2015. *www.designcurial.com/news/action-stations*

"The Dynamic Earth: Developing the Theory." USGS: Science for a Changing World, May 1999. Accessed 10 January 2015. *http://pubs.usgs.gov/ gip/dynamic/developing.html*

"The Fibonacci Sequence." *Science NetLinks.* Association for the Advancement of Science, no date. Accessed 17 February 2015. *www.sciencenetlinks.com/lessons/ the-fibonacci-sequence/*

"The Future of U.S. Manufacturing and the Importance of STEM Education." *Mid-Atlantic Technology, Research and Innovation Center*, no date. Accessed 29 January 2015. *www.matricinnovates.com/education/the-future-of-u-s-manufacturing-and-the-importance-of-stem-education/*

"The Limitations of Science." *Center for Independent Learning.* The College of DuPage, Sept. 2004. Accessed 22 January 2015. *www.cod.edu/people/ faculty/fancher/Limits.htm*

"The State of Our Union's 21st Century Workforce." *The Commerce Blog.* United States Department of Commerce, February 2012. Accessed 27 January 2015. *www.commerce.gov/blog/2012/02/06/ state-our-union's-21st-century-workforce*

"The Theory of pH Measurement." Emerson Process Management. Rosemount Analytical, November 2010. Accessed 15 January 2015. *www2.emersonprocess.com/siteadmincenter/PM Rosemount Analytical Documents/Liq_ADS_43-002 .pdf*

"Truss Bridges." Archaeology & History Preservation. Delaware Department of Transportation, no date. Accessed 11 January 2015. *www.deldot.gov/archaeology/historic_pres/ delaware_bridge_book/pdf/truss.pdf*

"Understanding the Birthday Paradox." *Better Explained*, no date. Accessed 29 January 2015. *www.betterexplained.com/articles/ understanding-the-birthday-paradox/*

"Understanding the Scientific Method." *Science Made Simple*, no date. Accessed 21 January 2015. *www.sciencemadesimple.com/scientific_method .html*

"Using the Rules of 69, 70 and 72: Doubling Time Shortcuts." *Had to Know*, no date. Accessed 1 February 2015. *www.had2know.com/business/rule-of-69-70-72-doubling-time.html*

Van der Krogt, Peter. "Development of the chemical symbols and the Periodic Table." Van der Krogt, no date. Accessed 20 January 2015. *www.vanderkrogt.net/elements/chemical_symbols.php*

Vollhardt, K. Peter C., and Neil E. Schore. *Organic Chemistry Structure and Function*. (New York: W. H. Freeman and Company, 2003).

Wallin, Nils-Bertil. "The History of Zero: How Was the Zero Discovered?" *YaleGlobal Online*. MacMillan Center, November 2002. Accessed 22 January 2015. *www.yaleglobal.yale.edu/about/zero.jsp*

Watkins, Denny. "10 Medical Breakthroughs That Sound Like Science Fiction." *Men's Health*, November 2014. Accessed 22 January 2014. *www.menshealth.com/health/medical-breakthroughs*

Weisstein, Eric W. "Trapezium." *MathWorld*. Wolfram, no date. Accessed 11 January 2015. *www.mathworld.wolfram.com/Trapezium.html*

Weisstein, Eric W. "René Descartes (1596–1650)." *Eric Weisstein's World of Scientific Biography*. Wolfram Research, no date. Accessed 20 January 2015. *http://scienceworld.wolfram.com/biography/Descartes.html*

"What is the pH of stomach acid when the stomach is not full of food?" UCSB ScienceLine, no date. Accessed 15 January 2015. *http://scienceline.ucsb.edu/getkey.php?key=275*

Whiting, David, et al. "Identifying Conifers." Colorado State University Extension, 2014. Accessed 1 February 2015. *www.ext.colostate.edu/mg/gardennotes/152.html*

"Why STEM Education Is Important for Everyone." *Science Pioneers*, no date. Accessed 27 January 2015. *www.sciencepioneers.org/parents/why-stem-is-important-to-everyone*

"Why the North pole is actually a South seeking pole." Physics.org, no date. Accessed 9 January 2015. *www.physics.org/article-questions.asp?id=65*

"X-rays and Uranium Rays." *Marie Curie and the Science of Radioactivity*. American Institute of Physics, no date. Accessed 9 January 2015. *www.aip.org/history/curie/resbr1.htm*

Zumbrun, Josh, and Nick Timiraos. "Q & A: What the $18 Trillion National Debt Means for the U.S. Economy." Real Time Economics. *Wall Street Journal*, February 2015. Accessed 2 February 2015. *http://blogs.wsj.com/economics/2015/02/01/qa-what-the-18-trillion-national-debt-means-for-the-u-s-economy*

Index